Literature as History

Continuum literary studies series

Related titles available in the series:
Translator as Writer edited by Susan Bassnett and Peter Bush

Literature as History

Essays in Honour of Peter Widdowson

Edited by
Simon Barker and Jo Gill

continuum

Continuum International Publishing Group
The Tower Building   80 Maiden Lane
11 York Road   Suite 704
London SE1 7NX   New York, NY 10038

www.continuumbooks.com

British Library Cataloguing-in-Publication Data
A catalogue record for this book is available from the British Library.

ISBN: 978-0-8264-3385-5 (hardback)

Library of Congress Cataloging-in-Publication Data
A catalog record for this book is available from the Library of Congress.

Typeset by Newgen Imaging Systems Pvt Ltd, Chennai, India
Printed in Great Britain by the MPG Books Group, Bodmin and King's Lynn

Airmail

A Poem for Peter

When parrots pass by night they drop a note
to say they've been. You find it in the morning,
a white patch on your doorstep, and still sticky
should you be fool enough to step in it.

If you're not often visited by parrots
or not at all, count yourself lucky.
Many's the enterprise that's been left yawning
for want of a bird-scarer. To inherit

good fortune's no mean feat, with the migrations
scheduled to start. Soon, soon will Hitchcock's dreams
become reality, as the air darkens
with endless flocks filling the sky in swarms
that block out daylight, squawking as they go,
drenching the landscape in a gooey snow.

Peter Widdowson

This collection of essays was conceived as a testimony to Peter Widdowson's life and work and was given to him in typescript a few weeks before his untimely death in June 2009. The editors and contributors decided to leave the text unchanged and to offer it to readers just as it was presented to him.

Simon Barker and Jo Gill

Contents

Acknowledgements

The editors are grateful for permission to reproduce Terry Eagleton, 'Tragedy and Revolution', in *Theology and the Political*, Creston Davis, John Milbank, Slavoj Zizek, eds, pp. 7–21. Copyright, 2005, Duke University Press. All rights reserved. Used by permission of the publisher. The figure in Chapter 7 of Joseph Mallord William Turner's *The Field of Waterloo* (exhibited 1818), is reproduced here by kind permission of Tate Britain, London, where it is held in the Turner Bequest collection.

We gratefully acknowledge the assistance of Diane Grosse (Duke University Press) and of Colleen Coalter and Anna Fleming (Continuum); in particular we have valued Anna's support for this project. We are grateful to Mr P. Muralidharan and his colleagues at Newgen Imaging Systems in India. We owe a special debt to the Widdowson family, and especially Jane and Tom. We also wish to thank Rosie Bailey, John Drakakis and everyone who has contributed to this volume.

Proceeds from the sale of this volume will go to Cancer Research UK, P.O. Box 123, Lincoln's Inn Fields, London, WC2A 3PX.

Notes on Contributors

Simon Barker is Professor of English Literature at the University of Gloucestershire. His publications include *The Routledge Anthology of Renaissance Drama* (2003), *Shakespeare's Problem Plays* (2005), *The Gentle Craft* (2007) and *War and Nation in the Theatre of Shakespeare and his Contemporaries* (2007).

Catherine Belsey is Research Professor in English at Swansea University. She first worked with Peter Widdowson on *Re-Reading English* (1982). Her books include *Critical Practice* (1980, 2002), *Desire: Love Stories in Western Culture* (1994), *Poststructuralism: A Very Short Introduction* (2002), *Culture and the Real* (2005) and *Why Shakespeare?* (2007).

Helen Carr is an Emeritus Professor in the Department of English and Comparative Literature, Goldsmiths, University of London. Her most recent book is *The Verse Revolutionaries: Ezra Pound, H. D. and the Imagists.* She is consultant to an AHRC funded project, 'Beyond the Linear Narrative' in the Goldsmiths Pinter Centre.

Simon Dentith is Professor of English at Reading University. He has published widely on nineteenth- and twentieth-century topics. For 13 years he was a colleague of Peter Widdowson at Cheltenham and Gloucester College, later the University of Gloucestershire, where he learnt immeasurably from Peter's example.

Tim Dolin is Associate Professor in the School of Media, Culture and Creative Arts at Curtin University of Technology in Perth, WA. He is the author of *George Eliot* (2005) and *Hardy* (2007), and is co-editor with Peter Widdowson of *Thomas Hardy and Contemporary Literary Studies* (2004).

Terry Eagleton is Professor of Cultural Theory at the National University of Ireland, Galway, Professor of English Literature at the University of Lancaster, and Distinguished Visiting Professor at the University of Notre Dame. He is author of over fifty works of literary criticism and cultural theory.

U. A. Fanthorpe was an Honorary Fellow of the University of Gloucestershire. She died in April 2009 while this volume was in preparation. 'U. A.' and her partner, the poet and academic Rosie Bailey, enjoyed a close friendship with Peter Widdowson. Her poem in this volume, 'Another "Last Signal"', a tribute to Peter in the voice of Thomas Hardy, was one of her last compositions.

Jo Gill is Lecturer in English at the University of Exeter. She is the author of *Anne Sexton's Confessional Poetics* (2007), *The Cambridge Introduction to Sylvia Plath* (2008) and the editor of *The Cambridge Companion to Sylvia Plath* (2006). Her Ph.D. was supervised at the University of Gloucestershire by Shelley Saguaro and Peter Widdowson.

John Lucas is Professor Emeritus at the Universities of Loughborough and Nottingham Trent. His publications include eight collections of poetry, most recently *Flute Music* (2006). He is the author of monographs on Dickens, Arnold Bennett, John Clare and Robert Browning and of *England and Englishness: Poetry & Nationhood, 1688–1900* (1990) and *The Radical Twenties* (1997).

Philip W. Martin is Professor of Literature and Pro Vice-Chancellor at De Montfort University, and author of *Byron: A Poet before His Public* (1982), *Mad Women in Romantic Writing* (1987), *Reviewing Romanticism* (joint-ed., 1992) and *English: The Condition of the Subject* (ed., 2007). He is an editor of *Literature and History* (since 1989).

Martin Randall is Senior Lecturer in Creative Writing at the University of Gloucestershire. His doctoral thesis on literary representations of the Holocaust was completed in 2005 under the supervision of Peter Widdowson. His book, *9/11 and the Literature of Terror* will be published in 2010 by Edinburgh University Press.

Professor R. C. Richardson began his career in 1968 at Thames Polytechnic where he worked with Peter Widdowson on *Literature and History* (of which he remains the longest serving editor) before moving to what is now the University of Winchester as Head of History in 1977. His publications include *The Debate on the English Revolution* (1998) and *The Changing Face of English Local History* (2000). His *Household Servants in Early Modern England* is forthcoming from Manchester University Press.

Shelley Saguaro is Head of Humanities at the University of Gloucestershire. Her research has had a recent emphasis on post-colonial landscapes. She is the editor of *Psychoanalysis and Woman* (2000) and the author of *Garden Plots: The Politics and Poetics of Gardens* (2006). An article, 'Telling Trees: Eucalyptus,

"Anon" and the Growth of Coevolutionary Histories', is forthcoming in the Canadian journal *Mosaic*.

Judy Simons is Professor of English and Pro Vice-Chancellor at De Montfort University. Her major publications include *Fanny Burney* (1987), *Diaries and Journals of Literary Women from Fanny Burney to Virginia Woolf* (1990), *Rosamond Lehmann* (1992) and *What Katy Read: Feminist Re-Readings of Classic Stories for Girls 1880–1920* (1995), co-authored with Shirley Foster.

Stan Smith holds the Research Chair in Literary Studies at Nottingham Trent University. His publications include studies of W. H. Auden, Edward Thomas and Yeats, as well as *History and Twentieth-Century Poetry* (1982) and the *Origins of Modernism* (1994). Recent books include *The Cambridge Companion to Auden* (2004) and (with Jennifer Birkett), *Right/Left/Right: Revolving Commitments, France and Britain 1929–1950* (2008). His first collection of poems, *Family Fortunes*, was published by Shoestring Press in 2008. Stan's poem for Peter evokes a 30-year intermittent correspondence about parrots following a joke Peter told at a boozy evening at Thames Polytechnic in 1978. No one can now remember the joke.

Peter Widdowson in London, 1984. Photograph taken and submitted by Jane Maxwell

Introduction

Simon Barker and Jo Gill

Literature as History: Essays in Honour of Peter Widdowson takes the retirement of Professor Peter Widdowson from a lifetime of scholarship, teaching, mentoring and enthusiastic debate as an opportunity for a reappraisal of the academic field which, some 40 years ago, he helped to nurture into being. The study of English at universities and colleges throughout the English-speaking world owes a debt to the pioneering work of Widdowson and his contemporaries – many of whom feature, or are acknowledged, in this collection – as they fought to redefine and thereby to open out the discipline.

Literature as History: Essays in Honour of Peter Widdowson seeks to do justice to Peter's work – both in terms of the quality of its contribution to the scholarly field and in terms of its cross-disciplinary and multivocal approach. The chapters that follow represent the work of a range of key contemporary thinkers and focus on the interdisciplinary study of literature and history – exemplified by essays on the history of the discipline of English Studies, the rise of theory and the current state of the field. The main themes of the book are as diverse as Widdowson's own scholarship, ranging from Oedipus and Shakespeare to the representation of the 'servant problem' in the eighteenth century and the poetry of war, to the work of Dickens and Hardy and on again to modernist and twentieth-century writers including Rosamund Lehmann, Edward Thomas and contemporary novelist, Toni Morrison. The unifying theme is the interrelationship between literary or cultural production and its historical moment. The essays in the collection are astute and exciting in terms of their engagement with ever-changing developments in critical and theoretical practice while retaining an invaluable focus on familiar and engaging texts and authors. Each of the contributions owes a debt to Widdowson's work, and each – in its originality, depth and rigour – pays tribute to his example.

Peter Widdowson took his BA in 1964 and his Ph.D. in 1969 at the University of Nottingham. His doctoral thesis was on the poetry and painting of the First World War. In 1968, he became a lecturer in English Literature at the University of Umeå, Sweden, but returned to England in 1971 to take up the post of Head of the Division of English at Thames Polytechnic (now the University of Greenwich). He was Head of the School of English at what is now Middlesex

University from 1986 until 1992 and Head of the School of Historical and Critical Studies at the University of Brighton from 1992 until 1993. In January 1994, he was appointed Professor and Reader in English at the University of Gloucestershire, previously Cheltenham and Gloucester College of Higher Education. Here he was the founder and general editor of The Cyder Press, which continues to publish new scholarly editions and reprints of long out-of-print and little known literary works, especially by writers with local regional connections.

Peter became an honorary Fellow of the English Association (2001) and was for many years a member of the English panel at the Council for National Academic Awards (CNAA). He also served on the national Research Assessment Exercise (RAE) panel for English in 1992 and 1996. He taught in the United States, held a visiting research fellowship at the Australian National University, Canberra, and lectured in various parts of the world for the British Council.

He was a founder editor with Peter Stigant, Roger Richardson and Peter Brooker of the internationally known journal *Literature and History*, the first issue of which came out in March 1975. The initial editorial preface explained that the journal had been 'founded to meet a need, in universities and poly-technics, for self-examination within history and literary studies and for dia-logue between them'. Now in its third series, *Literature and History* is currently published by Manchester University Press. A measure of Peter Widdowson's commitment to English in a range of institutions can be seen in the list of places where he continued to hold External Examining appointments virtually until the time of his retirement. These included the following: the University of Hertfordshire; King Alfred's College, Winchester; the University of Central Lancashire; the University of Sussex; the University of Salford; the University of Leicester; Falmouth College of Arts; the University of Sussex; and the University of Essex. He also examined upwards of 20 doctoral theses.

Peter's contribution to the subject will be remembered most widely by gene-rations of people from their encounters with him as a teacher. As several of the contributors to the 'Personalia' section of this book note, he had a lasting impact on countless undergraduate students. He was hugely successful as a research degree supervisor, and it is significant that this volume includes mate-rial from his former doctoral students, representing the many – including one of the co-editors of this volume – who went on from studying with Peter to gain appointments in the profession that he loved.

Peter's influence has been felt both on a personal level and in terms of his scholarly legacy. His principal areas of academic interest were nineteenth- and twentieth-century fiction (especially contemporary fiction), modernism, Thomas Hardy, literature in history, and contemporary theoretical develop-ments and the current state of 'English Studies'. Among his publications are the following: *E. M. Forster's Howards End: Fiction as History* (Sussex University Press, 1976); (ed.) *Re-Reading English* (Methuen, 1982); (ed.) *Popular Fictions: Essays in Literature and History* (Methuen, 1986); *Hardy in History: A Study in*

Literary Sociology (Routledge, 1989); (ed.) *D. H. Lawrence: A Critical Reader* (Longman, 1992); (ed.) *Tess of the d'Urbervilles: A New Casebook* (Macmillan, 1993); (with Raman Selden) *A Reader's Guide to Contemporary Literary Theory* (3rd edn, Prentice Hall/Harvester Wheatsheaf, 1993 and revised 4th edn with Peter Brooker, 1997); *A Practical Reader in Contemporary Literary Theory* (ed. with Peter Brooker; Prentice Hall/Harvester Wheatsheaf, 1996); a critical edition of *Thomas Hardy: Selected Poetry and Non-Fictional Prose* (Macmillan, 1996); *Thomas Hardy* (Northcote House/British Council, 'Writers and Their Work' series, 1996); a volume of his own essays, *On Thomas Hardy: Late Essays and Earlier* (Macmillan, 1998); *Literature* (Routledge: 'New Critical Idiom', 1999); an essay, 'Thomas Hardy and Critical Theory', in *The Cambridge Companion to Thomas Hardy* (Cambridge University Press, 1999, ed. Dale Kramer); and an introduction and notes for a reprinting of Patrick Hamilton's 1939 novel, *Impromptu in Moribundia* (Trent Editions, Nottingham, 1999).

Among many other essays in books and journals, three professorial lectures appeared as 'Terrorism and Literary Studies' (*Textual Practice*, 1988, 2:1); 'Newstories: Fiction, History and the Modern World' (*Critical Survey*, 1995, 7:1) and 'Editing Readers: The Craft of Literary Studies in the 1990s' (*English*, 1996, 45:182). Later publications included a special issue of *Critical Survey*, 'Poetry in English, 1800–2000', guest-edited by Peter Widdowson in honour of John Lucas (2000); an essay on Graham Swift in *Literature in Context* (ed. Rick Rylance and Judy Simons, Palgrave, 2001); and an article on Toni Morrison's novel *Paradise* in the *Journal of American Studies*, 35 (2001), 2, 313–35. Both his co-edited collection of essays, *Thomas Hardy and Contemporary Literary Studies* (with Tim Dolin; Palgrave – including a long essay by Widdowson on film versions of Hardy) and *The Palgrave Guide to English Literature and Its Contexts, 1500–2000* (a work in timeline form containing individual entries on history, politics, culture and literature for every year since 1500) were published in the spring of 2004, and the revised 5th edition of Selden/Brooker/Widdowson, *A Reader's Guide to Contemporary Literary Theory* in 2005.

'Thomas Hardy Goes Way Down East', an essay on early silent film versions of Hardy's fiction for the volume *Thomas Hardy on Screen*, edited by Terence Wright, was published by Cambridge University Press in 2006, and an essay on 'Contemporary Re-visionary Fiction' appeared in the summer issue of *Textual Practice* the same year. His volume on *Graham Swift* for the 'Writers and Their Work' series (Northcote House) was also published in 2006, as was his revised 2nd edition of *Thomas Hardy* for the same series. An essay on Hardy's short fiction and the late-Victorian literary market-place appears in the *Blackwell Companion to Thomas Hardy* (ed. Keith Wilson, 2009).

Over the course of his long career Peter was always busy. He always worked with a 'clean' desk rather than in the mess characteristic of many academics, but despite appearances there were always many projects being finished, underway or being planned, neatly arranged in folders or cabinets. Yet despite these commitments and his dedication to teaching and other university work, there was also always time in Peter's professional life for the day-to-day traffic of humanity, the 'buzz' (as he once put it) of the institution itself. Peter was on hand to help colleagues with advice and wisdom. In times of trouble he was a comforting but endlessly rational figure in any department, with a prodigious capacity to recall the details of the events in people's lives. He would remember what you said you were doing for the weekend, as well as what you were working on, or if your great aunt was sick. He would also want to tell you about his adventures on holiday or the latest domestic project or a film that he had seen. His enthusiasms were varied, but only seemed meaningful to him once shared with friends and colleagues, and the common ingredient was Peter's humour. In the later years of his career, when he was faced with a series of medical challenges, it would be only minutes before narratives that to most people would bring despair and sonority, were turned into a joke which in turn would become an anecdote.

In spite of his prolific academic accomplishments, Peter has always been able to find time to enjoy other areas of his life – time with his family (children, Patrick, Emily and Tom, grandchildren, Daisy and Ruby, and his wife Jane), pursuits such as home-renovation, walking, gardening and travel, and sharing good food and wine in the company of close friends. Jane has remarked that Peter could have had an alternative career as a football commentator. In 2008 and 2009 he was appointed to an Honorary Fellowship and Emeritus Chair at the University of Gloucestershire, nominations for which came from his colleagues in the Department of Humanities. These, like this book, are the more-than-willing testaments to an inspirational scholar, colleague, mentor and friend.

Part I

Essays in Criticism

Chapter 1

The Poverty of (New) Historicism

Catherine Belsey

I

In the early 1980s two schools of thought faced each other across the Atlantic Ocean. On the one hand, there was the new historicism, sleek, liberal, scholarly and, although an innovation, as its name announced, oddly reassuring; on the other hand, cultural materialism was sometimes awkward, always radical, driven primarily by conviction and determined to upset apple carts. These opposed points of view had come into being more or less independently and they entailed distinct assessments of the English department's agenda. Where they diverged most evidently was in cultural materialism's attention to the institution of English itself and the role of politics in the construction of the discipline. But they overlapped in their concern with the social and cultural context of the fictional work.[1] For both, the text was to be understood as a product of its moment. If cultural materialism also attended to the history of its subsequent reception, they shared, none the less, a commitment to the recognition of historical difference.

Between them, new historicism and cultural materialism have changed the nature of English studies on both sides of the Atlantic. In their wake we have become aware of the continuities between our own work and other areas of the curriculum, most notably history itself, as well as the history of visual culture. Historicism has generated politically aware studies of privilege on the basis of wealth, gender or race. Our knowledge has advanced into more arcane areas of the past, and brought to light obscure and neglected documents once dismissed as ephemeral or unworthy, with the effect of enriching our sense of past cultures. These developments undoubtedly represent major gains. To what extent can we, in consequence, afford to rest on our laurels?

Since the two schools came into existence a generation ago, American new historicism has retained its distinctive identity more sharply than cultural materialism. The British perspective was always more diverse. Where new historicism made its mark first in a monograph, cultural materialism inclined towards the essay form. Stephen Greenblatt's magisterial *Renaissance Self-Fashioning* (1980) focused its attention resolutely on anthropological readings of sixteenth-century works in their context(s); contributors to Peter Widdowson's influential *Re-Reading English* (1982) divided their collective energies between polemical accounts of 'History, Theory, Institutions' and 'Case Studies', the latter consisting mainly of theories of reading, or materialist interpretations of texts from a range of periods.[2] Against all probability, this more dispersed energy has proved remarkably pervasive. Cultural materialism has modified the practices of English departments without ever sinking into an orthodoxy. Instead, it has issued not only in the analysis of texts in history but also in histories of performance, the book, reading and, indeed, the discipline itself, turning the study of English into a wide-ranging cultural criticism so taken for granted that it barely recognizes a debt to the radical departures of three decades ago.

Conversely, after expanding into all periods of literary history, new historicism continues to flourish as separable category. Rooted in American anthropology,[3] the work of Greenblatt and his colleagues was taken up enthusiastically in the United states and then more gradually elsewhere. Perhaps because it is so much easier to define and differentiate,[4] for many scholars in English departments and beyond, new historicism has come to stand as the prevailing model for the historical location of fictional texts at the moment of their production. In those circumstances, and a generation after its inception, it might be valuable to take stock of the story so far, as well as the possibilities for the future. What does new historicism in its current incarnation do? Could it do more? What might it do in due course?

In order to assess the potential for future developments, let us go back to first principles. What is the project of making a historicist reading of a fictional work? I put the question not in order to generate a single definitive answer but rather to lay out the options. In the first instance, I suppose it might be generally agreed, we stand to gain a clearer sense of the text from an understanding of the conditions of its production and the conventions it invokes, as well as its range of conceivable allusions, attitudes, engagements, its likely evasions and moments of self-censorship, the sympathies it can count on and the hostilities it might generate. Its cultural context has explanatory value for the work in all these ways; a good sense of cultural history means better criticism.

But second, historicism also opens up the possibility of perceiving a relationship between a text and its background that might include difference, as well as the obvious resemblances. We can do more, in other words, than read off from the context what the work is likely to be saying. One slightly dispiriting impression it was possible to take away from the old historicism, with its *Elizabethan World Pictures* and *Discarded Images*, was that, sharing so much common ground, all the written texts of the period in question said the same thing again and again. Any given writer, it implied, must be read as taking a particular line because everyone else was. The history of fiction might be seen as supporting the exact opposite. In practice, fiction does not necessarily follow slavishly the fashions of its own time. On the contrary, it might intervene in its moment with a plea for a radical departure, the construction of a utopian vision or, indeed, an appeal to nostalgia, demonstrating that beyond the limitations of conventional thinking in the period a specific work may glimpse alternatives to its own present, if only in fantasy, if only for the duration, if only, precisely, as fiction.

Of course, any text might put forward an oppositional view, especially a political pamphlet, say, or a religious tract. And yet I think fiction represents a special case. Fiction offers a space where anything can happen. In self-proclaimed *tales* animals talk, magic spells work, the dead return, space ships travel the galaxies. Fiction allows pigs to fly, and this is so even in periods when the conventions of realism are at their most rigorous, most binding. The Victorians, for instance, who demanded in their stories the utmost fidelity to what might actually happen and deplored even coincidence as improbable, loved ghost stories and the Gothic – and not only in down-market genres. There are ghosts in Charles Dickens, as well as Emily Brontë and Henry James. Better still, when two conventions come into collision, rules are necessarily broken and the unexpected is free to make an appearance. As an example, I think of Shakespeare's comic heroines, girl-boys who move easily between genders, sometimes within a single speech. An emergent mimesis comes up against the all-male stage and, in the circumstances, cross-dressing offers an elegant solution, with the possible concomitant of cross-identification. But the resulting release of possibilities on the stage seems to run way ahead of real-life cross-dressed women, roaring girls like Mary Frith and Long Meg of Westminster, who enlivened the London social scene in the early modern period. Arguably, the plays also outdo in subtlety and flexibility our own most advanced theoretical accounts of gender as performative.

While fiction may, of course, confirm the existing convictions, it can also, then, project a vision that is in certain respects out of step with its moment. Geoffrey Chaucer's familiarity with the writings of the European Renaissance, for instance, meant his own poetry imported new values into the London of Richard II. In that sense fiction, not alone but most particularly, is capable, we might want to say, of anachronism. Or is it? Is such anachronism literally possible? Our readings, we recognize, made in the present, can certainly be anachronistic, bringing the perspectives of an unrelated epoch to bear on the historical text. But is any work, however eccentric, genuinely at odds with its own chronological moment? Don't we, instead, expect to stretch our understanding of the culture concerned to accommodate the texts it generates, however wayward?

If, in other words, culture not only forms the context but includes the work of fiction itself, that work can require us to complicate our image of the culture in question. If imagination is not distinct from society but a component of it, our model of culture itself will be one that allows incompatible perceptions to coexist in a heterogeneity that embraces the alternatives imagination invents. Shakespeare's cross-dressed heroines register a resistance to the constraints imposed by polarized early modern gender roles; Victorian ghosts point to the perceived limitations of nineteenth-century orthodoxy, whether religious or scientific. When fiction is understood as playing its part in the construction of culture, text and context become relative terms, shifting to localize one another according to the questions we ask of them, and the fictional text is acknowledged as able to be differentially constitutive for the culture of which it is also the outcome.

In this analysis, the interests of literary criticism and cultural history begin to converge. When fiction comes into its own as a constituent of culture and not just its proudest product, the more nuanced cultural history that results has a wider explanatory value when it comes to other fictional texts. In a feedback effect, the inclusion of fiction leads to better cultural history, which leads in turn to better criticism.

II

I am not sure how far the prevailing new historicism acknowledges this second feedback option. New historicists are notoriously economical with expositions of what they are setting out to do, stoutly maintaining (and with some justification) that they are practitioners, not theorists.[5] In one eloquent exception, however, Stephen Greenblatt's essay on 'The Circulation of Social Energy' promises to explain the cultural 'exchanges' that make Shakespeare's theatre possible. In the event, however, it turns out that these exchanges are effectively all one way: the stage borrows, appropriates, acquires and purchases stories, properties, references and modes of signification from the culture it inhabits. True, it reinvests them. But what it returns is no more than the emotions they generate in heightened form. Although he challenges the belief that fiction *does no more than* hold the mirror up to nature, Greenblatt's account of the relationship between the theatre and the world brings us back to a version of the text as no more than the reflection (with an added intensification of feeling) of meanings that are already to be found elsewhere.[6]

No place here, then, for the feedback effect that, treating fiction as constitutive, would lead to a more differential cultural history and a correspondingly more sophisticated criticism. My hopes of a reciprocal account of the relation between text and context were raised, however, when I came across the following observation in James Shapiro's widely acclaimed and prize-winning book, *1599: A Year in the Life of William Shakespeare*, published in 2005: 'it's no more possible to talk about Shakespeare's plays independently of his age than it is to grasp what his society went through without the benefit of Shakespeare's insights.' Here, perhaps, was something of the mutual disclosure I looked for: the times throwing light on the fiction and the fiction expanding our sense of the times. But again it turned out that the role of the stage was confined to condensing what was already there in its cultural world. 'He and his fellow players', Shapiro goes on, 'truly were, in Hamlet's fine phrase, the "abstract and brief chronicles of the time"'.[7]

Reflection theory seems pervasive in new historicist writing. Does it matter? I think it might. If all they do is reflect meanings and values determined outside them, the plays have no real life of their own: the new historicist project is to see the connection with their moment at the expense of their differences from it. And gradually, as so often in new historicist writing, the texts come to seem less exciting than the culture that produced them. When he brings to life Shakespeare's age, Shapiro does not disappoint: as social history, *1599* is a good and lively read. But the chapters on the plays seem curiously flat by comparison. Take *As You Like It*, for example. With one or two minor exceptions, Shapiro's account of this comedy could have been written at any time in the course of the past 150 years. The play shows, he maintains, how the wrestler Orlando moves under Rosalind's tuition from self-indulgent romance to mature and mutual love. We get an assessment of Rosalind's 'character' (intelligent, witty, capable of strong feelings) and an assurance that in her care Orlando learns to surrender sterile poetry for 'genuine intimacy'.[8]

This reading ignores the play's rapid transformations of its cross-dressed protagonist from sceptical lad to woman in love and back, and with them the sparkling alternations between cynicism and sexiness that challenge the audience to choose and choose again between attitudes to marriage. Instead, Shakespeare's disarming exposure of the many faces of courtship is replaced in Shapiro's account by a mass-market romance, where a rugged hero is taught to be worthy of winning the heroine. And popular romance, as we know, simply reduces to a formula the outlines of the Victorian novel (*Jane Eyre* or *Adam Bede* without the edgy bits). I should dearly love to see evidence that 'genuine intimacy' was an intelligible category in 1599.

I am reminded of a similar disappointment when it came to Greenblatt's curiously prim *Twelfth Night*, which toys with the question of gender only to conclude with the triumph of nature in heterosexual marriage.[9] Indeed, Victorian values seem to play a large part in the new historicist practice of interpretation and often in surprising places. At first glance, Greenblatt's interpretation of *Othello* looks very new and very much of its own moment in the Civil Rights movement. It puts race at the centre of the play and blames an oppressive society. European values have superimposed on Othello's passionate nature a prohibition of erotic pleasure that generates a 'deep current of sexual anxiety'.[10] And yet Greenblatt's protagonist here bears an uncanny resemblance to A. C. Bradley's. In 1904 Bradley proposed that Othello is left at the mercy of his own vehement passions by his ignorance of European women and his vulnerability to 'the corrupt products of civilised life'.[11] On the eve of modernism, at the culminating moment of the Victorian novel, Bradley assumed that all fiction aspired to the condition of psychological realism. In his account of Shakespearean tragedy, character is destiny and the protagonist's fall is dictated by his own tragic flaw. Greenblatt makes the anxiety that destroys the black hero the explicit effect of racial oppression, but he locates the source of the tragedy in the same strong feelings, the same status as outsider. His main change, in other words, amounts to updating the psychology and the social values.

III

Criticism as character study is not confined to Greenblatt's early work. A century after Bradley's book first appeared, psychological realism continues to feature widely in Greenblatt's biography of Shakespeare, *Will in the World*, published in 2004. But in case we see its prominence there as a concession to popular taste, the more scholarly *Hamlet in Purgatory*, published in 2001, also continues the Romantic tradition of blaming a 'corrosive inwardness' for delaying the prince in his obligation to kill Claudius.[12] While purgatory is depicted with great energy and conviction, the play has not substantially changed in consequence. Like the Victorians, Greenblatt identifies tragedy with psychological weakness and, conflating Hamlet's antic disposition, as they did, with the hero's own deepest convictions, gives us a protagonist who is very disturbed indeed.[13] He can act only when he lets go of the mourning process. And for good measure, Greenblatt adds some equally Victorian biographical speculation. Perhaps Shakespeare himself is here coming to terms with bereavement.[14]

This retreat into character and biography as explanation may be symptomatic. The newness of new historicism depended on the rejection of the prevailing models: on the one hand, the old historicism typified by the work of C. S. Lewis and E. M. W. Tillyard; and on the other, New Criticism, the 'close-grained formalism', as Greenblatt puts it, that revealed the work of art as a free-standing unity, a *Verbal Icon* or a *Well Wrought Urn*.[15] Forswearing both approaches, and effectively turning its back on the French theory that would have permitted another kind of close attention to textuality, new historicism had no obvious place to turn to for a critical model. If criticism does not simply happen in a magical, self-authorizing encounter between two psyches, we read in the light of the options we know. When it abjured both existing approaches, new historicism left itself open to whatever was available, even if that meant regressing to the habits of the nineteenth century.

The interpretation of Shakespeare from a Victorian perspective can only be seen, however, as radically *un*historicist. Historicism inevitably confronts the difficulty that we read from our own moment and in the light of current knowledges. We have no alternative: despite our most heroic efforts, we cannot entirely shed what we know to make another epoch fully present. But reading early modern drama in the twenty-first century through a nineteenth-century filter is only likely to push it further away. No wonder fiction has nothing to tell us in the present about its own epoch if the glass brought to bear on it has the effect of filtering out both its moment and ours.

In the specific case of Shapiro's Victorian *As You Like It*, while in this reading the play *adds* nothing I can detect to our understanding of early modern culture, it also seems to *owe* curiously little to the context that generated it. That context largely excludes Shakespeare's reading. It happens, for example, that a new and handsome folio edition of Chaucer had appeared the previous year, edited by Thomas Speght. Shakespeare, we know, admired his English predecessor and borrowed from him extensively. It is at least arguable that the influence was more pervasive than we have previously allowed, and that one aspect of it surfaced in three of the plays first performed in 1599. Is it possible that Chaucer's Geoffrey, forever slightly bemused, wide-eyed, out of his depth, and able by that very means to bring out aspects of his situation just as if they spoke for themselves, reappears in another guise as a succession of Shakespearean Williams, whose imperturbability throws into relief the eccentricity of *their* surroundings?

If so, Shakespeare was not above learning from the most theatrical of English poets a technique for inviting the audience to judge apparently for themselves, without the moralizing intervention of another character or the author himself in his own voice. As Charlie Chaplin also knew, a figure of fun who is the artist's own ironic persona constitutes more than a good joke: this innocent abroad throws into relief the absurdity of a world that treats guilelessness with contempt.[16]

IV

Shapiro's *1599* does not mention Speght's Chaucer or the possibility that Shakespeare learned from it. No doubt that would be source study, which Greenblatt, with whatever irony, once designated 'the elephants' graveyard of literary history'.[17] New historicism was never much interested in what writers were reading or the techniques they might have acquired in the process. Those formal features that constitute an author's repertoire of possibilities are inevitably a matter of indifference from a perspective that works mainly across distinct genres. The travellers' tales and merchants' reports that generate the anecdotes which enable new historicists to find their way into the fictional texts come from another part of the generic forest entirely. In consequence, the connections adduced, with whatever ingenuity, are largely thematic. Questions of form do not arise; the properties of genre – vocabulary, register, syntax, prosody, structure – all go the way of intertextuality itself.

If I'm right, the new historicist project is impoverished from the beginning by the neglect of its richest resource. Confined by anthropology to the quest for cultural homogeneity, it barely concedes the specificity of fiction, except as intensifying mirror; reacting against formalism, it all but ignores the features that define the difference of the text, the characteristics that would allow an insight into the complexity of its cultural moment. The understanding of cultural history can only be deepened by the disciplined analysis of fiction as a component of the culture that also produced it. Roland Barthes might have been anticipating the problem half a century ago, when he urged, 'Less terrorized by the spectre of "formalism", historical criticism might have been less sterile', adding, 'a little formalism turns one away from History, but . . . a lot brings one back to it'.[18]

The context of Barthes's observation makes clear that formal analysis is not to be confused with an aesthetic appreciation which holds the work of art aloft for admiring contemplation. Oddly enough, new historicism is by no means free from misty affirmations of 'wonder' in the face of fictional texts that have demonstrated a special intensity or an exceptional capacity for survival.[19] Thus revered, works of fiction come closer to New Criticism's free-standing verbal icons and well-wrought urns than we have been led to expect. Is this insistent veneration for the work of art a reaction against yet another critical school, this time new historicism's contemporary and rival, cultural materialism, with its rigorous interrogation of all value judgements? Even where value is in the end reaffirmed, cultural materialism has called for explicit criteria that can be assessed and contextualized. A proper respect for fiction's power to compel is no more than its due; I am inclined to share it. But reverence is no substitute for a close attention to the signifying practices that constitute the inscription of meaning.

Originating, ironically, in departments devoted to the study of literature, new historicism offers us fiction approached from a perspective that belongs neither to its own period nor to the present of the critic. The consequence is a cultural history which brings vividly to life out-of-the-way instances of social attitudes at the expense of the fiction that is capable of defining the values of the society in their most complex incarnation. Even where they do not overtly challenge existing values in the ways I have suggested, made-up stories not only invite their audiences to side with what they identify as virtue against vice, heroism against villainy: they also show how far these seeming opposites may encroach on one another's territory, facing the protagonist with dilemmas which, in extreme cases, are resolved in comedy by good fortune and in tragedy by death. What happens when love comes into conflict with money? What is the outcome when a rural community confronts the implications of industrialization? What ought to be done when a ghost demands murder in the name of filial piety? A culture that exposes such *un*certainties is intelligible in its internal differences. And if the issues are historically specific, they throw into relief one resemblance between past and present: earlier societies have been no less divided or ambivalent, no less heterogeneous than our own.

To understand the ways fiction represents such dilemmas, we surely need to exploit all the skills of reading and the critical resources that are or ought to be the special expertise of departments of English. Attitudes and values are inscribed in fine differences of vocabulary, register, syntax, rhyme, rhythm, precisely the concerns that are so readily bracketed when the common ground between distinct genres is no more than their content. Our success in locating the text in its culture depends on what we understand to be its mode of address. How does it invite an audience to assess what its characters say? Does the work produce the perspicuity and coherence it seems to seek, or are there moments when it inscribes a more ambiguous, more refractory world picture? Are there times when it recoils from the task of interpreting human interaction, or when it touches the outer edges of genre or the limits of language itself? And, beyond these imponderables, how do we define fiction? Are Shakespeare's Sonnets, for example, best read as the true record of actual events or as a radical experiment in a familiar form? These questions are not easily answered but they call on what critics do best. Taken into account, they lead to a mode of reading attentive to the twists and turns of the fictional text and one that is always ready to be surprised at the difference between text and context. Formal analysis allows us to recognize how far the work is out of step with orthodoxy to the degree that it 'permits the text to emerge as ideology's . . . interlocutor, rather than as its example'.[20]

Am I, then, proposing the replacement of historicism by the close-grained formalism the new historicists themselves have been so eager to supersede? Not if formalism isolates the text for veneration as an autonomous and timeless unity. We need history – not only in order to make sense of the texts but because it brings home to us the relativity of our own attitudes and values. Cultural history historicizes the present as well as the past; and in the process of developing an awareness of diachronic cultural difference, it also has the capacity to attune us to the synchronic implications of cultural distinctions in the globalized contemporary world. By exactly the same token, in order to understand our own moment, we need to take account of the distinct histories of empire, slavery and sexual oppression that historicist work has so resolutely fostered.

If, then, we are to read historically, we shall require a sense of linguistic change in order to know what the words mean; for that purpose, ideally we should be steeped in the texts of the period in question; at the same time, we should certainly know everything we can about how people lived and what went on; there is no doubt that we do well to come to terms with the distinctive values of the epoch that produced the work. But none of that is any substitute for a mode of interpretation that is, or ought to be, more difficult than either reading off from history what the text might be expected to say or, alternatively, retreating into ways of understanding and affirmations of admiration that have their roots in the nineteenth century.

My contention is simply that, whatever our motive for reading, or whatever histories we set out to construct, we shall do so more effectively if we interpret more skilfully. Of course, any number of heroic individuals have never abandoned the attention to form. They are the exception that proves the rule. My anxiety concerns the prevailing new historicist model that seems to me to privilege context over text. Text and context, I have suggested, are exchangeable. In my view, closer attention to the formal properties of fiction means better cultural history, which leads to better criticism, which leads to better cultural history. That history is inscribed in stories and poems at least as fully as it is elsewhere. Perhaps in due course a historically attuned criticism will come to do it more widespread justice.

Notes

[1] I have opted to identify the primary material of the discipline as fiction, in order to avoid the value judgements inscribed in 'literature' (or 'Literature'), as these are laid out by Peter Widdowson in *Literature* (London: Routledge, 1999), 1–92.

[2] Where Greenblatt's book marks the emergence of new historicism, the development of cultural materialism is harder to date, but early instances would include the collected papers from the Essex conferences, the first of these published as *Literature, Society and the Sociology of Literature*, ed. Francis Barker et al. (Colchester: University of Essex, 1977). A number of journals were involved in the debates at about that time, including *Screen, Ideology and Consciousness, m/f* and *Literature and History*. The phrase 'cultural materialism', duly attributed to Raymond Williams, was first used as defining in the subtitle of *Political Shakespeare*, ed. Jonathan Dollimore and Alan Sinfield (Manchester: Manchester University Press, 1985).

[3] I have argued that the new historicist debt to Foucault has been greatly exaggerated ('Historicizing New Historicism', *Presentist Shakespeares*, ed. Hugh Grady and Terence Hawkes (London: Routledge, 2007), 27–45).

[4] And also, no doubt, because, since most of the 'international' journals are in practice American, the United States plays a major part in setting the academic agenda.

[5] See, for example, Stephen J. Greenblatt, *Learning to Curse: Essays in Early Modern Culture* (New York: Routledge, 1990), 146–60. See also Catherine Gallagher and Stephen Greenblatt, *Practicing New Historicism* (Chicago: University of Chicago Press, 2000), 1–2, 18.

[6] Stephen Greenblatt, *Shakespearean Negotiations: The Circulation of Social Energy in Renaissance England* (Oxford: Clarendon Press, 1988), 1–20.

[7] James Shapiro, *1599: A Year in the Life of William Shakespeare* (London: Faber and Faber, 2005), xv–xvi.

[8] Shapiro, *1599*, 241–2, 232.

[9] Greenblatt, *Shakespearean Negotiations*, 66–93.

[10] Stephen Greenblatt, *Renaissance Self-Fashioning: From More to Shakespeare* (Chicago: University of Chicago Press, 1980), 250.

[11] A. C. Bradley, *Shakespearean Tragedy* (London: Macmillan, 1957), 154.

[12] Stephen Greenblatt, *Hamlet in Purgatory* (Princeton, NJ: Princeton University Press, 2001), 208.

[13] See also 'The Mousetrap', in Gallagher and Greenblatt, *Practicing New Historicism*, 136–62.

[14] As is Greenblatt himself, he tells us, in writing this book about the play.

[15] Greenblatt, *Shakespearean Negotiations*, 3, 95.

[16] See Catherine Belsey, 'William and Geoffrey', *Shakespeare without Boundaries: Essays in Honor of Dieter Mehl*, ed. Christa Jansohn, Lena Cowen Orlin, and Stanley Wells (Newark: University of Delaware Press, forthcoming).

[17] In an earlier version of 'Shakespeare and the Exorcists', *Shakespeare and the Question of Theory*, ed. Patricia Parker and Geoffrey Hartman (New York: Methuen, 1985), 163–87, 163. Greenblatt's admirers may have taken the comment too literally: *Hamlet in Purgatory* studies the sources of Shakespeare's play.

[18] Roland Barthes, *Mythologies* [1957], trans. Annette Lavers (London: Cape, 1972), 112.

[19] See, for example, Greenblatt, *Shakespearean Negotiations*, 127–8; *Learning to Curse*, 161–83.

[20] Ellen Rooney, 'Form and Contentment', *Modern Language Quarterly*, 61 (2000), 17–40, 34.

Chapter 2

Re-Reading English, Re-Reading Modernism

Helen Carr

In 1982, when *Re-Reading English*, Peter Widdowson's first edited collection, appeared, Margaret Thatcher had been in office for three years.[1] No one, as far as I remember, guessed how long she would remain there, but the support engendered that year when her armada won back the Falklands ensured that the left would not, as had been hoped, rapidly be rid of her. The 1980s were to be a decade of fiercely oppositional politics, both in the wider social scene and in the academic literary world; the miners' strike, the Wapping disputes, the growth of Militant, Section 28, the rise and fall of the Greater London Council were all happening as the so-called theory wars, between a predominantly young, left-wing generation and the more established traditionalists, were in stormy process in the country's departments of English Literature. Not that the left was unified, either in or out of the academy, and its different groupings spoke very different political languages. I remember during the miners' strike, when the University of Essex students and staff welcomed picketing miners from neighbouring Wivenhoe on to the campus, a feminist meeting was organized to explain to the miners why they shouldn't say 'hello, love' to women entering the student bar; I was a very part-time Ph.D. student then, and not at the meeting, though sometimes in the student bar, but reports suggested that it ended in mutual non-comprehension. It didn't seem to make much difference to what happened in the bar. Of course, there was a certain sector of the left within the academy who felt that women's issues were a distraction from the class struggle (I remember one of Peter's colleagues at Thames Polytechnic, a stalwart of the Socialist Workers Party, explaining this to me at some length).[2] Many male left-wing academics were indifferent to much more blatant examples of sexist language than 'hello, love', which happily no one seems to object to any more. Yet in broad terms, in the wide-reaching changes which were occurring in the discipline of English, and which *Re-Reading English* both charted and influenced, issues of class, gender and race would all shape the new terrain of English studies.

Many of the questions that were raised in *Re-Reading English* had been debated in *Literature and History*, the journal that Peter, along with Peter Brooker,

Paul Stigant and R. C. Richardson, had started at Thames Polytechnic in 1975. Signs of change in the discipline of English, in fact, had become increasingly evident since *Literature and History*'s first issue appeared. Jonathan Culler's *Structuralist Poetics* was published in 1975, Terry Eagleton's *Marxism and Literary Criticism* as well as his *Criticism and Ideology* in 1976, and Methuen launched their New Accents series in 1977, in which *Re-Reading English* would be published, leading off with Terence Hawkes' *Structuralism and Semiotics*, and introducing the student world, and many academics, to the heady excitement of this French-inflected, left-wing criticism. Elaine Showalter had published *A Literature of Their Own* in 1977, and Edward Said's *Orientalism* appeared in 1978; feminist theory and, as it would later be called, post-colonial studies, would gradually make their way into the academy. Works by Derrida, Foucault, Barthes, Lacan and Benjamin were appearing in paperback translation, and by 1982 British Althusserianism had come and gone; the polemic launched against it by E. P. Thompson's 1978 *Poverty of Theory* and his conviction of the unflagging opposition of 'theory' and 'history' was the subject of a symposium in *Literature and History* in the autumn of 1979. The symposium itself (to which Terry Eagleton, Alison Assiter and Gregor McLennan contributed, Assiter memorably commenting that the 'mole-hill – Althusserianism – crumbles under the mountainous weight of Thompson's invective') was preceded by an editorial note which said it was to be seen as the 'beginning of what needs to become a sustained and continuous debate about "Literature" "History" and "Theory"'.[3]

The first time many people heard of 'Theory', largely then in the guise of 'Structuralism', was when the dissension about the appointment of Colin MacCabe broke out at the University of Cambridge in 1980. Yet in fact the interest in French theory or feminism or what would later be called post-colonial issues developed in the 1970s largely in the new universities introduced in the 1960s, or in the polytechnics, or in extramural or adult classes. At the time that Peter's book appeared, I was still a new and green spectator of the various controversies that were gripping the discipline, but because of the particular institutions with which I was in touch, I found myself in the maelstrom of some of the changes that were occurring. I had been a late returner to higher education, only enrolling for an MA when my second child started at school, having taken my BA in the 1960s in a securely Leavisite English Department. While the children were small I had taught University of London extramural classes in literature, which I loved doing, and which I always felt was my real education. The most ground-breaking areas of the London extramural department then were in women's history, with pioneers such as Sheila Rowbottham and Sally Alexander opening up the field, and film studies, a new and exciting area in itself, which introduced its students to semiotics and Lacanian psychoanalysis. The literature tutors were deeply split over the possible introduction of new ideas, with an old guard denouncing any kind of theorizing that interfered with their well-tried teaching practices, and a younger generation eager at least to find out about what was going on, and the department obligingly put on

training sessions in structuralism and post-structuralism. In 1982, having moved
on from my MA to a Ph.D. at the University of Essex, I discovered the very
influential Sociology of Literature conferences, which had been running since
the late 1970s. I was also teaching part-time in the English division at Thames
Polytechnic (now the University of Greenwich), where Peter Widdowson was
then Head, and where several of the contributors to *Re-Reading English* also
worked; at Thames, the new ideas were not simply something on which
academics wrote research papers, but were incorporated into the syllabus, and
I was able to teach feminist literary criticism, which must have been very rare
in those days.

   Now that we have reached a period when books are published with names
like *life. after. theory*, or indeed simply *After Theory*, one might ask what was the
legacy of that period of black leather jackets, bitter dissension between Marxists
and post-structuralists, and wave after wave of French theory. What happened
in the 1980s has been interpreted in very disparate ways. I was discussing the
period recently with someone who went up to Cambridge in 1980 to see at first
hand as a first-year undergraduate the vicious wrangling over Colin MacCabe's
appointment, or non-appointment; he insisted to me that the 'theory wars'
were all about jobs. I would not agree in any simple way, but they were certainly
at one level a power struggle which would determine which people's work
would accumulate symbolic capital (to invoke Bourdieu), and the possession of
such symbolic capital would inevitably and intimately affect their employment
chances. The Leavisite revolution (by 1980 the bourgeois literary criticism
denounced by Marxist critics) had been, as Francis Mulhern had by then already
made clear, the ascendancy of a largely lower-middle-class group of critics (*petit
bourgeois* as he puts it) at the expense of the gentleman scholar, as well as the
establishment of the primacy of the Leavisite mode of literary criticism at the
expense of both *belles-lettres* literary writing and the philological study of literary
texts.[4] At one level, what was going on in the 1980s could be described as a challenge to the hegemony of an established white male Oxbridge, or Oxbridge-
educated, scholarly elite by young critics from the polytechnics and the new
universities, by women and non-whites. (Though given one of the leading figures, Terry Eagleton, was at Oxford, even that is an overgeneralization.) But
to see the embrace of theory only in terms of career enhancement would be to
return to a version of vulgar Marxism, or indeed vulgar Capitalist cynicism, that
the 1980s wanted to leave behind. When I started teaching courses on feminist
literary criticism at Thames, I certainly had no thought that that might make
me more employable in the future, though, now I come to think about it, in the
end it probably did. Reading again the left-wing literary criticism of the early
1980s, as I have been doing to write this article, it is true that some of the
denunciations of bourgeois attitudes by indubitably bourgeois academics now
seem irresistibly comic – though, indeed, they often seemed quite comic at the
time. But perhaps even more, what can seem woefully dated in its rhetoric is
the application of a nineteenth-century model of a society divided solely by

class, when even then divisions of ethnicity, race, gender and sexuality were making such an analysis inadequate, as feminist, black and proto-post-colonial critics were already pointing out. Indeed, what one could argue is undoubtedly the legacy of those years is the way the canon has been transformed since the 1970s: women's writing, post-colonial literature, diasporic writing, popular fiction, comic books, all are now taught in higher education, and all are the subject of literary criticism.

Something else that could be said to come out of those turbulent 1980s was a renewed awareness of the multiplicity of possible critical viewpoints, as well as of their implicit and explicit politics, an awareness which Peter Widdowson's work did much to encourage. Following that call in 1979 in *Literature and History* for a debate about 'Literature', 'History' and 'Theory', the next year Peter published an article there titled '"Literary Value" and the Reconstruction of Criticism'. Looking back at it now, one can see that it pointed, not only to the way in which Peter's own work would develop, but to significant developments in the discipline as a whole. Among other things, he called for more work on the history of the rise of English studies, criticism that read literary texts in their 'historical and ideological contexts', analysis of the way those perceived as major authors are 'produced' for readers and students (one thinks of his own book on *Hardy in History*), and the study of contemporary and subliterary writing and its cultural impact.[5] Both the reading of texts in their historical and intellectual contexts (even if the word 'ideology' is now unlikely to be evoked) and the expansion of the critical field to include the contemporary are central features of English studies today, but here I want to look at Peter's emphasis on what one might call historicized metacritical analysis, the attempt to understand the historical and political matrices out of which critical attitudes emerge. Such analysis has been important to his own work, and in addition has again been a productive strand in literary criticism; in the rest of this article I want to make some observations on this 'metacriticism', and relate it to some of the re-readings of modernism that would emerge later in the decade.

Many of the essays in *Re-Reading English* were concerned with 'metacriticism' in one way or another, most directly the opening one by Brian Doyle, on 'The Hidden History of English Studies'. The story of emergence of 'English' has since then been more fully charted, both by further work from those involved with *Re-Reading English* and by others.[6] The next year, 1983, saw the publication of Terry Eagleton's *Literary Theory*, with a chapter titled, 'The Rise of English Studies', and Chris Baldick's *The Social Mission of English Criticism, 1848–1932*, which traced the development, from Arnold to the Leavises, of the idea of the study of literature as a humanizing and civilizing force, mapping its history, from the nineteenth-century view of English literature as particularly fitted for training women, artisans and colonial subjects to absorb the culture of their betters, to the Leavisite conviction that, taught in the right terms, English would produce a cultural 'counter-elite' that would be, as Baldick puts it in the title of one of his chapters, 'Armed Against the Herd'.[7] The teaching of English literature as a tool of colonialism was investigated in more detail in Gauri Viswanathan's *Masks of Conquest: Literary Study and British Rule in India* (1990), and in Robert Crawford's *Devolving English Literature* (1992), which moved the promotion of the study of English Literature as a civilizing instrument back to the eighteenth century, and north to Scotland, in the wake of the Act of Union of 1707, claiming that as a university subject English Literature was a 'Scottish invention'.[8] More generally, the way the canon that was in place in the 1970s had been framed by gender, class, racial, nationalist and colonialist assumptions was widely critiqued, as were the terms in which those texts had been interpreted. Such a critique had in fact been mounted by feminists since Kate Millett's *Sexual Politics* in 1969, and a different kind of questioning of accepted judgements had begun even earlier in post-colonial rewritings of major literary texts, such as Chinua Achebe's *Things Fall Apart* and Jean Rhys's *Wide Sargasso Sea*. It is perhaps a striking example of the repeated re-readings of those years that in 1966, when Rhys's reworking of Charlotte Brontë's novel appeared, *Jane Eyre*, though widely read, was in fact by and large critically dismissed, along with the rest of her work, as too 'mawkish' and melodramatic for serious study; Emily was quite another case, and was one of the only three women writers taught on my university course, at any rate outside the medieval period, the other two being Jane Austen and George Eliot. 'It is tempting to retort', Leavis says in a note on the 'Brontës', 'that there is only one Brontë', and it was in fact an early feminist critic, Kate Millett, who used the word 'mawkish' of Charlotte's writings; the only one of Charlotte's novels in which either Leavis or Millett can find anything to praise is not *Jane Eyre* but *Villette*.[9] During the 1970s *Jane Eyre* was reclaimed as a feminist classic, most notably in Sandra Gilbert and Susan Gubar's *tour de force* of 1979, *The Madwoman in the Attic*, where it provided the book's central organizing image, only to have its exemplary status called in question again in 1985 in Gayatri Spivak's analysis of its colonialist assumptions in the light of the critique in Rhys's novel.[10]

The Brontës had earlier been subject to more than one Marxist analysis, one of the striking facts of the left-wing criticism of the early 1980s being that there was so much more political critique of the ideological shortcomings of well meaning nineteenth-century liberal or at least socially concerned texts than of the deeply dubious right-wing attitudes of many modernist writers.[11] By the end of the decade this would have markedly changed, but, in spite of a series of critiques, and notwithstanding the emergence of post-modernism in the United States, and of the undoubtedly anti-modernist Movement in Britain, the high prestige of modernist poetics and poets that had been established before the Second World War still remained to a large extent unquestioned in academic literary criticism.[12] As early as 1932, T. S. Eliot's pre-eminent position among contemporary poets had been uncompromisingly asserted by Leavis in his *New Bearings in English Poetry*, and grudgingly conceded by Sir Paul Harvey's much more gentlemanly *Oxford Companion to English Literature*. Pound and Eliot had quite self-consciously set out to be the arbiters of good literature in the place of what Pound referred to in 1912 as 'the appalling fungus of our "better magazines"', and as Gail McDonald has convincingly shown, their campaign against the way literature had been taught in American universities played an important part in determining how the subject was taught in the academy for many decades, particularly by the New Critics.[13] The modernists' own tale of their emergence, which was repeated, with varying nuances, first by traditional and later by post-structuralist critics, was the story of the heroic break from Victorian sentimentality and convention, a break that was signalled by a 'revolution in poetic language', in Kristeva's phrase, the use of experimental techniques which guaranteed the work's worth. The reactionary politics of some high modernists were largely ignored: even the storm over Pound and the Bollingen Prize in 1949 could be said only to have highlighted the acceptance of a hermetic seal between poetry and politics. The value, one might almost say the correctness, of the modernist aesthetic continued to be accepted by critics on the right and on the left. For the right, the aesthetic placed the work beyond politics: for some at least on the left, the aesthetic was a sufficient politics in itself. In *Re-Reading English*, one contributor quoted approvingly Herbert Read's comment that 'the true revolutionary artist today is not any artist with a Marxist ideology; it is the good artist with a revolutionary technique.'[14] As late as 1985, a left-wing post-structuralist critic writing in *Literature and History* could say of Pound's *Cantos*: 'They do contain some mid-Western anti-Semitic right-wing hysteria but only at the superficial level of conscious opinion: their actual operation as text is mainly progressive.'[15] By some alchemy, Pound's avant-garde form purged his political intentions, turned fascist dross to literary gold.

The version of modernism in place in those years was, as Bonnie Kime Scott would make clear in her 1990 compilation *The Gender of Modernism*, a deeply masculinist one, both in terms of tone and in the choice of the writers who merited inclusion. Even Virginia Woolf, now the subject of a vast critical industry, only began to be recuperated in the later 1970s, and someone like H. D. rather later. (Woolf's work had been dismissed by Leavis as 'the equivalent of Georgian poetizing', therefore quite the opposite of the 'new bearings' in literature that he admired.)[16] Many male modernists, like Pound, Hulme and Lewis, had indeed been very consciously macho, anxious to escape from the charge of effeminacy that clung to writers and artists in the wake of the aesthetes, especially after Wilde's disgrace. Pound always abused his enemies in the 'better magazines' in the most misogynist of terms; the editor of the *Atlantic Review* was a 'male hen', and others he referred to more generally as the 'little old ladies, male and female, of the aged editorial offices'.[17] Hulme demanded a newly 'virile' poetry, and began to have doubts about Bergson when he realized how many women attended his lectures.[18] Eliot's magisterial and elegant prose, his emphasis on restraint and control, offered a very different kind of masculine authority, but one no less clearly gendered. This uncompromising masculinity undoubtedly appealed to the still mainly male critical world of the mid-century, anxious to dispel the widespread view of English as a women's subject, though the chief exemplum of masculine vigour from the modernism era that Leavis came to embrace, so to speak, was not Pound or Hulme but Lawrence; in particular, as Chris Baldick points out, the Leavises strove to 'elevate the heterosexually "fecund" Lawrence against the reviled homosexual W. H. Auden'.[19] Leavis by now was less enamoured at least of Eliot's critical work, and saw Lawrence in his great tradition of largely nineteenth-century writers, one reason perhaps why the focus of re-reading was often there. Yet more generally, the followers of Leavis in postwar literature departments, which were also shaped by versions of New Criticism, could line up their tough-minded, rigorous analysis with the virile and authoritative modernists in opposition to the effete, well-bred Georgians or Bloomsburyites, who stood in for the gentlemen-scholars they were ousting. (This point emerges very clearly in Boris Ford's 1961 guide to *The Modern Age* where Woolf is found to have 'the weakness of the liberal intellectual', a 'lack' of 'vitality', insufficiently able to probe 'that polite liberal culture which [was] radically incommensurate with challenges confronting it in the twentieth century'.)[20] In addition, the notion of modernist work as difficult, complex, elitist, indeed highbrow, could usefully confirm the intellectual and demanding rigour needed for its explication and appreciation; English could not in these terms be considered a 'soft' subject.

Such an analysis of Leavisite criticism would have not met with much dissension either in the 1980s or more recently, but when Lisa Jardine – very controversially and to noisy dissension – suggested at the Sexual Difference Conference at Southampton in 1985 that the left embrace of 'theory' was a continuation of this drive to prove that English was a 'tough specialism', there was outrage at her suggestion 'that "progress" in English Studies . . . is, for the male Left, explicitly a matter of growing "toughness" (machismo): a sloughing off of the "feminine", marginalising origins of Lit. Crit., and an insistence on the "rigour" . . . of Left Eng. Lit'.[21] Lisa Jardine presumably did not have modernist studies in mind – her own interest at that stage, Renaissance studies, was one of the most productive areas of left criticism at the time. But as Raymond Williams suggested not long after, literary critics who wrote of modernism continued to think in modernism's own categories, and it was undoubtedly the case that one of those categories had been, at any rate in the received version of modernism, the macho struggle.[22] But during the 1980s that version of modernism was steadily undermined.

I have not room here to do now more than briefly indicate some of the re-readings that began to emerge in those years. Eagleton's chapter on 'The Rise of English' in his 1983 *Literary Theory*, turned from a vigorous hatchet job on Leavisite criticism to Eliot, whose map of acceptable English literature he points out had deeply influenced it, and attacks the authoritarian stance of Eliot's poetics and the ultimately fascist leanings in Pound's.[23] This was just a few pages, but in 1984, Michael Levenson published his *Genealogy of Modernism*, which, although for the main only concerned with the male canon of modernists, established in careful detail how they moved from an anti-traditional and individualist libertarianism to a traditionalist authoritarianism. This had perhaps been the main crux of the left's difficulty with modernism; there had been an ambiguous shared structure of feeling between the literary and political revolutionaries of the early twentieth century; modernism was both revolutionary and reactionary, like the left attacking the bourgeois world, desiring to change it radically, but with very different aims.[24] For the rest of the 1980s it would be modernists' reactionary side that critics highlighted.[25] Maud Ellmann in *The Poetics of Impersonality* (1987) showed incisively the move from individualism to conservatism, reading Eliot and Pound's poetry alongside their criticism, particularly highlighting their anti-Semitism. The modernists' status as a radical movement was undermined further by Peter Bürger's *Theory of the Avant-Garde* (1984, originally published in German in the 1970s) and Andreas Huyssen's *After the Great Divide: Modernism, Mass Culture and Postmodernism* (1986). Bürger's argument that only movements that deconstructed the institution of art could be considered truly avant-garde, while other forms of modernism implicitly reinforced the bourgeois status quo, threatened to deprive literary Anglo-American modernism at a stroke of its revolutionary credentials; Huyssen repeated this distinction, seeing modernism as irrevocably opposed to mass culture, while the avant-garde creatively engaged with it. Modernism was also under siege from post-colonial and feminist critics. The early post-colonial attack on modernism, which began in the field of the visual arts, equated the modernist fascination with non-Western forms with imperialist plunder, the spoils of colonial wars, while one influential feminist attack put forward by Gubar and Gilbert in their three-volume *No Man's Land*, construed the period as a battle between the sexes; in each case the violence of the metaphors very much mirrored the modernists' militaristic self-imaging, the 'agon' as, Michael Levenson described it, of their fight against the 'tyrant', whether seen as 'the Editor, the Lady, the Public, the Banker, the Democrat'.[26] (Levenson interestingly does not mention one of the most central versions of the tyrant, the Bourgeois, the factor that had earlier complicated left-wing responses to the movement.) But there were other post-colonial and feminist interventions that would offer a much more nuanced understanding of modernism. The reassessment of other writers of the period, women, African-Americans and others, would eventually lead to a recognition that there was a range of modernisms, not all reactionary.[27]

The 1980s saw the British intellectual left move from the authoritative certainties of Althusser's Marxist science to the disarray following the collapse of the Soviet empire, and the dream of revolutionary change that had been part of early modernism became perhaps an unwelcome reminder of its own lost political direction. Yet the 1980s was also culturally an immensely rich decade for literary studies, which with the addition of women's writing, and post-colonial and diasporic literature, was by the end of the decade much more closely engaged with the cultural energies of the modern world than it had been before. The transformation of the discipline for which *Re-Reading English* had called had come about to a remarkable extent. The 1980s, as I began by saying, was a decade of polarized positions; the sweeping nature of the critiques of modernism that were launched then, important though they were in disrupting the earlier established story of the movement, were only a beginning in a reassessment of a period that Eagleton had earlier acknowledged as the 'highpoint of literary creativity in the twentieth century'; but that critical attack made it possible to think again what modernism's value might be.[28]

Notes

[1] Peter Widdowson (ed.), *Re-Reading English* (London: Methuen, 1982).
[2] I do not want to suggest that all SWP members held this view.
[3] Terry Eagleton, Alison Assiter, Gregor McLennan, 'E. P. Thompson's *Poverty of Theory*: A Symposium', *Literature and History* 5.2 (1979), 139–64.
[4] Francis Mulhern, *The Moment of 'Scrutiny'* [1979] (London: Verso, 1981).
[5] Peter Widdowson, '"Literary Value" and the Reconstruction of Criticism', *Literature and History* 6.2 (1980), 138–50.
[6] Brian Doyle developed his work further in 'The Invention of English' in Robert Colls and Philip Dodd's edited collection, *Englishness, Politics and Culture, 1880–1920* (London: Croom Helm, 1986) and in *English and Englishness* (London: Routledge, 1990).
[7] Chris Baldick, *The Social Mission of English Criticism, 1848–1932* (Oxford: Clarendon Press, 1983). This was the publication of his doctoral thesis, on which Eagleton drew in his own account, so the work for this book predates *Re-Reading English*. I am not suggesting influence, just that Peter Widdowson had recognized that such work needed to be done. Chris Baldick has a note when he mentions *Re-Reading English* as a 'belated recognition' of the 'paralysing anti-historical tendencies' of structuralist attacks on the discipline (16, 3).
[8] Gauri Viswanathan, *Masks of Conquest: Literary Study and British Rule in India*, (London: Faber & Faber, 1990), and Robert Crawford, *Devolving English Literature*, (Oxford: Oxford University Press, 1992).
[9] F. R. Leavis, *The Great Tradition* [1948] (London: Chatto & Windus, 1960), 27, and Kate Millet, *Sexual Politics* [1969] (London: Sphere Books, 1971), 146.
[10] Gayatri Spivak, 'Three Women's Texts and a Critique of Imperialism', *Critical Inquiry* 12.1 (1985).
[11] Feminist criticism also concentrated on the nineteenth century though in terms of resurrecting women's writing. I have written on this in 'A History of Women's Writing', *A History of Feminist Literary Criticism*, ed. Susan Sellers (Cambridge: Cambridge University Press, 2007).
[12] See the excellent introduction to Peter Brooker's edited collection *Modernism/Postmodernism* (London: Longman, 1992) for a discussion of postwar responses to modernism.
[13] Ezra Pound, *Patria Mia* (Chicago: Ralph Fletcher Seymour, 1950), 38 (first published in the *New Age* in 1912). Gail McDonald, *Learning to be Modern: Pound, Eliot and the American University* (Oxford: Oxford University Press, 1993); her study was concerned with the States, but the same was true in Britain.

[14] John Hoyles, 'Radical critical theory and English', in *Re-Reading English*, 46. The quotation is from Read's 'Picasso and the Marxists'.

[15] Anthony Easthope, 'Alan Durrant, *Ezra Pound: Identity in Crisis*, Harvester, 1981' (review), *Literature and History* 11/1 (1985), 152. This comment sums up the argument he put forward in his chapter on Pound in *Poetry as Discourse* (London: Methuen, 1983), also in the New Accents series. Alan Durrant, to do him justice, did see Pound's Fascism as a problem, though his Lacanian reading in the end seems to ascribe Pound's politics largely to his lack of post-structuralist sophistication.

[16] Leavis, *The Great Tradition*, 129.

[17] 'Those American Publications', *The Egoist*, 15 October (1914), 390.

[18] 'A Lecture in Modern Poetry', Karen Csengeri, *The Collected Writings of T. E. Hulme* (Oxford: Clarendon Press, 1994), 51.

[19] Baldick, *Social Mission of English Criticism*, 217. Queenie Leavis was one of the exceptions to this male dominance, though both in her life and work she seems to have internalized a very traditional view of gender roles; see Jan Montefiore's fascinating interview with her daughter, Kate Varney in Jan Montefiore, 'A Conversation about Q. D. Leavis', *Women: A Cultural Review* 19/2 (2008).

[20] John Holloway, 'The Literary Scene', *Pelican Guide to English Literature*, Vol. 7, The Modern Age, ed. Boris Ford (Harmondsworth: Penguin, 1961), 74.

[21] Lisa Jardine, '"Girl Talk" (for Boys on the Left)', *Oxford Literary Review: Sexual Difference*, special issue, 8/1&2 (1986), 209–10.

[22] Raymond Williams, *The Politics of Modernism*, ed. Tony Pinkney (London: Verso, 1989).

[23] Terry Eagleton had already pointed out the conservatism that lay behind Eliot's use of myth in *Exiles and Emigrés: Studies in Modern Literature* (London: Chatto & Windus, 1970), but that overall was a much less damning attack.

[24] I touch on this shared structure of feeling further in my book *The Verse Revolutionaries: Ezra Pound, H. D. and the Imagists*, published in 2009 by Jonathan Cape.

[25] Peter Widdowson and Peter Brooker included a brief but perceptive account of the critical standing and political stances of the modernists in 'A Literature for England' in Colls and Dodd, *Englishness, Politics and Culture*.

[26] Michael Levenson (ed.), *The Cambridge Companion to Modernism* (Cambridge: Cambridge University Press, 1999), 2.

[27] There would of course be many other influences on those further re-readings of modernism, but in this context, one might mention the increasing interest in Benjamin and Adorno.

[28] Eagleton, *Exiles and Emigrés*, 14.

Chapter 3

'I would have her whipped': *David Copperfield* in its Historical Moment

Simon Dentith

In this essay I explore the relationship between text and intertext in *David Copperfield*, in particular in relation to the extraordinarily virulent language used by Rosa Dartle towards Little Emily. Drawing on Bakhtin's notion of heteroglossia, I suggest the immersion of the novel's texture in the myriad linguistic and discursive contexts of its immediate historical moment. Yet the essay will also suggest that the violence of Rosa Dartle's language draws more from historically distant models of punishment, better explained in classically Foucauldian terms. Analysis of the novel's language and rhetorical strategies thus leads to an account of its complex situatedness in overlapping historical rhythms.

To talk of the 'myriad linguistic and discursive contexts' for the novel is at once to recognize that 'context' cannot be understood as organic or non-conflictual. On the contrary, discursive conflict, at all levels of discourse from the word upwards, is characteristic of all developed social formations, and it is to this pervasive discursive conflict that Bakhtin's notion of heteroglossia is addressed. This term suggests that what is characteristically novelistic is linguistic rather than plot- or character-based. In other words, conflict in the novel (not just *David Copperfield*, but all novels) does not solely appear as a matter of passive representation – we need not only see those moments of actual conflict as the most characteristically novelistic way of representing conflict. So, for example, George Osborne being shot at the Battle of Waterloo in *Vanity Fair*, or Adam Bede and Arthur Donnithorne engaging in fisticuffs over Hetty Sorrel in *Adam Bede*, are both examples of 'conflict', and behind them one can indeed see the military and class-and-gender conflicts of the nineteenth century. Bakhtin's notion, however, allows us to see conflict in more pervasive terms: the conflicts and struggles of a culture appear mediated via the complex utterances of the novel, in which differing and indeed conflicting valuations are simulta-neously present in the novelistic word. The model for the kind of analysis to be made here is Bakhtin's account of *Little Dorrit* in 'Discourse in the Novel', which uses the wonderful phrase 'washed by heteroglot waves from all sides' to describe the linguistic texture of the novel.[1]

To be sure, this is to read the notion of heteroglossia in a particular way: to stress the conflictual and competitive potential of the term more than its initial apparent indication of mere diversity of language. The term as used by Bakhtin in 'Discourse in the Novel' certainly does more than merely suggest the way in which the novel includes the multiple voices of the culture from which it emerges. In Bakhtin's model of language use and change, there is a permanent struggle between the centralizing and official forces on the one hand, and the destabilizing, unofficial and 'centrifugal' forces on the other hand. Every utterance is to be understood as a nexus of these conflicting social forces realized through language. The notion of heteroglossia thus has conflict rather than mere diversity as its conceptual centre.

The movement in 'Discourse in the Novel', from language to novel, also deserves comment, since it entails a particular understanding of the novel's immersion in its historical moment. Bakhtin first establishes, in relatively abstract theoretical terms, a model of language, and then offers the novel as the artistic form best placed to exploit language as he understands it. Indeed, it is not just that the novel is 'best placed' – the genre's very existence is predicated upon its use of, or emergence from, the multiple and conflictual nature of language. The kind of novelistic analysis that the essay suggests, therefore, is at once formally specific and gestures towards the discursive environment which surrounds it. That is to say, attention to the novel as such requires, in the same gesture, attention to the surrounding linguistic world. One could say that Bakhtinian analysis in this mode is both formalist and historicist at the same time.

The analytical possibilities are suggested by Bakhtin's own account of sections of *Little Dorrit* in 'Discourse in the Novel'. Despite the off-putting technical-sounding formulations ('pseudo-objective motivation', 'hybrid construction', and so on), the force of these analyses of the actual speech of the novel is to direct the reader to the linguistic environment of mid-nineteenth-century England, from which the multiple echoes, parodies and stylizations emerge. Thus Bakhtin quotes a section from Dickens's novel to this effect:

> That illustrious man and great national ornament, Mr Merdle, continued his shining course. It began to be widely understood that one who had done society the admirable service *of making so much money out of it*, could not be suffered to remain a commoner. A baronetcy was spoken of with confidence; a peerage was frequently mentioned.

Bakhtin comments upon this in this way:

> The epithet 'who had done society the admirable service' is completely at the level of common opinion, repeating its official glorification, but the subordinate clause attached to that glorification ('of making so much money out of it') are the words of the author himself (as if put in parentheses in the quotation). The main sentence then picks up again at the level of

common opinion. We have here a typical hybrid construction, where the subordinate clause is in direct authorial speech and the main clause in someone else's speech. The main and subordinate clauses are constructed in different semantic and axiological conceptual systems.[2]

Bakhtin's analysis is formally very precise, differentiating even different clauses of the same sentence, indicating their differing provenance and the way that the evaluative accent with which they are written alters. It presumes an acquaintance with the linguistic milieu of mid-century England in the confidence with which it characterizes the majority of the extract from Dickens as belonging to the level of 'common opinion'.

Yet it is of course not the case that Bakhtin was widely read in this milieu – quite apart from the fact that he scarcely had access to any library resources when he wrote the essay, there's some uncertainty as to whether he even read English. So the heterogeneous and conflictual discursive world of mid-Victorian Britain has, in a very real sense, to be deduced or intuited from the linguistic texture of the novel. This certainly raises questions over the kind of research programme suggested by 'Discourse in the Novel'. On the one hand it appears to suggest that it ought to be possible to go out and find the surrounding voices from which any novelistic text is at once constituted and from which it takes its distance. This is a programme of onerous but doubtless manageable scholarship. On the other hand we need to recognize that the stuff out of which the novel is constructed is in principle anonymous, unsourceable, more like the unceasing buzz and hum of a culture than punctual, autographed documents. This possibility – with which we are familiar from any serious consideration of the notion of 'intertextuality' or from *S/Z*[3] – certainly holds within it the danger that afflicts many versions of historicism, in which the historical horizon is deduced from the literary text and then read back into it as explanatory external term. The account of *David Copperfield* which follows is doubtless caught somewhere between these two alternatives.

I nevertheless pursue an enquiry of this kind in relation to *David Copperfield*, and particularly in relation to the way that this novel includes conflicts over sexuality and class as part of its topic – though this is an odd way of putting it, since these were an inevitable aspect of Dickens's writing and were not included as a matter of conscious choice. The language of Rosa Dartle is especially revealing, since she gets to articulate the most unsettling and violent attitudes towards Little Emily and the Peggotty family that are included in the novel. What is the discursive context for these aspects of the novel, and how are they mediated in the linguistic texture of the novel itself? Following Bakhtin, the analysis seeks to move between the linguistic texture of the novel itself and its discursive context as a way of locating that language initially in its immediate moment.

One substantial formal departure from the passages from *Little Dorrit* discussed by Bakhtin is that all the passages that I shall be looking at are the character's own words rather than being written in the narrative voice. This certainly makes a difference in terms of the local analysis that the text requires; but direct speech in a novel is no less 'double-voiced' than indirect speech, for in it can still be heard two value-systems. This is most obvious in the case of irony, though it is often the case, as with all ironic statements, that its precise nature and even its direction is difficult to establish – sometimes, indeed, remain permanently inscrutable. I do not think this is the case with Rosa Dartle's speech, though she does indeed initially appear ambivalent.

For Rosa Dartle is an unsettling presence in the novel not only because of the violence of her speech but because she is at first an enigmatic figure, and it is uncertain how both David, and we as readers, are expected to react towards her. In David's first encounter with her, for example, she questions Steerforth's easy patronage of working-class people, in a way that will remain an open possibility in the text until after Emily's elopement with Steerforth clarifies matters:

> 'Oh, but, really? Do tell me? Are they, though?' she said.
>
> 'Are they what? And are who what?' said Steerforth.
>
> 'That sort of people. – Are they really animals and clods, and beings of another order? I want to know so much.'
>
> 'Why, there's a pretty wide separation between them and us', said Steerforth, with indifference. 'They are not to be expected to be as sensitive as we are. Their delicacy is not to be shocked, or hurt very easily. They are wonderfully virtuous, I dare say – some people contend for that, at least; and I am sure I don't want to contradict them – but they have not very fine natures, and they may be thankful that, like their coarse rough skins, they are not easily wounded.'
>
> 'Really!' said Miss Dartle. 'Well, I don't know, now, when I have been better pleased than to hear that. It's so consoling! It's such a delight to know that, when they suffer, they don't feel! Sometimes I have been quite uneasy for that sort of people; but now I shall just dismiss the idea of them, altogether. Live and learn. I had my doubts, I confess, but now they're cleared up. I didn't know, and now I do know; and that shows the advantage of asking – don't it?'[4]

Since Rosa Dartle's speech is itself sarcastic, the ironies of this passage are especially hard to decode – in her case we have an example of irony ironically presented. Steerforth's speech is perhaps a simpler starting point, since the nature of the double-voiced discourse is clearer. When he says 'They are not to be expected to be as sensitive as we are. Their delicacy is not to be shocked, or hurt very easily', his speech is subject to a straightforward irony. When he continues with a concession ('They are wonderfully virtuous, I dare say – some people contend for that, at least'), he does so to what he acknowledges to be a recognizable opinion abroad in the culture – though the most famous proponent of the virtues of the poor at mid-century is surely Dickens himself. But the concession is short-lived and he goes on to speak in a way that we are to presume is symptomatic not only of his own disposition but of a wider discursive possibility or attitude. This is certainly what Rosa herself assumes in her response, her sarcasm exposing the consolatory mystification involved in the attitudes that Steerforth has lightly articulated. Yet it is hard for the reader to remain easily in this riposte either, since the aggressive sarcasm of Rosa's speech does not provide a comfortable concluding resting-place for the reader to inhabit.

So after David's first meeting with Rosa Dartle the reader is left in some uncertainty as to the polemical direction of her speech. There is even a suggestion that David might fall in love with her. However, the uncertainty is definitively dispelled after Steerforth's seduction of Little Emily, and Mr Peggotty's visit to Mrs Steerforth in search of news. As he and David leave the house they are accosted by Rosa Dartle, who verbally attacks Emily and the Peggottys in the following ferocious terms:

> 'I do him [Mr Peggotty] no wrong', she returned. 'They are a depraved worthless set. I would have her whipped!'
> Mr Peggotty passed on, without a word, and went out at the door.
> 'Oh, shame, Miss Dartle! Shame!' I said indignantly. 'How can you bear to trample on his undeserved affliction!'
> 'I would trample on them all', she answered. 'I would have his house pulled down. I would have her branded on the face, drest in rags, and cast out in the streets to starve. If I had the power to sit in judgment on her, I would see it done. See it done? I would do it! I detest her. If I ever could reproach her with her infamous condition, I would go anywhere to do so. If I could hunt her to her grave, I would. If there was any word of comfort that would be a solace to her in her dying hour, and only I possessed it, I wouldn't part with it for Life itself.' (478)

These too are double-voiced words, because the reader can hear in them two 'conflicting axiological conceptual systems': that of Rosa Dartle herself, with an uncertain general resonance, and that of the author, given the irony that we presume surrounds this speech. There is no doubt that Rosa's words are presented as pathological here, since they encompass both Emily and the Peggotty household, and so are aimed at all the pious memories of David's childhood as much as the girl herself. The novel certainly proposes a psychological or character-based explanation for Rosa's violence: we are to see it as the product of her fraught history with Steerforth and of her sexual jealousy of Emily. However, such an explanation does not take us beyond the novel itself to consider its discursive context; is Rosa's speech in any way symptomatic of comparable utterances in the culture which surrounds the novel?

This is clearly not just a matter of sexual resentment; Rosa also articulates a strident class hostility towards Mr Peggotty and his family. This emerges as clearly on the next occasion of David's visiting her, when she has news of Emily's whereabouts gained from Littimer:

'This devil whom you make an angel of, I mean this low girl whom he picked out of the tide-mud', with her black eyes full upon me, and her passionate finger up, 'may be alive, – for I believe some common things are hard to die. If she is, you will desire to have a pearl of such price found and taken care of. We desire that, too; that he may not by any chance be made her prey again. So far, we are united in one interest, and that is why I, who would do her any mischief that so coarse a wretch is capable of feeling, have sent for you to hear what you have heard.' (679)

The hurtful phrases in this passage also seem aimed exactly at David's most heartfelt sentiments, and with them part of the very point of the book – the tender memories surrounding his holidays in the upturned boat at Yarmouth, represented so touchingly and piquantly by Dickens as part of his strategy of winning sympathy for those members of society normally outside the orbit of novelistic sympathy. Yet one remarkable thing about this speech of Rosa's is that its last sentence includes the phrase 'any mischief that so coarse a wretch is capable of feeling': exactly the belief (that the poor cannot feel as sensitively as 'us') that she had subjected to such withering sarcasm earlier in the novel. She herself uses as a hurtful barb at David the very notion that she had exposed as a consolatory fiction in a previous passage of arms with Steerforth. Rosa has become the mouthpiece for all the words about class and gender in the book that its wider narratives are keenest to controvert.

Dickens is thus embarked upon a very surprising rhetorical strategy in the novel, by which Rosa Dartle articulates with a particular vehemence precisely those opinions which most threaten the author's own dearest purposes. This strategy and its dangers are most visible in that extraordinary chapter towards the end of the novel when Rosa Dartle is given the opportunity of insulting Little Emily at length while David is obliged to overhear. This occurs in chapter 50 of the novel, and concludes part XVI – the chapter ends with Mr Peggotty being reunited with Little Emily, a scene chosen for illustration by Hablot Browne. On this occasion Rosa Dartle actually addresses Emily herself; she is overheard by Copperfield and Martha while they are waiting for Mr Peggotty to arrive. In other words, Dickens so arranges the narrative that Little Emily is subjected to a stream of insult from Rosa, while David must overhear the abuse but is powerless to intervene – he has to hear it out. Furthermore, Mr Peggotty, as in the previous scene that I quoted, is protected from hearing the words of direct insult to his niece and his family. Rosa variously describes Emily as 'the bold, flaunting, practised companion of persons like James Steerforth' (723); a 'purchased slave' (724); an 'earth-worm' (725); 'this piece of pollution, picked up from the water-side'; and 'that carrion' (726). She describes the Peggotty household as 'that low place', and scornfully suggests that Emily was 'part of the trade of your home, and were bought and sold like any other vendible thing your people dwelt in' (725). She threatens Emily in various ways: 'If you try to evade me, I'll stop you, if it's by the hair, and raise the very stones against you!' (723); 'Why don't they whip these creatures!', she exclaims; 'If I could order it to be done, I would have this girl whipped to death' (726); she promises to pursue and proclaim Emily wherever she goes unless she hides herself completely or marries Littimer; 'if this will not do either', she suggests to Emily that she 'die! There are door-ways and dust-heaps for such deaths and such despair – find one, and take your flight to Heaven!' (726).

This is remarkable in its virulence; Dartle gets to articulate a particularly violent and horribly malicious account of Emily and the Peggotty family. What is particularly hurtful, and what should cause the reader to start up in indignant denial, is the imputation cast by Dartle on the Peggotty household: Emily was in some sense sold to Steerforth. There is surely no construction of the earlier scenes in the novel which would allow this charge, despite the remarkable way in which the book suggests the mixture of class condescension, lady-like ambition, and social awkwardness that propels Emily's seduction. The twin conflicts of gender and class emerge in Rosa Dartle's discourse in especially malignant form; the violence of her speech expresses both extreme class and sexual hostility which Emily's modesty and penitence in the scene only inflames.

One initial explanation of this is to do with the rhetorical economy of the novel; Rosa Dartle's outbursts are perhaps to be read as prophylaxis, as Dickens deliberately including these vehement, malicious and flagrantly unjust outbursts in order to prompt the reader into indignant denials and thus towards sympathy towards Little Emily. In this connection the timing of Rosa's most sustained attack on Emily is significant; it occurs immediately before, indeed delays, Mr Peggotty's reunion with his niece. That is, the culmination of one of the most romantic narrative strands in the novel is prepared for by an extended calumny of its affective significance. Mr Peggotty's protection from the violence of Rosa Dartle's language is also relevant here; he never gets to hear what David (and the reader) is forced to hear. The benign and forgiving patriarch is protected from hearing what would rob his quest of its meaning. The text appears compelled to utter calumnies of its own best feelings, but also to protect the idealized masculine focus of those feelings from hearing them. This suggests the instability of the rhetorical strategy that Dartle's invective embodies. Nevertheless, and despite this instability, clearly we can go some way to explaining the inclusion of Dartle's extraordinary discursive violence by reading it as a rhetorical strategy designed to forestall critical and hostile interpretations of Emily and her story.

This wider rhetorical account of these sections of the novel is really designed to supplement the Bakhtinian approach already suggested. Rosa's speech remains 'double-voiced discourse', carrying two simultaneous valuations – that of the character herself and that of the narrator; it is subject to a particularly visible irony. Thus when she says; 'If I could order it to be done, I would have this girl whipped to death' (726), we can recognize in this both a particular pathology and behind it the narratorial repudiation of the attitude that this pathological character has expressed. The question raised by both a Bakhtinian analysis and a rhetorical one is this: what wider social or ideological current is speaking through Rosa Dartle? Or better: what discursive conflicts in the world that surrounds *David Copperfield* are echoed in the double-voiced discourse of her speech? – that is, in its harshly punitive violence to illicit sexually active lower-class women, and the condemnation of that harshness implicit in the irony surrounding its articulation. We can put the same question in rhetorical terms: what condemnation of Emily and the Peggotty household is Dickens anticipating and seeking to deflect by including such a virulent version of it in the text of the novel?

This is the moment, then, when the transition from text to history is required by the very notion of heteroglossia, though the 'history' is here to be understood specifically in discursive terms, as the essentially conflictual to and fro of competing voices, accents and valuations: 'different semantic and axiological conceptual systems', to repeat Bakhtin. So I should say at once that I have not found anyone in the Britain of the 1840s articulating attitudes towards the lower classes, towards fallen women, or towards prostitutes, that at all approach the violence of Rosa Dartle's invective.

An instructive parallel can perhaps be made with the double-voiced discourse which accompanies Dora's friend Miss Mills, where there is irony of an altogether softer kind, and where the conflicts in question (over the language of sentiment) are much less ideologically acute or threatening. In the following passage, for example, David has gone to meet Miss Mills at a particularly difficult moment in his courtship of Dora:

> Miss Mills had a wonderful flow of words, and liked to pour them out. I could not help feeling, though she mingled her tears with mine, that she had a dreadful luxury in our afflictions. She petted them, as I may say, and made the most of them. A deep gulf, she observed, had opened between Dora and me, and Love could only span it with its rainbow. Love must suffer in this stern world; it ever had been so, it ever would be so. No matter, Miss Mills remarked. Hearts confined by cobwebs would burst at last, and then Love was avenged. (562)

The double-voiced discourse here too can be described as ironic; when Miss Mills says 'and Love could only span it with its rainbow' we are clearly to recognize both her speech and the sceptical voice which has already recognized the 'luxury' and the 'petting' that is enjoying the afflictions of the lovers. Dickens is alluding to, and ambivalently mocking, a language of sentiment that is alive in the culture in the form of keepsakes, albums and verse. Although this does indeed connect with one of the central strands of the novel (David's undisciplined heart, and his failures and mistakes with Dora and Agnes), Dickens can permit himself a wholly affectionate and sympathetic parody of what we take to be a real cultural presence in the world surrounding the novel. The contrast with the way that the novel sets up the language of Rosa Dartle is clear.

It is hard to imagine anyone in the 1840s actually saying or believing what Rosa Dartle says. Yet the violence that Rosa Dartle suggests should be visited on the body of Emily, and which indeed she volunteers to inflict, does of course have precedents in the historical record of the legal treatment of prostitution, from which Dartle draws her imaginative repertoire of fantasy punishments, especially those of branding and whipping. So rather than seeking precedents for her speech in the immediate synchronous context of the novel, perhaps we should be looking to a longer discursive history, in which a punitive regime of violent and visible physical punishment was replaced by one of penitential and spiritual reform.

Classically Foucauldian accounts of this kind are fortunately not wanting; I have used Linda Mahood's *The Magdalenes: Prostitution in the Nineteenth Century* from 1990 since it gives a helpful general characterization of the relevant context:

> Therefore, [the prison inmate's] punishment took the form of penitence and prayer combined with periods of solitary confinement. This was part of the new philosophy of punishment that emerged in the prison reform movement between 1775 and 1840. The new form of corporal discipline, directed at the mind with large doses of scripture and hard labour, replaced a cluster of punishments directed at the body such as whipping, dunking, and branding used in previous centuries.[5]

It is true that Rosa Dartle does not suggest dunking for Emily, but she does, as we have seen, suggest whipping and branding. She repeatedly articulates, it seems, the response of an older discursive order to the kind of transgression that Emily represents.

On this reading, the text of *David Copperfield* becomes part of what Mahood describes, for a period exactly coincident with the publication of the novel, as a 'struggle to cast the "prostitute" as a worthy object of charity and compassion'.[6] The familiar reference, in this context, is to Dickens's work with Angela Burdett-Coutts on the management of Urania Cottage, the moral-penitentiary institution which the heiress established, and upon which Dickens advised her about the management in 1847, two years before he began to publish *David Copperfield*. We are all now alert to the resonances of the management regime which he proposed:

> The design is simply, as you and I agreed, to appeal to them by means of affectionate kindness and trustfulness, – but firmly too. To improve them by education and example – establish habits of the most rigid order, punctuality, and neatness – but to make as great a variety in their daily lives as their

daily lives will admit of – and to render them an innocently cheerful Family while they live together there. On the cheerfulness and kindness all our hopes rest.[7]

And again:

One great point that I try to bear in mind continually, and which I hope the clergyman will steadily remember, is, that these unfortunate creatures are to be tempted to virtue. They cannot be dragged, driven, or frightened. You originate this great work for the salvation of these women who come into that Home; and I hold it to be the sacred duty of every one who assists you in it, *first to consider how best to get them there, and how best to keep them there.* Every other consideration should fade before these two . . .[8]

Kindness backed by firmness; 'how best to get them there, and how best to keep them there', in a phrase that Dickens himself emphasized – these are both passages which indicate that while 'Salvation' is aimed at, management is required. Not that Dickens was simply uncritical of modern managerial regimes; he was strongly hostile to the system of solitary confinement in prisons, a hostility which features very prominently at the end of *David Copperfield* with the false repentances of the two model prisoners Heep and Littimer.

In the novel, Martha clearly represents the preferred outcome for the reformed prostitute, in her eventual marriage. Yet the sheer attractiveness of the Urania Cottage material has led to a shift in emphasis from Little Emily to Martha, from the 'fallen woman' to the 'prostitute'. Rosa Dartle's virulent speech is directed at the former; in the final scene she addresses a penitent woman, and still does not relent. For the reformed prostitute, a married future in Australia can be imagined; for the penitent fallen woman, only a life of service which definitely does not include marriage. And yet, to return to the conundrum of Rosa Dartle, it is Emily and not Martha who is subjected to the most extended verbal violence with its powerful echoes of the judicial punishments characteristic of the *ancien regime*.

I have sought to explain this violence as a kind of prophylaxis: *David Copperfield* represents a clearing of the ground for more 'progressive' regimes of knowledge/power to be brought to bear upon the fallen woman. The 'conflict' in question then turns out to be a secular one, to replace one discursive regime with another. An analysis which began with Bakhtin has concluded with Foucault, the latter called upon in order to describe one of the discursive horizons within which the novel falls. He may also be invoked to direct our attention to the historicity of the novel; where the Bakhtin of 'Discourse in the Novel' looks to the immediate heteroglossic context, Foucault rather points us to the longer epochal shifts that a novel's language can nonetheless invoke. This in turn should lead us to recognize the extraordinary complexity of any 'heteroglossia', made up not only of the minute-by-minute specificities of what

Bakhtin calls the 'slogans of the hour', but shot through also with longer diachronic strands marked with older histories and emerging from more ancient
discursive and generic legacies. In this sense the novel participates in differing
historical moments and navigates its own way among them.

But a profound difference between Bakhtin and Foucault obviously remains
in the attitudes towards the novel that they encourage; where Bakhtin seeks
to read with the grain of Dickens's writing, indeed entirely celebrates it, a
Foucauldian analysis of the novel (rather than its discursive context), doubtless
provokes deep suspicion of it.[9] I am not inclined to be suspicious of *David
Copperfield*, though I have been provoked by Rosa Dartle's violence to see it as
enacting, in specifically novelistic ways, one of the central conflicts of the nineteenth century. Peter Widdowson's own inflection of the idea of the 'literary'
perhaps enables us to square this particular circle; while 'Literature' can be
understood to provide a monumental record and fixed positions, the 'literary'
can allude to a space in which the multiple stories of a complex culture can be
told and retold, continually reinflected for differing social purposes.[10] At this
distance of time those purposes are bound to appear to us ambivalently marked,
if only by hindsight; yet Bakhtin's celebration of the energetic work performed
by Dickens's writing upon the multiple discursive resonances of his culture
must surely count as one of the prime instances of that positive power of the
literary to which Widdowson alludes.

Notes

[1] Mikhail Bakhtin, 'Discourse in the Novel', in Michael Holquist, ed., *The Dialogic
     Imagination: Four Essays*, trans. Michael Holquist and Caryl Emerson (Austin
     Texas: University of Texas Press, 1981), 307.
[2] Bakhtin, 'Discourse in the Novel', 306. Bakhtin's emphasis is indicated in his
     quotation from *Little Dorrit* (1855–7).
[3] For the instability in the usage of the term intertextuality, see Jonathan Culler,
     The Pursuit of Signs: Semiotics, Literature, Deconstruction (London: Routledge and
     Kegan Paul, 1981). See also Roland Barthes, *S/Z*, trans. Richard Miller (London:
     Cape, 1975).
[4] Charles Dickens, *David Copperfield*, ed. Jeremy Tambling (London: Penguin Books
     2004 [1850]), 302–3. All subsequent references are from this edition and appear
     parenthetically in the body of the text.
[5] Linda Mahood, *The Magdalenes: Prostitution in the Nineteenth Century* (London:
     Routledge, 1990), 83.
[6] Ibid., 56.
[7] Charles Dickens, *The Letters of Charles Dickens*, ed. Graham Storey and K. J. Fielding
     (Oxford: Clarendon Press, 1981), Vol. 5, 178–9.
[8] Dickens, *The Letters of Charles Dickens*, 183.
[9] As classically in David Miller's *The Novel and the Police* (Berkeley: University of
     California Press, 1988).
[10] See Peter Widdowson, *Literature* (London: Routledge, 1999).

Chapter 4

On Hardy's Realism, Again

Tim Dolin

'Art is a disproportioning . . . of realities, to show more clearly the features that matter in those realities. . . . Hence "realism" is not art.'[1] Could Thomas Hardy have been any more explicit? This is, for him, an uncharacteristically matter-of-fact statement, and about as close as he came to a declaration of aesthetic principles: realism is not art, and Hardy's art – the art of his fiction, at least – is not the art of the realist. Yet before the publication of Peter Widdowson's ground-breaking *Hardy in History: A Study in Literary Sociology*, first as an article in *Literature and History* in 1983, and then as a book in 1989, few readers and critics were actually prepared to go along with it. '[R]eceived and naturalized notions of "Literature"',[2] Widdowson argued, associated literariness with realism; and Hardy, therefore, if he was a great writer, was a great realist: *the* great tragic realist of rural England in decline. Widdowson was not the first to question this orthodoxy. Among the 'openly and self-consciously politically interested' practitioners of literary and cultural theory in the 1970s and early 1980s, Marxist and feminist, it had long been a vital question.[3] Most notably, Terry Eagleton, whose materialist theory and criticism is an obvious and important influence on Widdowson's study, argued in *Criticism and Ideology* (1976) that, although the 'typically "impure" Hardyesque compounds of pastoral, mythology, "classical" tragedy and fictional realism' did find 'formal consummation' in the 'fully elaborated realism' of *The Woodlanders* and *Tess of the d'Urbervilles*, the unresolvable ideological and formal contradictions of *Jude the Obscure* took that novel, and the English novel, to the 'limits of realism itself'.[4] And in 1982 Penny Boumelha took up this line of argument for Marxist feminism. In Hardy, she wrote, 'pastoral is disrupted by tragedy, and the tragedy subverted by elements of realism that cannot be stabilised within its mythical perspective'.[5] After *Tess*, however, realism is 'in turn pushed against its limits by the disintegration of the cohering power of character and by radical dissonances of narrative voice and point of view. The disjunction of such varied modes resists the organization into a hierarchy of discourses that would endorse a particular ideological position.' For Boumelha, Hardy's experimental fiction is driven not, as it is for Eagleton, predominantly by class alienation and instability, but by gender. The 'radicalism of Hardy's representation of women resides . . . in their resistance to reduction to a single and uniform ideological position'. Their resistance to the dominant sexual ideology is homologous, in this argument, to the text's resistance to classic realism, which naturalizes ideology as part of 'its project to effect an imaginary resolution of actual (but displaced) social contradictions'.[6]

The goal of *Hardy in History* was to expose and critique this project further, substantiating and extending earlier observations about Hardy's unstable heteroglossic forms using what Widdowson called a 'critiography'. A politicized form of critical historiography (and, in this respect, a version of the cultural materialism also coming to the fore at this time in work on Shakespeare), the critiography is interested in the ways that the (literary) past is 'constituted by criticism (and other related social processes)'.[7] Its aim is to expose 'the history which has carried [Hardy's novels] down to us in the present as "readable" and "profitably readable"': that is, as realist. Widdowson noted and deplored the 'striking absence within formalist–humanist criticism of work dealing with Hardy's manifestly non-realist discourses', and sought to trace the history of this ideologically motivated absence, and the social and political forces underlying the critical and popular construction of Hardy as a humanist–realist icon of English national culture.[8] In practice, the Widdowsonian critiography combines theoretical, literary critical, historical, and empirical approaches and methods in now familiar ways: through detailed analyses of the various texts and techniques which perpetuated the myth of Hardy's tragic realism, including photographic images and artworks used on book covers, questions in examination papers, period details and scenery in films and TV serials, and the tourism industry's investment in the realism of the 'Hardy Country', wherein Wessex and Dorset coexist happily as interchangeable names for the one knowable (because visitable) place.

Hardy in History goes further than either Eagleton or Boumelha, therefore: Hardy's anti-realism was the 'core of [his] fictional aesthetic', Widdowson argued, 'which makes it perversely inappropriate to critically recast his fiction in the formal-realist mode'.[9] In a brilliant polemical reversal of that perverse enterprise, an enterprise that had been carried out with assiduousness and unity of purpose by the custodians of the critical establishment and the popular cultural imagination alike, *Hardy in History* begins with a provocation. Did Thomas Hardy write any bad novels? That no critic could now answer that question as they once might have (without hesitation in the affirmative) – indeed, that such a question no longer makes a lot of sense – is a measure of the book's lasting influence. On the first page Widdowson declared that *The Hand of Ethelberta* was every bit as significant as *Tess of the d'Urbervilles*. If this claim has not been borne out by the comparative number of copies sold, films and TV serials produced, or scholarly words devoted to each novel, then that is, ironically, a vindication of Widdowson's argument that the silent naturalizing processes of the dominant cultural apparatuses are indeed formidable. And the claim has achieved an undeniable critical orthodoxy. In fact, if I began by suggesting that *Ethelberta* was *not* as significant as *Tess* it would now beg a number of important questions. For the terms on which we value Hardy these days are decisively post-Widdowsonian. We value his disturbance of the complacencies of late-nineteenth-century realism by certain alienation effects: a 'mannered and intrusive style; the improbable use of chance and coincidence; the "sensational", "melodramatic", and "gothic" modes; the self-conscious and self-reflexive obsession with the artifice of art, the fictiveness of fiction, the ambiguity of illusion and reality, the "veracity" of appearances'.[10] These qualities are more immediately evident in the uncanonical *Ethelberta* than the canonical *Tess*.

For the earlier Marxists, Hardy's fiction only gradually reached the point of formal-ideological impasse after a career-long 'series of alternative relations between text and ideology'. Hardy had used realism, after all, to throw pastoral ideology into 'radical self-question' in *Far from the Madding Crowd*, as Eagleton shows, and only the 'dramatic internal dislocations and contradictions' of *Jude the Obscure* are finally so contortive that nineteenth-century realist form is utterly incapable of accommodating or resolving them.[11] For Widdowson, however, *Ethelberta* (published immediately after *Far from the Madding Crowd* in 1876), and the other experimental or 'artificial' romances and 'novels of ingenuity' that appeared throughout Hardy's novel-writing in parallel with the novels of character and environment, testify to an anti-realist strain that had been there from the start – from before the start, in fact, in the inflammatory 'socialistic' romance, *The Poor Man and the Lady*.[12] In this unpublished novel – 'a sweeping dramatic satire of the squirearchy and nobility, London society, the vulgarity of the middle class, modern Christianity, church restoration, and political and domestic morals in general' – the youthful Hardy had tried his hand at the 'affected simplicity of style' and 'naive realism' of Defoe (failing, as he admitted, by pushing it all too far).[13]

In Widdowson's argument, Hardy's realism, read aright, remained satirical (in this sense of 'double') because he was always acutely conscious of the tension between his tenuous class position in the metropolitan writing profession (which rewarded orthodoxy) and his forfeited position in the rural intermediate class about which he wrote with such knowledge (a knowledge which always threatened to give away his origins). Chief among the formal tactics he adopted to cope with the stifling conditions of late-Victorian serial and circulating-library fiction production was the deployment of different modes of address for different constituencies of readers. The novel form, as Franco Moretti has argued, 'is always commodity and artwork at once: a major economic investment and an ambitious aesthetic form',[14] and in the period when Hardy was writing, this double identity gave rise to what John Frow describes as 'a double standard of legitimacy' determined by 'upper- and lower-middle-class "taste cultures"'.[15] For Widdowson, realism is the favoured mode of lower-middle-class taste cultures. The realism/anti-realism binary, cardinal in Hardy studies after *Hardy in History*, therefore operates to reinforce the antithesis of a radically interrogative (academic) Hardy, focused on a politics of representational form, and a conventionally humanist–realist (popular) Hardy, focused on a represented world – Wessex. Lurking behind this, in turn, is an unresolved double characterization of Hardy himself as both 'purist' and 'profiteer' (in Peter McDonald's useful terms):[16] simultaneously an audacious proto-high-modernist insurrectionary and a pragmatic petit bourgeois conformist who played a duplicitous (and increasingly strained) role in the promotion/ironization of the myth of the 'novels of character and environment'. Although very much a 'party' to the constitution of '"Thomas Hardy" as a body of work which colludes with the dominant social and cultural ideology', Hardy also constantly destabilizes the realism he appears to promote: he operates 'within a realist paradigm', but 'flaunts its very speciousness'.[17] Having taken Meredith's advice in 1869 that no aspiring writer could reasonably expect to succeed by scandalizing or ridiculing the ruling classes, the *Poor Man*'s political disturbance of the established social order was displaced into the formal dissonances that constantly obtrude into, and qualify, the realist narrative.

Realism is therefore 'not merely a literary mode but a crucial representation of bourgeois individualism'. It disguises its fictionality by 'purporting to tell a true story, a "history" which is absolutely convincing in its verisimilitude', in order to 'show in its concrete experiential "reality" how human beings can transcend their social environment and fulfil themselves as free individual subjects. . . . [It] helps people to understand and sympathize with their fellow human beings in order to improve their own moral altruism and hence the condition of life generally.' Literary realism is at once the expression of liberal-humanist ideology, then, and a prime agent in its naturalization. That ideology is summed up as 'the authority of the individual human subject as the source of social efficacy': the deconstruction of realism is focused primarily on the dismantling of the illusion of coherent *character*.[18] Widdowson's conclusion to a later essay on *Tess* – again, a strategic provocation[19] – is exemplary in this regard: 'Tess *has no character at all*: she is only what others (most especially the author) construct her as.'[20]

The antithesis between literary realism and its others ('romance', 'fantasy', 'ingenuity' and 'experiment'),[21] grounded as it is in the ideological antithesis between 'verisimilitude' and 'artificiality', therefore had its origins in Hardy's own discernibly uneven fictional practice: his career-long tendency to alternate 'the fiction we tend to call "realist" simply because we get carried along by it' with the more venturesome and reader-unfriendly formal experiments.[22] But it was the dominant regimes of reading that privileged the 'safe' liberal-humanist-realist Hardy, rejecting the 'potentially disruptive discourses' of *Ethelberta*, and ignoring the 'profound alienation which marks all Hardy's work – the clash of modes, the mannered style, the derisive irony, the "satires of circumstance" – [which] is determined by the *anomie* of his class and professional contradictions'.[23] And *Hardy in History*, as its title suggests, was principally concerned with these regimes. Realism is *what happens to* Hardy's novels, and is no part of what they are trying to achieve.

Widdowson was not alone in observing an 'unequivocal anti-realistic bias' in Hardy's aesthetics, nor, of course, in regarding realism as a strategy for naturalizing the social order – it is a version of the prevalent 1980s post-structuralist argument against 'classic realism'.[24] The originality of *Hardy in History* lies in its extensive analysis of the underlying dynamics of post-Hardyan culture, which privileged Hardy's realism because it 'participates in and reinforces the dynamics of consumption'.[25] Quoting from Martin Wiener's influential polemic, *English Culture and the Decline of the Industrial Spirit, 1850–1980* (a book taken up by the Thatcherite new right in the 1980s, curiously), Widdowson associates the canonization of the realist Hardy with the project to revive pastoral myths of rural England and its heritage and 'establish a cohesive national consciousness in a period [immediately prior to the First World War] deeply riven by domestic and international tensions'. But that is only the beginning. Wiener notes how 'The "Wessex Worshippers" . . . shaped their own version of Wessex and made it into a mythic image for England itself. . . . In such ways, Hardy's complex and realistic fiction was reduced to a one-dimensional, repetitious chronicle of an appealingly timeless and nonmaterial way of life under siege.'[26] Widdowson is not explicitly concerned with tourism in this section of the book, but his restatement of Wiener's assumptions about the complacent gaze of the mass tourist is telling: this is the worst kind of reader of Hardy, exemplifying 'an ideology "drenched in anxiety about change", which desperately requires an "essential" national identity; that is, one which is beyond the depredations of historical process'.[27] The rise and rise of the popular Wessex and its ignorant hordes is a clear example, from this point of view, of the triumph of Theodor Adorno's reviled culture industry: no 'homeland can survive being processed by the films [and tourist industries, we might add] which celebrate it, and which thereby turn the unique character on which it thrives into an interchangeable sameness'.[28]

It is little wonder that few critics after *Hardy in History* have made a case for Hardy's realism – or even, as Eagleton did, a case for his 'laborious and uneven . . . movement towards a fully-developed critical realism' which comprehends 'pastoral, melodrama, social realism, naturalism, myth, fable [and] classical tragedy'.[29] Yet as Boumelha had already recognized by the end of the 1980s, the 'classic realism' orthodoxy was problematic. Reconsidering the position she had taken in *Thomas Hardy and Women*, Boumelha reminded critics, first of all, that realism was 'the means by which so many nineteenth-century women writers staked a claim to speak of the public issues lying outside the constricted sphere of traditional feminist concerns'.[30] Then, and at other historic moments of ideological resistance, realism was a 'deliberate – even militant – extension of form rather than [an] effort at literal representation or record'.[31] The customary manoeuvre of the critique of classic realism – 'the collapse into and on to one another of realism as an epistemology and realism as a mode of writing' – was oblivious to the political significance of any such extension of form, and dismissive of a criticism that give realism credence: 'By a conceptual sleight of hand, a critical practice that values [realism as a mode of writing] is made complicit in [realism as an epistemology].'[32] Boumelha argued, moreover, that the proliferating arguments against classic realism shared the common assumption that

> realist texts can only be read productively by contestatory or oppositional criticism in so far as they are disrupted by other modes of writing; that is, . . . we can only value a realist text for those moments when and where it shows the traces of other modes (whether those be chronologically prospective, as in the dislocations of early modernism, retrospective, as in half-repressed persistences of the gothic, or simply lateral).

As we have seen, *Hardy in History* proceeds in just this way. Realism 'is characterised by an inability or refusal to know itself as writing', and its 'major ideological tactic' is 'illusionism, a kind of wilful self-blindness destined to induce in its reader a reciprocal self-blindness'.[33]

The aim of this essay, therefore, is to make the argument again for the critical realism of Hardy's fiction; or rather, to make a start on making the argument, for what follows is necessarily preliminary. It proposes only to re-examine Hardy's sketchy remarks on realism, showing that, for him at least, it was not a mode disrupted by or showing the traces of other modes, but one the more real for its strategic disproportionings of the real. His purpose was here, as in other aesthetic choices, polemical: a declaration and rejection of the conventionalism that marks cultural verisimilitude, demanding, in Christine Gledhill's words, 'representation of what has not been seen before, what has been unthinkable because unrepresentable'. In each generation, realism repeats the gesture of putting behind it the ossified realisms of the past, as 'the new signifiers of the real in their turn solidify into the established codes of cultural verisimilitude and become open to further challenge'.[34] For Hardy – 'continuously aware of the disparity between the human imagination of the real and the possibilities of the real itself' – realism is the mode of disenchantment.[35] His is a 'progressive or critical realism', in Fredric Jameson's understanding of it: one that does not simply 'reflect or express the phenomenology of life under capitalism',[36] but makes visible 'the process whereby consciousness becomes distorted or concealed by the proliferation of discourses and images that objectify reality'.[37] Not unsurprisingly, Hardy's progressive realism, and the increasing pressure that his writing begins to exert upon the cultural verisimilitude in mainstream middle-class fiction, developed from a sustained inquiry, beginning in the early 1880s, into the new ideas and artistic movements of the time. Throughout the 1880s and early 1890s he spent much of his time in London during a period of intense debate over the nature of art, and his slowly forming conception of

Wessex – as a partly real and partly imagined place, where observation ends and art begins – coincides with his reassessment of his artistic concerns and practices against established and emerging aesthetic ideas and principles:[38] the competing convictions that 'art should be grounded in the natural world and that it should be edifying'; and 'that the value of art lies in the autonomy of its formal and decorative effects'.[39]

Inevitably, much of Hardy's attention was directed to the controversy in the reviews and journals, and in the public sphere, over French scientific naturalism. Indeed when Hardy uses the word 'realism' in his notebooks, he is often referring to naturalism. He describes Zola in 'The Science of Fiction' (1891), for instance, as both the 'most devoted apostle of realism' and 'the sheerest naturalist'; and is clearly referring to the sexual explicitness of naturalism when he writes in the same essay that 'realism is an unfortunate, an ambiguous word, which has been taken up by literary society like a view-halloo, and has been assumed in some places to mean copyism, and in others pruriency'. Hardy was publicly disdainful of Zola, whom he also pointedly describes in 'The Science of Fiction' as a 'romancer' who 'abandons in practice' the naturalist (i.e. 'copyist') dictum 'that the novel should keep as close to reality *as it can*'.[40] To Florence Henniker he wrote: 'You mistake in supposing I admire Zola. It's just what I don't do. I think him no artist, and too material';[41] and later again he denied Zola's influence, claiming, in mischievous allusion to "The Science of Fiction", that George Crabbe, not Zola, was the 'apostle of realism who practised it in English literature three-quarters of a century before the French realistic school had been heard of'.[42] Yet as Mrs Henniker no doubt divined, and as is well known, Hardy's writing after 1885 was significantly influenced by Zola's naturalism.[43] The tremendous forces that sway humanity to their purposes 'as the tide sways the helpless weed' in the later novels are the same calamitous forces that drive naturalist fiction: determinism and chance, unbending social and natural laws, hereditary personality, and physical drives and instincts.[44] The influence is most evident in *Tess of the d'Urbervilles* and *Jude the Obscure*, but these concerns are already present in Hardy's ironic idyll of déraciné modernity, *The Woodlanders* (1887). Many critics have noticed the Zolaesque quality of that novel's descriptions of the 'saps . . . beginning to heave with the force of hydraulic lifts inside all the trunks of the forest' and the narrator's insistence that here,

> as everywhere, the Unfulfilled Intention, which makes life what it is, was as obvious as it could be among the depraved crowds of a city-slum. The leaf was deformed, the curve was crippled, the taper was interrupted; the lichen ate the vigour of the stalk, and the ivy slowly strangled to death the promising sapling.[45]

The adoption of the rhetoric of naturalism in these and other descriptions of nature was carefully considered. Zola's mission (it became Hardy's) was that of generations of realists before them, including, most famously, the generation of Courbet and Flaubert: to contest 'the definition of the real and force changes in the codes of verisimilitude', and to speak out on public issues, giving voice to the unheard and making visible what had not been seen before.[46] When in 'Candour in English Fiction' (1890) Hardy writes that it is because life is 'a physiological fact' that 'its honest portrayal must be largely concerned with, for one thing, the relations of the sexes', he is taking up the scientism but also the radical dissidence of naturalism. In 1889, the English publisher Henry Vizetelly was tried and jailed for indecency for his translations of Zola's notorious fiction (Hardy signed a petition to the Home Secretary for his release). This trial was a scandalous climax to nearly a decade of public suspicion and censure of the new French realism in Britain: suspicion at what it had 'brought into the field of the visible and made available to a wide audience'.[47] It was intellectually ambitious, but also luridly sensationalist and unashamedly populist and democratic. Its 'materialistic, analytical, mechanistic vision that assimilates man to nature's deterministic laws' ostentatiously disposed of the regulatory moral framework of the bourgeois novel.[48]

But because naturalism was uninterested in the 'invisible truths and values that underlie the visible world' – because it applied the 'language and procedures of dissection and analysis . . . merely to make the material world more open to view' – Hardy was also acutely conscious of its artistic limitations.[49] In 'The Science of Fiction' he passionately defended creativity, 'in its full and ancient sense' of 'the making a thing or situation out of nothing that ever was before', against the new 'realism, that is, . . . an artificiality distilled from the fruits of closest observation'.[50] In a note on style from early 1881, Hardy put this in Romantic terms:

> Consider the Wordsworthian dictum (the more perfectly the natural object is reproduced, the more truly poetic the picture). This reproduction is achieved by seeing into the heart of a thing (as rain, wind, for instance), and is realism, in fact, though through being pursued by means of the imagination it is confounded with invention, which is pursued by the same means. It is, in short, reached by what M. Arnold calls 'the imaginative reason'.[51]

Hardy concludes 'The Science of Fiction', predictably, by cautioning the naturalists that: 'A sight for the finer qualities of existence, an ear for the "still sad music of humanity", are not to be acquired by the outer senses alone, close as their powers in photography may be.'[52] Here he echoes the sentiments, and repeats the metaphors, of his contemporaries. One of the entries in his literary notebook from this period paraphrases George Meredith's preface to *Diana of the Crossways* (1885): 'real pictures of human life [are] neither photographs, *unfaithful in their very accuracy*, nor daubs, unfaithful through lack of knowledge.'[53] Even George Moore, chief among those who had championed naturalism in England, was by 1888 railing against 'mere facts', and would describe realism in the *Fortnightly Review* in 1892 as 'the disease from which art has suffered most in the last twenty years'. In the important early essays appearing at this time, further, Oscar Wilde deplored 'the monstrous worship of facts' in naturalism (and in the science fetishism of romance – in Stevenson and Rider Haggard) and argued in 'The Decay of Lying' that 'No great artist ever sees things as they really are. If he did, he would cease to be an artist.'[54] Hardy's Wordsworthian advocacy for the 'power of observation informed by a living heart' was alien to Wilde's aestheticism, however; and Hardy retained that strong sociological impulse to preserve 'a fairly true record of a vanishing life'[55] while privileging 'the true realities' over the 'old material realities'.[56]

These ideas were also in accord with the post-naturalist thinking in France, which Hardy kept up with through the *Révue des deux mondes* and other periodicals. In 1888 he made notes from an article about the emerging 'Symbolistes et Décadens', whose attack on the dominance of Zola's scientific naturalism raised many of his own reservations: 'At a time when, under pretext of *naturalism*, art had been reduced to being no more than an imitation of the exterior contour of things, the Symbolists . . . appeared to teach that things have also a soul, of which the bodily eyes only seize the envelope, or the veil, or the mask.' Still, the writer goes on, 'it is very necessary to bear in mind that, if there is something beyond *nature*, we can only express it with nature's means . . . & only observation is able to make us masters of those means of correcting, mending, & transforming nature. Our symb.[sts] and Decadents seem to forget this . . . to believe that art consists of getting away from nature. . . . Imitation of nature, wh. is not the whole of art, is at least its beginning.'[57]

In a later entry Hardy noted down a term Edward Dowden had coined for the work of the decadent novelist J.-K. Huysmans – 'spiritual naturalism' – and remarked that it 'nearly defines my own old idea of the principle of novels of the future', an idea described in a note in the *Life* which is dated from the period of *The Woodlanders* in 1886: 'Novel-writing as an art cannot go backward. Having reached the analytic stage [i.e. of scientific naturalism] it must transcend it by going still further in the same direction. Why not by rendering as visible essences, spectres, etc. the abstract thoughts of the analytic school?' A diary entry from January 1887 expands on this:

> After looking at the landscape ascribed to Bonington in our drawing-room I feel that Nature is played out as a Beauty, but not as a Mystery. I don't want to see landscapes, i.e., scenic paintings of them, because I don't want to see the original realities – as optical effects, that is. I want to see the deeper reality underlying the scenic, the expression of what are sometimes called abstract imaginings.

The entry continues by linking these reflections back to the Romanticism of the late Turner, for whom the

> exact truth as to material fact ceases to be of importance in art – it is a student's style – the style of a period when the mind is serene and unawakened

to the tragical mysteries of life; when it does not bring anything to the object
that coalesces with and translates the qualities that are already there, — half
hidden, it may be — and the two united are depicted as the All.

Hardy contrived an elaborate dramatic–poetic technique for the presentation
of this dialectical interplay between mind and material world in *The Dynasts*,
where he renders 'abstract imaginings' and 'tragical mysteries' as 'visible
essences', making 'the old material realities' mere 'shadowy accessories' of 'the
true realities of life . . . hitherto called abstractions'.[58]

In the fiction, meanwhile, Hardy adapted from naturalism techniques to 'aes-
theticize, transfix and transform into static verbal pictures the disintegrating
reality that is being depicted',[59] and grafted them on to a Romantic aesthetics
interested in representing abstract imaginings and tragical mysteries as visible
essences. On a Sunday in July 1888 he imagined the real lives of the church-
goers around him 'spinning on beneath [their] apparent one of calm, like
the District Railway-trains underground just by – throbbing, rushing, hot, concerned with next week, last week'. He had a vision of these 'true scenes' being
'brought into church bodily with the personages, . . . jostling phantasmagorias
crowded like a heap of soap bubbles, infinitely intersecting, but each seeing
only his own'. Modern life, he concluded, was a kind of sleep-walking: 'the
material is not the real only the visible, the real being invisible optically. That it
is because we are in a somnambulistic hallucination that we think the real to be
what we see as real.'[60] The Coleridgean atmosphere of this imaginary scene
recalls how, in the *Lyrical Ballads*, Coleridge and Wordsworth contrived a series
of poems of two sorts – the 'uncommon and the ordinary' (in Hardy's phrase).
The first, by Coleridge, were supernatural: 'the excellence aimed at was to con-
sist in the interesting of the affections by the dramatic truth of such emotions,
as would naturally accompany such situations, supposing them real. And real in
this sense they have been to every human being who, from whatever source
of delusion, has at any time believed himself under supernatural agency.'
Wordsworth's poems, however, aimed to give 'the charm of novelty to things
of every day' and in doing so to 'excite a feeling analogous to the supernatural,
by awakening the mind's attention from the lethargy of custom, and directing
it to the loveliness and the wonders of the world before us'.[61] Hardy's methodi-
cally reasoned explanation of what constitutes reality in fiction (in a note from
1881) takes up this Romantic dyad of uncommonness and ordinariness:

> The real, if unavowed, purpose of fiction is to give pleasure by gratifying the
> love of the uncommon in human experience, mental or corporeal.
> This is done all the more perfectly in proportion as the reader is illuded to
> believe the personages true and real like himself.
> Solely to this latter end a work of fiction should be a precise transcript of
> ordinary life: but, . . .
> The uncommon would be absent and the interest lost. Hence, . . .

The writer's problem is, how to strike the balance between the uncommon and the ordinary so as on the one hand to give interest, on the other to give reality.

In working out this problem, human nature must never be made abnormal, which is introducing incredibility. The uncommonness must be in the events, not in the characters; and the writer's art lies in shaping that uncommonness while disguising its unlikelihood, if it be unlikely.

The process of shaping that plausible uncommonness demanded radical alterations in

the actual proportions and order of things, so as to bring out more forcibly than might otherwise be done that feature in them which appeals most strongly to the idiosyncrasy of the artist. The changing, or distortion, may be of two kinds: (1) The kind which increases the sense of *vraisemblance*. (2) That which diminishes it. (1) is high art: (2) is low art.

'Art', he concluded in this note from July 1890, 'is a disproportioning – (i.e., distorting, throwing out of proportion) – of realities, to show more clearly the features that matter in those realities, which, if merely copied or reported inventorially, might possibly be observed, but would more probably be overlooked. Hence "realism" is not Art.' Once again Turner is the exemplar, for he 'recognizes the impossibility of really reproducing on canvas all that is in a landscape; then gives for that which cannot be reproduced a something else which shall have upon the spectator an approximative effect to that of the real'. For Turner, and for Hardy, 'Art is the secret of how to produce by a false thing the effect of a true.'[62]

Taken together, these notes amount less to a 'defiant flouting of verisimilitude',[63] and much less to an anti-realist manifesto, than an attempt to reclaim a narrative fiction 'done from the real – that is to say, [with] something real for its basis, however illusively treated' – from the extreme materialism of scientific naturalism.[64] At the same time, the disproportioning energies of Hardy's realism owe much of their power to the sensationalism with which naturalism radicalized the representation of actuality. The realism that is *not* art is quite clearly, in Hardy's mind, the pure naturalism that merely copies or reports inventorially. The realism that *is* art is, for him, 'quite accurately a going to Nature' which is, however, 'no mere photograph, but purely a product of the writer's mind'. Hardy's realism, in rejecting the positivism of the naturalists and the facile literality of consumer realism, recognizes the imperative to falsify what it imitates, in order to represent the 'deeper reality underlying the scenic'.[65] In this, it is true to what Jameson calls the 'constitutive tension and incommensurability' between realism's epistemological and aesthetic claims. If realism 'validates its claim to being a true or correct representation of the world, it thereby ceases to be an *aesthetic* mode of representation'; if its artistic devices are foregrounded, it risks falling into 'the sheerest representation and illusion'. Yet, as Jameson concludes, no 'viable conception of realism is possible unless both these demands or claims are honored simultaneously, prolonging and preserving – rather than "resolving" – this constitutive tension and incommensurability'.[66] In the two decades since *Hardy in History* appeared, the orthodoxy of the anti-realist Hardy has for the most part obscured this progressive realism of Hardy's, which constantly throws into question 'the world we seem to know',[67] and by doing so challenges its social relationships, moral values and power structures.

Notes

[1] Quoted in Florence Emily Hardy, *The Early Life of Thomas Hardy, 1840–1891* (London: Macmillan, 1928), 299.

[2] Peter Widdowson, *Hardy in History: A Study in Literary Sociology* (London: Routledge, 1989), 4.

[3] Penny Boumelha, 'Penny Boumelha on Realism and Feminism', *Realism*, ed. Lilian R. Furst (London: Longman, 1992), 319–33, 319.

[4] Terry Eagleton, *Criticism and Ideology: A Study of Marxist Literary Theory* (London: NLB, 1976), 95.

[5] Penny Boumelha, *Thomas Hardy and Women: Sexual Ideology and Narrative Form* (Brighton: Harvester Press, 1982), 7.

[6] Boumelha, *Thomas Hardy*, 7, 6.

[7] Widdowson, *Hardy in History*, 13. See Jonathan Dollimore and Alan Sinfield, eds, *Political Shakespeare: Essays in Cultural Materialism* (Ithaca: Cornell University Press, 1994).

[8] Widdowson, *Hardy in History*, 5, 38.

[9] Ibid., 164.

[10] Ibid., 219.

[11] Eagleton, *Criticism and Ideology*, 95, 94, 95.

[12] Florence Hardy, *Early Life*, 75.

[13] Ibid., 81.

[14] Franco Moretti, ed., *The Novel* (Princeton, NJ: Princeton University Press, 2006), ix.

[15] John Frow, *Marxism and Literary History* (Oxford: Blackwell, 1986), 252, n.14.

[16] Peter D. McDonald, *British Literary Culture and Publishing Practice, 1880–1914* (Cambridge: Cambridge University Press, 1997); see also Jonathan Freedman, *Professions of Taste: Henry James, British Aestheticism and Commodity Culture* (Stanford: Stanford University Press, 1990).

[17] Widdowson, *Hardy in History*, 154, 74. Neither *Hardy in History* nor Joe Fisher's *The Hidden Hardy* resolve the question of the creative artist's freedom to control the relationship between authorized and the subversive texts. Even Fisher's characterization of Hardy as a 'trader' presupposes a degree of clandestine autonomy, and characterizes the market-place as a sphere of individualism (expressed in Hardy's 'wilful flourishes and dangerous "dares"'). See *The Hidden Hardy* (Basingstoke: Macmillan, 1992), 15. But even the 'subversive' Hardy is compelled to act within the constraints of subversiveness set by the artistic field.

18 Widdowson, *Hardy in History*, 23, 73, 75, 76.
19 See, for example, Valentine Cunningham, 'Tess of the d'Urbervilles', Moretti, ed., *The Novel*, 548–58, 557.
20 Peter Widdowson, *On Thomas Hardy: Late Essays and Earlier* (Basingstoke: Macmillan, 1998), 133.
21 Widdowson, *Hardy in History*, 49.
22 Mieke Bal, 'Over-Writing as Un-Writing: Descriptions, World-Making, and Novelistic Time', Moretti, ed., *The Novel*, 571–610, 572.
23 Widdowson, *Hardy in History*, 76, 138.
24 Lennart Bjork, 'Critical Introduction', Thomas Hardy, *The Literary Notebooks of Thomas Hardy*, ed. Lennart Bjork (London: Macmillan, 1985), xiv–xxxi, xxiv. See also Catherine Belsey, *Critical Practice* (London: Methuen, 1980).
25 Edward Barnaby, 'The Realist Novel as Meta-Spectacle', *JNT: Journal of Narrative Theory* 38.1 (2008), 37–59, 37.
26 Martin J. Wiener, *English Culture and the Decline of the Industrial Spirit, 1850–1980* (Cambridge: Cambridge University Press, 1981), 51.
27 Widdowson, *Hardy in History*, 63.
28 Theodor W. Adorno, *The Culture Industry: Selected Essays on Mass Culture*, ed. J. M. Bernstein (London: Routledge, 1991), xxx.
29 Eagleton, *Criticism and Ideology*, 131.
30 Boumelha, 'Realism', 322.
31 Martin Price, *Forms of Life: Character and Moral Imagination in the Novel* (New Haven: Yale University Press, 1983), 27.
32 Boumelha, 'Realism', 323.
33 Ibid., 320, 323.
34 Christine Gledhill, 'Genre and Gender: the Case of Soap Opera', *Culture, Media and Identities*, ed. Stuart Hall (London: Sage/Open University, 1997), 337–86, 361.
35 George Levine, *The Realistic Imagination: English Fiction from Frankenstein to Lady Chatterley* (Chicago: University of Chicago Press, 1981), 238.
36 Fredric Jameson, *The Political Unconscious: Narrative as a Socially Symbolic Act* (Ithaca: Cornell University Press, 1981), 134.
37 Barnaby, 'The Realist Novel', 43.
38 See Hardy, *Literary Notebooks*.
39 Charles Harrison, Paul Wood and Jason Gaiger, *Art in Theory, 1815–1900: An Anthology of Changing Ideas* (Oxford: Blackwell, 1998), 834.
40 Thomas Hardy, *Thomas Hardy's Public Voice: The Essays, Speeches, and Miscellaneous Prose*, ed. Michael Millgate (Oxford: Clarendon Press, 2001), 107, 108, 109.
41 Thomas Hardy, *The Collected Letters of Thomas Hardy*, ed. Richard Little Purdy and Michael Millgate, 7 vols (Oxford: Clarendon Press, 1978–88), 2.157.
42 Florence Emily Hardy, *The Later Years of Thomas Hardy, 1892–1928* (London: Macmillan, 1930), 114.
43 Donald George Mason, 'The Doll of English Fiction: Hardy, Zola and the Politics of Convention.' Ph.D. thesis (Canada: McMaster University, 1994).
44 Thomas Hardy, *Tess of the d'Urbervilles*, ed. Tim Dolin (London: Penguin, 1998), 190. See also William A. Newton, 'Hardy and the Naturalists: Their Use of Physiology', *Modern Philology* 49.1 (1951), 28–41 and Lyn Pykett, 'Representing the Real: The English Debate about Naturalism, 1884–1900', *Naturalism in the*

European Novel: New Critical Perspectives, ed. Brian Nelson (New York: Berg, 1992), 167–88.

45 Thomas Hardy, *The Woodlanders*, ed. Patricia Ingham (London: Penguin, 1998), 52.

46 Gledhill, 'Genre and Gender', 360.

47 Pykett, 'Representing the Real', 175.

48 David Baguley, 'The Nature of Naturalism', *Naturalism in the European Novel: New Critical Perspectives*, ed. Brian Nelson (New York: Berg, 1992), 13–26, 15.

49 Pykett, 'Representing the Real', 173–4.

50 Hardy, *Thomas Hardy's Public Voice*, 108.

51 Florence Hardy, *Early Life*, 190.

52 Hardy, *Thomas Hardy's Public Voice*, 109.

53 Hardy, *Literary Notebooks*, 1.165 n. 1350.

54 Oscar Wilde, *Intentions* (London: Methuen, 1934), 44.

55 Hardy, *Thomas Hardy's Public Voice*, 109; Thomas Hardy, *Thomas Hardy's Personal Writings. Prefaces, Literary Opinions, Reminiscences*, ed. Harold Orel (London, Melbourne: Macmillan, 1967), 46.

56 Florence Hardy, *Early Life*, 232.

57 Hardy, *Literary Notebooks*, 1.225.

58 Florence Hardy, *Early Life*, 232, 242.

59 Baguley, 'The Nature of Naturalism', 19.

60 Florence Hardy, *Early Life*, 276, 243.

61 Vincent B. Leitch, ed., *The Norton Anthology of Theory and Criticism* (New York: Norton, 2001), 677.

62 Florence Hardy, *Early Life*, 193–4, 299, 283–4.

63 Eagleton, *Criticism and Ideology*, 95.

64 Hardy, *Thomas Hardy's Personal Writings*, 46.

65 Florence Hardy, *Early Life*, 198, 242.

66 Fredric Jameson, 'The Existence of Italy', *Signatures of the Visible* (New York: Routledge, 1990), 158.

67 Belsey, *Critical Practice*, 51.

Chapter 5

Tragedy and Revolution

Terry Eagleton

Oedipus, broken and blind, stands before Colonus. As he once gave an answer
to the Sphinx, his presence now poses a question to the nearby city of Athens.
Is it to gather this unclean thing to its heart, or cast it out as so much garbage?
Just as Oedipus himself, solver of riddles, detected the image of humanity –
itself the ultimate conundrum – in the Sphinx's portrait of a monster with four
legs, two legs and then three, so Athens is being asked to recognize the image
of the human in this monstrosity at its gates. Four, two and three in one is the
enigma of identity and difference, the garblings and doublings of incest, the
scrambling of subject positions, and the giddy exchange of symbolic roles.
Oedipus is the *pharmakos* at the threshold, the impossible homeopathy of poi-
son and cure. He is both guilt and innocence, king and beggarman, stranger
and brother. Indeed, the very tragic theatre in which he appears, according to
its earliest theorist, is itself a kind of homeopathy, a *catharsis* in which we take a
pinch of the noxious ingredients of pity and fear in order to purge ourselves of
these poisons. Now, however, Oedipus must wait while Theseus, ruler of Athens,
weighs the perils of excluding the sacred against the dangers of assimilating the
polluted. Since the *pharmakos* is both in one, holy and defiled, contradiction
incarnate, this is scarcely a simple choice.[1]

Tragedy is said to be about pity and fear, and pity and fear are a question of
identity and alterity. We can, it would seem, pity only what is akin to us, just as
we fear what is strange. Both are political notions: pity enjoyably cements the
social bond from the inside, while fear austerely reinforces it against external
threats, and is what we feel in the presence of authority. For another vein of
aesthetics, this sado-masochistic fusion of pleasure and horror, the daunting
delights of an infinite sovereignty, goes by the name of the sublime. Only if our
imaginary social bonds are founded upon the Real, upon a certain horror at
the heart of the social itself, will they prove sufficiently durable. Only if the
Furies are installed within the city-state itself will it be secure – which is to say
that only if the terrorism of the law is turned inwards as well as outwards, to
become domesticated as hegemony as well as armed and helmeted as military
might, will the social contract stand. Oedipus himself will end up as such a tute-
lary power, his death made fruitful for the future life of the *polis*, so that his

death-in-life existence, once embraced by the city, will prove fertile for its flourishing. 'Surely a just God's hand will raise him up again', exclaim the Chorus.

A tragedy like that of Oedipus, however, also turns Aristotle's logic of pity and fear on its head, scrambling its dichotomies by showing us that nothing is more fearful and opaque than ourselves and those akin to us, and nothing more pitiable than a humanity deformed alarmingly out of recognition. It is, indeed, only when we are 'out' of recognition that we are fully 'in' it. Confronted with the parricidal Oedipus, the demented Lear or the tortured Christ, we are asked to couple these classical responses to tragedy together, and come to pity what we fear. It is not just a matter of pitying whatever is still human in these poignant figures, whatever residual humanity has survived their monstrosity, but of feeling for them in that very deformity, grasping them as most human when inhuman, and hence of seeing them in the Real rather than the Imaginary. It is to perceive that what is most intimately human about them is also what is most frightful to gaze upon, and that no power can enable us to look upon them and live but an answering inhumanity in ourselves. The moment of recognition of this more-and-less-than-human in ourselves is the moment traditionally known as repentance.

These, then, are not men travestied, dehumanized, violently disfigured, but signs of the violent disfiguration which is humanity itself. In inviting the vagrant Oedipus into the city, Theseus is not simply divining a blessing within an apparent curse, but recognizing in this beggarly sovereign an image of the monstrosity of himself and his city. When it comes to human affairs, the aberrant is the normative. What more graphic image of power than the powerless, since tyrant and vagrant are both beyond the law? And what could more forcefully testify to the failure of power and so to its ironic kinship with the dispossessed, than the flayed, butchered bodies of its victims?

'I come to offer you a gift – my tortured body – a sorry sight', Oedipus tells Theseus, 'but there is value in it more than beauty'. Truth is unaesthetic, a mangled body; it reminds us of beauty only by negation. The cynic is the one for whom value is so much shit, whereas it is in shit – the detritus of a repressive social order – that the revolutionary finds value. The Fool is a figure who hovers somewhere between the two. Sophocles's meditation on Oedipus broods upon impossible arithmetical calculations – on incestuous paradoxes of two or more in one, of one plus one making four or more, on defacements and illegibilities at the heart of the symbolic order. Incest lays bare the guilty secret of that order, which is that all of its places must be arbitrarily interchangeable simply for it to function. Like any structure, the price it pays for working all by itself is the perpetual possibility of transgression, which is to say the possibility of not being itself at all. Incest is an abomination which confounds essential boundaries and obscenely commingles distinct categories; yet since desire itself does nothing less, the vilified, accursed Oedipus, as Freud will later instruct us, is simply representative of the way of the world, the social unconscious, the truth that transgression is our routine business. Incest is the Real of the symbolic order, to which Sophocles's art will place us in an imaginary relation.

Incest presses through the logic of the symbolic order to the point of a surreal, scandalous deconstruction, which is at once a garbling of all orthodox social relations and the unspeakable truth of them. If you are to be free to permutate the roles of, say, husband and father, then there is nothing in the structural grammar of the symbolic order itself to rule out the hybridity of being your own mother's spouse. Comedy seizes on this recognition as well, noting as it does that desire is no respecter of rank or difference, and playing off our anxiety that social order will thereby be undermined against our deliciously vindictive desire for exactly that. Shakespeare's *King Lear*, in a way not entirely removed from Sophocles, rings changes on the tragic calculus of more, less, all, something and nothing, of cyphers, creative surpluses and destructive superfluities, notions which resound through the poetry of the play just as they run as a riddling subtext beneath some of Shakespeare's other works.

Incest, monstrosity, is the place where exact calculations and distinctions break down, and so also is the wager of Theseus as he stands before this besmirched parody of his own kingship. Oedipus himself knows that an unspeakable power for good will flow from welcoming the immigrant, embracing the excremental remainder, assimilating into the political order the sign of its own non-identity. To do this, however, is not to be 'inclusive' (that magical postmodern word) but to encompass what that order is forced to exclude simply to be itself and thus to transform it beyond recognition. The astonishing irony of class-society is that this excluded remnant is not some postmodern margin or minority, but the actual majority. This power for good, or magnificent flourishing of life, is known as sacrifice, the dialectical movement by which the very dissolution of the unclean thing becomes fertile and life-bearing. In modern political parlance, it goes by the name of revolution – the project, in Marx's words, of a class which is the dissolution of all classes, a total loss of humanity in the name of a total gain of one, and which thus represents in its very decomposition the shape of the classless future.

To acknowledge this thing of darkness as one's own, whatever name it happens to go under, is to thrown the projective act of scapegoating into reverse, confessing that this savage travesty of humanity was cast out of the city not because it was alien but because it was too familiar. A similar interplay of the alien and the overintimate characterizes the act of incest. The scapegoat or *pharmakos* must be shifted from the metonymic to the metaphorical register – from being that fragment of the *polis* on which the people project their crime and guilt, driving it out and thereby disavowing it, to being the mirror in which they can recognize themselves for the monsters that they are ('Man' is the answer to the Sphinx's riddle), and by that recognition transcend their own deformity.

The scapegoat wins our compassion because it is the terrifying Real in the humanizing shape of suffering flesh and blood. But it is also suffering flesh and blood *as* the Real, as dehumanized and atrociously disfigured, and thus as placing so implacably anonymous a demand on our own humanity that only that within ourselves which is beyond the personal – whatever it is that lies non-subjectively at the root of our subjectivity, rather than simply falls within its frame – can hope to answer to it at all adequately. Only the ruthless abstraction of love, which is no respecter of persons because it attends equally to the needs of any old person, could suffice to repair the ravages of a desire which is similarly indifferent to individuals in its impeccably egalitarian ambition to maim and madden them all. Only a Real which was beyond humanity, and so terrible, but at the same time friendly to humanity, could prove sufficient.

Love differs in this sense from friendship, or indeed from the 'romantic' version of itself, both of which are nothing if not particular. But this is not to contrast an abstract universalism with a sensuous specificity, in that hoariest of all antitheses to which the solution (we know it even before the words are out) is art. For one thing, particularism in these postmodern times is itself a full-bloodedly universal creed, just as nationalism is a thoroughly international phenomenon, and a highly parochial view of the world has come to be known as globalization. A universalized particularism is postmodernism's goal, whereas justice and charity involve that very different condition, a particularized universalism.

This is universal in so far as everyone has a claim to love and justice, but this claim is empty unless it is this or that individual's uniquely particular being which is granted recognition, and his or her irreducibly specific need attended to. Every individuality must be acknowledged, regardless of whose individuality it is. As far as that goes, any old individuality will do. When it comes to difference, one has to be grandly indifferent. This is why neither early-bourgeois abstraction nor late-bourgeois particularism will do – a traditional enough socialist case, to be sure, since socialism has insisted all along that the universal commonwealth must be constructed in and through the developed, uniquely individual powers and capacities bequeathed to us as an opulent heritage by middle-class society. One can tell the difference between a Marxist and a postmodernist by the former's unabashed admiration for the bourgeoisie.

In any case, there can surely be no genuine opening of our eyes to the particular, no grasping the situation as it actually is in all its densely determinate reality, which does not at some level implicate a kind of infinity – whether in the Christian sense that this hard-headed realism, *pace* the bankers and burghers, is the most difficult thing in the world and possible only by the power of grace (a novel variant on the ancient theme that virtue and knowledge have an internal bond), or simply as a kind of Kierkegaardian marvelling at the fact that things are eternally given as what they are – that in purely gratuitous style God fashioned you and not someone else. In this perspective, individuality is the claim of the infinite on the finite, the mind-shaking mystery of the uniquely self-identical. To see eternity in a grain of sand is to see a grain of sand, not to see through it. Being is the way to see beings, not an entity to be seen in itself.

To discern the workings of a non-subjective Real in the subject is to see the subject as it is, constituted to its core by what is unnervingly alien to it. To understand political oppression is to grasp that this particular group of men and women is what it uniquely is exactly by virtue of its place in some more universal context. To say that those with freckles or pony-tails are not oppressed as such is to say that their distinctive features can be understood well enough without recourse to such a global setting.

To return to the scapegoat: sacrifice, *pace* the right-thinking liberal, is not an evil to be kept to a minimum, but an action which grows more beneficent the more it is universalized. For sacrifice to be general and reciprocal is just what a communist ethics urges. It is for each to find his or her life in being the means of life for others, to adapt the language of *The Communist Manifesto* a little. Shakespeare's *Measure for Measure* recognizes that a reciprocal scapegoating and condemnation can be flipped over at a stroke, with no momentous alteration of structure, into a community of forgiveness – induced, as it were, to cancel all the way through, as a futile round of tit-for-tat or moral exchange-value gives way to a mutual forbearance. Sacrifice is the authentic alternative to the bogus ruling-class conspiracy of pity and fear, by which an imaginary, endlessly circular sympathy for those identifiably of one's own kind (one which in fact depends on their abstract exchangeability) is buttressed by the intimidatory terrors of the Real.

Sacrifice, seen as the inner structure of authentic social relations, replaces fear of the death-dealing alien with the more fruitful death of the act of self-giving. Only on a universal 'death' of that kind can a community of the living be durably founded. Such a death retains all the uncanny force of the Real, in contrast to the liberal humanist illusion that the social bond can be cemented by sympathy alone; but at the same time it helps to unburden that Real of its terrors. Death is now in the service of life, as the very form of an emancipated sociality, rather than life pressed into the service of a deathly annihilation. It is the latter which we observe in the unstaunchable capitalist Will, which can conceive of nothing more vigorous, dynamic and bouncily robust than itself, and which would be outraged to be informed that it is in reality a form of ascetic otherworldliness.

'Am I made a man in the hour I cease to be?', Oedipus cries, pondering the tragic or revolutionary reversal by which genuine power can spring only from humanity's embrace of its own shit-like negativity. Only less can become more; only humanity at its nadir can be redeemed, since if what is redeemed is not the worst then it would not be a question of redemption. This is why the dispossessed are the sign of the future, a negative image of utopia. They testify to that future simply by what they are, and so stay faithful to the ban on fashioning graven images of it, manufacturing blueprints, idols and fetishes. 'Nothing will come of nothing', Lear warned Cordelia, but the truth turns out to be just the opposite. In the arithmetic of redemption, two negatives make a positive: only by knowing that you are nothing, like the Fool, redoubling your negativity in ironic self-awareness, can you achieve an ironic edge over the fools who believe themselves to be boundless. Only by tracing the limits of one's finitude from the inside can one transcend it. *Pace* the paranoid Lear, something will *only* come of nothing, a founding identity spring only from an openness to death and destitution; but this truth is so terrible that it proves hard to survive it, so that Lear has no sooner passed from the illusory nothingness of 'all' to a lowly but determinate 'something' than he passes into nothingness once more.

It would be a mere inversion of this process to see the disposed as passing *tout court* from nothingness to power. 'We once were nought, we shall be all', chant the proletariat in the *Internationale* – but there can be no authentic revolution if the 'all' in question is simply what you lacked when you were nought. It is not just a question of restoring Oedipus to his kingship, but his transcending this status to achieve a form of sovereignty which, like Jesus's carnivalesque, mock-heroic entry into Jerusalem, transforms the very meaning of the term. Had Lear struggled through, this would no doubt have been the measure of his achievement as well. The revolutionary passage from nought to all, like that from all to nought, involves a change in the meaning of the terms themselves, so that the power of the proletariat is not of the same species as the power that it overthrows. Lenin makes the point in *The State and Revolution* by insisting that what is at stake in the workers' struggle is not a change of state-power, but a transfiguration of the state itself.

It is not just a matter of appropriating an existing power and turning it to new ends; but nor is it a matter of disclaiming power altogether. Only the privileged liberal can afford to do that. Or, indeed, the privileged Lear of the play's first scene, who imagines in his megalomaniac fashion that he can divest himself of his sovereignty while remaining untouched in his authority. It is rather that the power which has passed through weakness is not one in substance with the power which thrust it there. The signifier 'power' conceals a change in substance. Hence the difference between a superstitious view of sacrifice and a revolutionary one. In the former case, you consume the flesh of the sacrificial victim in order to brim yourself full of its mysterious strength, drawing life directly from its death. In the latter case, what you identify with (in the case of the Christian Eucharist, by literally absorbing it into your flesh as nourishment) is the transfigurative power of the victim's very weakness, the scapegoat as living death, not as a creature slain in order that you may hijack its vital force and live more vigorously at its expense. There is no simple passage from death to life here, but rather a movement from a living death (that of the destitute, the scapegoat) to a life which can flourish all the more richly because it has absorbed this death into itself in the form of an abiding awareness of human frailty, neediness and dependency. Only the political action which maintains this fidelity to failure can bear fruit. Only in the knowledge that failure is definitive of us can we succeed.

In the tragic calculus of all, something and nothing, there can be no such thing as a global identity. They told me I was everything, the repentant Lear reflects bitterly, but it was false: 'I am not ague-proof'. What has forced him into a sense of finitude is the fragility of the body. Power can wreak the damage it does because it is bodiless, swaddled from material need by a thick skin of property and privilege. When we are out of our senses we are out of our mind. Now Lear has to 'see feelingly', think with the body, just as the blinded Gloucester must smell his way to Dover. One cannot be human without overreaching the body (hubris is what makes us human), yet this is also the source of our inhumanity. The contradictions of an Oedipus, who like the rest of us has knowledge only by virtue of the flaw which blinds him to the secret sources of his own flesh, come to a head in our own day in the military generals who can bomb at will because they are too remote to smell the burning flesh of their victims. But to speak of original sin as *felix culpa* is to remind ourselves that this blind spot is also the source of our creativity, as Oedipus or Gloucester can see only when they are eyeless.

A global identity, of the kind which the United States is intent on achieving today, is an oxymoron, since there are none so blind as those who see only themselves. The most narcissistic nation is the one with its gunboats in every continent. You cannot roll over difference in the name of securing your identity, since in doing so you scupper the very conditions of identity itself. Like Oedipus, the West ends up blinded by an enormous knowledge, undone by its own forensic powers. Nothing more graphically illustrates this paradox than its confrontation with Islamic fundamentalism, in which one crazed textual literalness (Texan) encounters another (Taliban). The less the West is able to decipher its own bloodstained image in the monstrosity of terrorism, discern the fruits of its own political actions in this festering despair, the more it can complacently define terrorism as absolute otherness; but the more it does this, the more justified it feels in suppressing the liberties and violating the rights of its own citizenry, thereby losing grip of its own dog-eared liberal-democratic identity and turning into an image of what it opposes, which, one need hardly add, is exactly what its opponents hope to achieve. What swifter way of forcing the West once more into fascism then driving it to defend its democratic freedoms?

Yet terrorism is far from absolutely other. Like most moral obscenities, it begins at home. As a self-conscious cult of political violence, a specialized form of politics all of its own rather than just the kind of common-or-garden ravaging and plundering which runs back into the mists of time, terrorism is a thoroughly modern phenomenon, one which comes to birth at the origin of European middle-period modernity, the French Revolution. For Hegel, that revolution was the triumph of absolute freedom, or 'freedom in a void'; as he scathingly called it. It was the very epitome of bourgeois liberty – the fantasy of a freedom so utterly absolved of constraint that it could not even bear to be restricted by itself, and thus turned logically to devouring itself once it had consumed its enemies.

Such liberty is bound to be self-destructive because it harbours a virulent hatred of material limit, and so cannot tolerate even its own concrete self-realization. The force which drives this most crassly materialist of all social orders is secretly anti-materialist, horrified by the unfinishedness and impurity of matter, enraptured by annihilation. It is, in a word, the death drive, a ferociously pure idealism which is in love only with itself, which accumulates for the sake of the obscene pleasure of voiding and negating, and which is known admiringly by Western ideology as the all-affirmative will. It is bourgeois society itself, so Hegel recognizes, which is the ultimate anarchist, the very figure of what it fears. The destruction from which it protects itself springs straight from its heart. This is literally so today, when Islamic terrorism represents a Western violence come home to roost, the reimagined as the abominable and outlandish, market forces reconfigured as the monstrous.

Tragic or revolutionary: the terms are more usually contrasted than coupled. For tragedy is supposed to be the most patrician of all the art forms, heroic and high-minded, more preoccupied with the death of princes than with anything as drably quotidian as car smashes or concentration camps. The aesthetics of tragedy are seized less by human suffering than by its sublime transcendence. For this cadet-corps ideology, only *affirmative* suffering passes muster as the genuine tragic article, as opposed to the merely miserable or drearily dejected. Only that anguish which is exultant and auratic need apply for tragic status, just as only a humour which steers clear of belly laughs may qualify for classical French theatre. No artistic form, at least according to its conservative champions, is more fastidiously pure, rank-conscious, remorselessly idealist or jealous of its honour. Tragedy is life-enhancing rather than dispirited – a quality which proves precious to those ruling classes for whom pessimism is somehow subversive. In few places has this been truer than in the United States, that profoundly anti-tragic culture (though the source, so to speak, of tragedy in others) whose ideological orthodoxy regards scepticism as a thought crime and negativity as unpatriotic.

The exaltation of suffering in much classical tragic theory is at root a device for disavowing it. What it refuses to countenance is that tragedy, so to speak, is itself tragic. It is indeed true, as Yeats observes, that nothing can be sole or whole that has not been rent; but one might at least have the decency to add, in order to distinguish this Christian and Marxist orthodoxy from the Boy Scout syndrome, that it would be far preferable if this were not the case. If tragedy is a kind of value, then it is the kind of value we could do without, rather as it is a crying shame that we ever had to have anything called socialism. What we have in the theory of tragedy is for the most part an ideology, which is thus exactly the opposite of what is taking place in *Oedipus, Lear,* or *Death of a Salesman.* It is, moreover, for the most part a sort of religious ideology, in all the most objectionable senses of the word.

It is not only the modern age which makes an ideology out of tragedy. As a state apparatus, tragic art was harnessed to political dominion from the outset. For Aristotle's *Poetics,* it performs the politically vital service of draining off from the *polis* a perilous surplus of pity and fear, both socially enfeebling emotions. It is a kind of public therapy for a citizenry in danger of emotional flabbiness.

The anti-ideological version of this is something like the crucifixion of Jesus, that sublime tragic scenario in which it is neither a question of our morbidly indulging nor briskly dispelling our pity and fear, but – absurdly – of the scapegoat himself taking compassion on us and pleading fearfully that the punishment we deserve for this cowardly political murder should not fall on our heads.

The reason Jesus himself gives to get us off the hook is, exactly, our ideological mystification – the fact that we cannot possibly know what we are doing, any more than any historic event can know itself other than in retrospect. By which time, of course, it cannot be undone, so that the knowledge is in a strict sense useless. We live forwards and understand backwards. Establishing a symbolic solidarity with this kind of scapegoat means accepting his pity by coming to have pity for ourselves, confessing our weakness and thus being freed from guilt. To grasp that this monster is of our own making is not just to acknowledge that it is we who have reduced him to this lamentable condition, but that in doing so we have turned him into a living image of ourselves.

To be able to look upon this frightful image of ourselves and live is to confess that the power by which we have brought the world to such a sorry pass is in fact no genuine power at all, but the reflex of frailty. It is to recognize that aggression, dominion, hatred and greed have their root in fear. To discern the lineaments of true power in weakness – in the political actions of those who have nothing much left to lose – also involves discerning the pathos and bogusness of the power they challenge, even though it might well end up by blowing us all to pieces. Jesus is the figure of the *anawim*, the destitute or shit of the earth, those whose fate is to be divested even of themselves; but it is not just a question of acknowledging our responsibility for this fate, as class-society might confess in a spasm of self-recrimination that hunger and poverty are its own creations. It is only when we recognize our own countenance, rather than just our own actions, in the disfigured and dispossessed, when we acknowledge that their weakness signifies the fundamental failure of our own power system, that we can shift from liberal guilt to revolutionary politics.

Tragedy in the epoch of modernity has fulfilled rather different ideological functions from those proposed by Aristotle. For one thing, it has acted as a secularized or aestheticized version of theodicy. If tragedy is the art-form which plucks affirmation, even joy and ecstasy, from human anguish, then it promises to offer yet another account – this time one conveniently unexplicated, shown rather than said – of the problem of evil. In fact, a great deal of tragic art is either silent on this score, or like much ancient tragedy stubbornly refuses to let the gods off the hook. Far from making suffering seem cosmically explicable, it allows its raw shrieks to resound unredemptively around the stage. It is for the most part tragic theory, not tragic practice, which seeks to reconcile us to our suffering as mysteriously providential, in notable contradiction to the attitude of the New Testament. For the New Testament, it would seem that suffering is an evil, which if it cannot be repaired is best avoided. If you cannot avoid it, then that is an evil as well – which is not to say that the confrontation may not issue in some good. It is preferable, however, not to have to snatch value from the jaws of pain and heartache if you can conceivably do otherwise. It is only because the world is as oppressive as it is, and will seek to destroy you if you challenge it in the name of justice, that such avoidance is sometimes tragically impossible.

For some of its apologists, tragedy is also a displaced form of religion in being a trace of the numinous in a naughty world, a residue of the mysterious, mythological and metaphysical in a disenchanted age. It can talk of the transcendent without the embarrassment of having to put a name to it, hijack its high-toned glamour while ditching its tedious doctrine. Tragedy is where the gods, blood guilt, cosmic destiny and the mystery of evil can still find a precarious foothold – and find it moreover, in yet another ideological function of the tragic, in the form of a critique of modernity as such. Tragedy is the mythology which upbraids a modernity from which myth has been banished. As an aristocrat among art forms, it does what the aesthetic in general accomplishes in the modern period, but in a way that is exalted, writ large, raised to the second power. To claim, as critics frequently do, that tragedy is the most precious of aesthetic forms is really to propose that it is most typical or paradigmatic of the arts in the age of modernity, a distillation of their very essence and function.

In its unfathomable depths and starkly absolutist claims, tragic art is an antidote to the callow rationalism of modern culture, a critique of hubristic Reason. It represents the dark underside of Enlightenment, the obscurely suggestive shadow cast by an excess of light. Its gods, princes and virile protagonists recall us to an heroic era before we lapsed into the squalor of democracy and the catastrophe of egalitarianism. Tragedy celebrates the sovereignty of power and fate over human agency, unmasking sentimental humanitarianism for the contemptible sham that it is. In disdain of all brittle doctrines of Progress, it rubs our noses in the eternally irreparable. No mere medicine could patch up Philoctetes's foot, no social engineering retrieve Phaedra from her doom. Tragedy in this view of it is the most unabashedly Tory of modes, valuing wisdom over knowledge, eternity over history. In affirming human powers in a way beyond the ken of the petit bourgeois suburban scientists, it also humbles them before some transcendent truth. Man has a dignity beyond the political mob or the scientific laboratory, but one entirely compatible with reverent submission. He is autonomous enough to rebut the scientific determinists, but subject to cosmic law in a way that equally confounds their middle-class colleagues, the liberal individualists.

Indeed, the question of freedom and determinism is another of tragedy's ideological functions, at least in the eyes of the great German theorists of the mode from Hegel and Hölderlin to Schelling and Schlegel. Tragedy is an aesthetic solution to a philosophical contradiction – to the Kantian dualism of phenomenal determinism and noumenal freedom. Here, perhaps, is one solution to the puzzle of why tragedy, that most absolutist, aristocratic, anti-reformist of modes, should loom so large in the thinking of a buoyantly progressivist bourgeoisie, if by no means quite so large in its dramatic practice. Why does the topic crop up in one modern European philosopher after another, from Schopenhauer to Sartre? One might do worse than respond that it is an answer (though, once again, more as a showing than a saying) to the problem of how we are apparently at once free and unfree.

Like any interesting philosophical problem, this is not of course in the first place a philosophical problem. It runs right to the heart of a bourgeois social order for which the political realm – one of freedom as collective self-determination – is at loggerheads with the economic domain, in which we are shuttled around like so many inert bits of matter by unmasterable market forces. A knowledge of necessity is the dream of the human sciences, since then we would be able to calculate our actions more exactly, and hence be more free to realize our projects. The fantasy of the stockbroker is to be able to foresee the behaviour of others while remaining impenetrably unpredictable himself, appropriating Kant's noumenal realm for himself while consigning his competitors to the phenomenal. Yet such predictive knowledge is also the ruin of freedom, which thrives on the incalculable. This is why the American movie *Minority Report* must finally dismiss such precognition as the enemy of freedom rather than the enablement of it. Freedom and order are not really compatible. The human sciences are necessarily self-undoing, scuppering the very liberty whose conditions they investigate.

One might also post the question of freedom and unfreedom in a familiar Marxist form. Why is it that in these social conditions, our apparently free actions are confiscated from us, congeal into iron laws, and come to confront us in unrecognizable form as an implacable destiny? By what fatal mechanism does freedom warp into the image of its opposite, just as equality veers on its axis to become exploitation? This, to be sure, is scarcely a question peculiar to capitalism, though it is one mightily magnified there. Among other things, it is the *cri de coeur* of Oedipus himself, who discovers like the rest of us that the Other returns an estranging response to the question of who he is. Philippe Lacoue-Labarthe argues that Oedipus, before becoming with Freud the 'figure of desire', was the figure of the scientist or philosopher (though epistemophilia can be assumed to unite the two).[2] He is thus, one might claim, the allegorical signifier of the West twice over, first as daylight and then as darkness. Oedipus is knowledge at the end of its tether, the transparently obvious ruin of self-transparency, the starkest possible illumination of the obscurely unfathomable roots of selfhood. It is only after Kant has revealed the contradictions into which human reason falls when it seeks to transgress its own limits that Oedipus, with his hubristic hunger for a knowledge which will finally blind him, stages his reappearance in philosophy, with Hegel, Hölderlin, Schelling, Schlegel and their *confrères*.

Yet tragedy is not just a salutary upbraiding of Enlightenment, a matter of traditionalist prudence against an upstart bourgeois eagerness. On the contrary, it is both the realization and the ruin of Enlightenment, which is no doubt one reason why it proves so alluring to a German philosophy as conscious of the baffling of Enlightenment in its national history as of its pressing relevance to it. On this view, tragedy portrays the defeat of the protagonist, crushed by a sublime Reason which brooks no rebellion. Yet in bowing to this Absolute, or indeed in resolutely embracing it in the manner of Shakespeare's Antony or Kleist's Prince Friedrich von Homberg, the tragic protagonist both obediently ratifies that Law and reveals at the same time a freedom which raises him to equality with it – which demonstrates, in fact, that his resolute submission is itself the secret work of the very Law or Reason which seems so oppressive.

If the insurgent hero's Oedipal strike against the Name of the Father is punished by death and destruction, hence expiating his guilt, it is also what ushers him into mature equality with that Law. His very failure yields us a glimpse of an infinite order of freedom and justice – one which, as in the Kantian sublime, can be illuminated only by negation, in the devouring flames which lay bare the hero's finitude. The power to relinquish one's creaturely existence could only spring from beyond it, so that the hero, as both priest and sacrificial victim, presides over the ritual of his own destruction with an authority which outlives it. The freedom by which he accepts his own finitude disproves it at a stroke. The act of being able to draw a limit to one's power must inevitably be self-undoing. The tragic act is in this sense a performative contradiction, transcending in its very freedom the limit to which it submits. Vulgar determinism is elevated to the rather more august status of providence, and the deepest liberty lies in a knowledge of necessity. The Absolute graciously permits the hero to struggle against his doom, and in doing so pays tribute to his freedom. Without transgression, the Law is out of business.

If this promises to resolve the Kantian schism of freedom and determinism, it is because what seems an oppressive fate turns out to be Reason itself in phenomenal disguise, but also because what seems to be submission to this Law is in fact freedom. By choosing the inevitable in a spirit of *amor fati*, running towards one's death (as Shakespeare's Antony vows that he will) as a bridegroom to a lover's bed, one reclaims it for human liberty, making one's destiny one's decision. Nothing more cogently demonstrates your freedom than the act of gratuitously giving it away. Reason, moreover, has always-already incorporated the hero's free action into its majestic teleology, and Necessity itself turns out to have the free self-determination of a subject. Tragedy also dismantles the distinction between freedom and necessity in a different sense, by demonstrating, all the way from Antigone to Willy Loman, that the commitments which most deeply constitute the self are not really of the kind it can easily choose. There is an inner as well as an outer necessity, a moral as well as a material destiny, as the ancient Greeks were well aware. There is a sense in which we are most free when we have no choice – when not to do what we must do is to violate the selfhood which is the very source of freedom.

It is not hard to read in this version of tragedy the allegory of a prematurely insurgent bourgeoisie – one conscious of the truth that political absolutism is still too powerful to break, but which can console itself with the knowledge that Reason is secretly on its side and will bring it to fruition in the fullness of time. Schiller's *Don Carlos* ends on just such a note. Neither is it difficult to see in this theory of tragedy a secularized version of the theology of the Crucifixion, to which it is faithful in almost every detail. For Schelling, the paradox of law and liberty is most graphically revealed when the tragic protagonist is an innocent figure who gratuitously embraces guilt and punishment, demonstrating his freedom through the loss of it. Indeed, the oxymoronic figure of the guilty innocent is the very stuff of tragedy from Oedipus onward. Yet it is also possible to decipher in this model of tragedy the dialectical movement by which, for the Georg Lukács of *History and Class Consciousness*, the working class comes to transcend its own commodity-like status in the act of confronting this very degradation, so that only a consciousness which has actively taken on the ultimate status of thinghood or sheer meaningless materiality can redeem that facticity as a general condition. Which is to say, for orthodox Marxist doctrine, that only an immanence can become transcendence.

Scapegoats, blood sacrifice, hubris, the *anawim*: no discourse could be less archaic, no language more insistently relevant to our political world. The postmodern discourse which might find all this a touch mythological or metaphysical is for the same reason embarrassed by talk of revolution. What we face, politically speaking, is a choice between one kind of death-in-life and another. On the one hand there is the hubristic Western will, a form of 'bad' infinity, shimmering with the hectic vitality of the terminally diseased. It is a form of life secretly in love with annihilation, and all that saves it from evil is the fact that it genuinely mistakes this nihilism for energy. Evil is far more clear-eyed about the matter: it knows that the point is to unmask the portentous sham of all apparent vitality by searching out the nothingness at its heart and revelling in it, creating even more of the stuff by destroying for the sheer delight of it. The imperial Western will is the death drive in the guise of the life-giving.

On the other hand, there is the alternative form of death-in-life which is the existence of the dispossessed, who know that only a life which has passed through death, finitude and failure, and continues to nourish these things at its heart, has any final chance of flourishing. In the meantime, the West continues to prove incapable of tragedy. It cannot recognize its own visage in the raging fury at its gates. It is unable to decipher the symptoms of weakness and despair in that fury, and therefore is capable only of fear rather than pity.

Notes

[1] I have discussed these questions more fully in *Sweet Violence: The Idea of the Tragic* (Oxford: Wiley Blackwell, 2003).

[2] See Philippe Lacoue-Labarther, 'Oedipus as Figure', *Radical Philosophy* 118 (2003).

Chapter 6

'The Weight of History': Poets and Artists in World War Two

John Lucas

Paul Nash's famous letter of 1917, in which he hoped that his 'message', however feeble and inarticulate, would burn the lousy souls of those prolonging and glorifying in the war, was written from the Western front at a time when, as an official war artist, he was painting 'The Menin Road' and 'We Are Making a New World'. These two great paintings between them sum up much of the horror of the First World War. In the Menin Road we are made to stare at a series of apparently directionless tracks zigzagging through a churned-up landscape of broken trees and crater holes, most filled with water the colour of mustard, across which random figures pick their way, trudging hopelessly from nowhere to nowhere. And in the other painting, a sun rises – or falls – through blood-red clouds, fitfully illuminating a landscape devoid of any life, human or natural. 'We' is inclusive, although not all are equally to blame. There is a difference between the lousy souls of those who ordered the fighting and those who took their orders and died. But the experience of war is for Nash overwhelmingly one of destruction.

A little more than 20 years later, Nash was again appointed to act as an official war artist, and again produced some of the most memorable paintings to come out of the war against Germany. The dead sea of 'Totes Meer' (1940–1) depicts a dump of wrecked German aircraft at Cowley, Oxford, wings and fuselages heaped together in a litter of steel waves over a waning half moon. Writing about the painting to Kenneth Clark, who as chairman of the War Artists' Advisory Committee was charged with commissioning and purchasing war art, Nash commented that 'the only moving creature is the white owl flying low over the bodies of the other predatory creatures, raking the shadows for rats and voles'.[1] The owl reasserts the primacy of nature over the wrecked man-made killers. And that the title should be in German makes plain Nash's conviction that Hitler's Germany is responsible for making a new world of death. To the experience of war has now been added a judgement in which the meaning of history is involved. The rearming of Germany, the appeasement of Hitler, has brought us to this.

And there is another matter to consider. In the previous world war, Nash had to travel to France to see the new world that was being created. But now the lousy souls of the nazis threaten the British mainland. The odour of death has offended the very heart of England. Bombing raids were meant to soften the nation up for invasion. It hardly needs saying that the extraordinary courage and skill shown by British pilots during what became called the Battle of Britain led to a cancelling or anyway postponement of Hitler's plans. Nash's painting, 'Battle of Britain' (1941) attempts, in his own words, 'to give the sense of an aerial battle in operation over a wide area, and thus summarize England's great aerial victory over Germany'.[2] 'England's', not 'Britain's'. Patriotism is confined to his native country. It is even more notably confined to the southern counties as his painting, 'Oxford in Wartime' (1943), reveals. I touch on the implications of this in a poem, 'Other Houses, Other Lives':

> *Oxford in Wartime.* Nash's premonitory oil
> views Hopkins's 'towery city' from a hill
> up which lumber numerous tanks, massed steel
> to cull the White Roses of Death
> that Hitler's planes would scatter and let fall
> on the Heart of England, poisoning the sweet breath
> of Culture.[3]

The full horror of the German dead sea can only be fully registered, Nash hints, when you realize that the marish is lapping at Oxford. Like many artists, writers and intellectuals of his generation, Nash instinctively thought of England as an essentially rural, ancient land. Home Counties England. It was *this* England which was under threat, *this* 'immemorial' way of life which men and women must fight to protect. It is so in David Gascoyne's short lyric 'Oxford: A Spring Day', written in 1941, in which Gascoyne remarks on spring's 'swift tremulous instant of rebirth and peace', and then,

> Tremulous – yet underneath, how deep its root!
> Timelessness of an afternoon! Air's gems, the walls' bland grey,
> Slim spires, hope-coloured fields: these belong to no date.[4]

Oxford stands as metonymy for an England that is or anyway ought to be outside history or in which history is an endless – dateless – repetition. And it is true that the Battle of Britain was fought above fields of the southern shires from where agricultural workers stared up at tiny, flickering, fast-wheeling objects seemingly no bigger than skylarks. But it is also true that it was the cities of the industrial midlands and north, which, London apart, took most of the pounding from Hitler's bombers.

I do not however want here to make much of this undoubted fact. That would require a different essay. Of more immediate relevance is Nash's sense that

England's security is threatened as never before. Not that invasion threats were new. But previously they had come from the sea. This time, they came as much from the air. And how defend against those? Anyone now in their seventies will remember how, for the duration of a war at the outset of which the entire civilian population had been kitted out with gas masks, we were urged to keep a lookout for German paratroopers, those White Roses of Death as the Spanish republicans dubbed the storm troopers Hitler sent to help Franco, who might at any time fall silently from the sky, thereby signalling the start of the expected air-and-sea invasion of our shores. And though the threat of airborne invasion dwindled as the war went on, it never went away. (Owen Sheers' novel, *Resistance* plausibly imagines England and Wales under a German army of occupation.)[5] Some 2,000 English people had been killed by air-raids in the First World War. It was clear that flying machines would be integral to any future war, able to deliver death and destruction on an entirely new scale. By the middle 1920s there was talk of the need to construct underground cities to protect at least some of the population from gas bombs which enemy aircraft would, it was widely assumed, drop in large quantities. The *London Illustrated News* featured illustrations of one such imagined city. There was even a certain amount of construction, which, if it didn't extend to the building of entire cities, certainly provided well-fortified and extensive bunkers.[6]

Eric Ravilious's magical, mysterious watercolour, 'Train Landscape', painted in 1939, may not at first appear to have anything to do with invasion fears. It is one of a series in which Ravilious made good his interest in 'mapping' prehistoric or ancient features of the English countryside, an interest he shared with Nash and John Piper, all of them alert to the writings of the archaeologist, Jacquetta Hawkes and to H. J. Massingham, 'whose books Downland Man, 1926, and English Downland, 1936', Alan Powers tells us, 'described the chalk country of southern England as the most essentially English of the country's varied landscapes, speculating on the historical formulation of an English people in this region.' But Powers suggests that 'Ravilious was not visibly affected by Massingham's pessimism.'[7] I disagree. The very fact that Ravilious spends so much time painting this landscape surely testifies to a compulsive need to record it before it disappears or comes under new/enemy ownership. In suggesting that Ravilious 'captures perfectly the antinomy' of landscape and railway train in his landscape, Powers refers to Ian Carter's *Railways and Culture in Britain: The Epitome of Modernity* and he adds that 'Ravilious undoubtedly had a deep feeling for the "country" which in his own lifetime was coming under increasing threat from suburbanisation.'[8] But that isn't where the threat lies. Neither in 'Train Landscape' nor its companion piece 'The Westbury Horse' (1939), where a train is seen crossing a stretch of land below the hill on which the horse is carved and which it seems massively to guard, is the railway a threat. On the contrary, it is easily accommodated into the landscape. The train in 'The Westbury Horse', seen in the distance, is a kind of child's train, and in 'Train Landscape' our view, as though from that same train, is now across a third-class carriage out onto the landscape with the horse in the distance, while the carriage itself, with its patterned carriage-cloth and wooden-framed windows, seems as cosy and rustic-feeling as a cottage interior.

Powers tells us that after the war, Ravilious's son James, 'continued the family tradition of silent witness to the integrity of rural working life'.[9] But in 'The Westbury Horse' and 'Train Landscape' there is no such life. Nobody is shown at work, in fact there are no humans in either landscape, and the carriage of 'Train Landscape' is itself empty, which, given that it is marked 3, is very unusual. Or is this the point? Life has drained away from the land. Its very emptiness inevitably carries a melancholy charge or, conceivably, is a discreet portent of what may soon be England's fate. And we have then to note the widely held belief that the white horse of Westbury had been carved to celebrate Alfred's decisive victory over the Danes at Edington in Wiltshire in 878. (The white horse is equidistant between Westbury and Edington.) It was a symbol of England's ability to withstand invasion. A foolish poem of 1940 by Dorothy Sayers welcomed the opportunity given Britain, after the fall of France, to resist Hitler's plans, although instructively she thinks of it as purely English resistance:

This is the war that we have known
　　And fought in every hundred years,
Our sword, upon the last, steep path,
Forged by the hammer of our wrath
　　On the anvil of our fears.

Send us, O God, the will and power
　　To do as we have done before,
The men that ride the sea and air
Are the same men their fathers were
　　To fight the English war.[10]

But few of those who had to do the fighting welcomed this opportunity. There was precious little of that mood of innocent exultance which had led Julian Grenfell and others into battle in 1914. First, and as I have already noted, *this* war might well be fought on home soil. Second, there was no doubting the power and resources of Hitler's armed forces. Third, the coming of war proved the folly, if not downright wickedness, of liberal governments trying to appease fascist dictators. And for members of the Communist Party of Great Britain (CPGB), who almost alone had argued against such appeasement, who had supported the Republican government in Spain against Franco, and who rightly saw the fascist threat to Europe as both real and pressing, there was the problem that the Molotov-Ribbentrop Pact left King Street to argue that communists should keep out of fighting a war between corrupt capitalist nation-states.

What everyone agreed, at least in hindsight, was that this war had been coming. The weight of history now bore down on all. No matter where you put down a marker for the war's inception – the treaty of Versailles, the collapse of the Weimar Republic, the Anschluss, the Italian invasion of Abyssinia, Britain and France's non-interventionist policy at the time of the Spanish War (which obligingly guaranteed Franco's victory) – even before Chamberlain's declaration of war on 3 September, 'the sirens cry in the dark morning / and the lights go out and the town is still / And the sky is pregnant with ill-will', as Louis MacNeice commented in *Autumn Journal*.[11] Or, as Geoffrey Matthews wrote in 'War has become Official, old Friend', 'Time's come at last to stop and rope in all my / Friends and memory and say goodbye'.[12] 'Old Friend' may be overdoing it, given that Matthews had been born in 1920, but he was among those, including E. P. Thompson and Arnold Rattenbury, who as committed communists took for granted the need to fight the forces which all too plainly had for years been preparing to overwhelm the liberal democracies of Europe.

It is this sense of commitment to a just cause which makes the Second World War so different from the first. But there is no sense of exultation about having to fight this war. For many of those who accept that the war is inescapable also know that what happened in the years 1914–18 will almost certainly be repeated: once again millions will die, official bungling and failed military plans are to be expected, and bullshit can be guaranteed. The mood at war's outbreak was therefore predominantly anti-heroic and often fearful, too. This was part of the weight of history and anyone who thought or said otherwise was talking bullshit. Bullshit was what the artist James Boswell made his especial subject. Not an official war artist – as Richard Cork has remarked, 'no Committee was ever going to vet his response to the war, let alone purchase his work' – Boswell was free to 'allegorise the war as a bestial farce conducted by bulls. These Orwellian animals, often dressed in generals' uniforms, heave their obese bulk through page after page [of three sketchbooks]. They ride on the backs of exhausted Tommies, pause with a watering-can to sprinkle a flower-pot containing the grotesquely dismembered skeleton of a soldier, and sit on a hideous pile of corpses and buildings while they type out a mass of documents which sail ridiculously into the sky.'[13] Given that Boswell was a member of the communist party, had been an enthusiastic member of the AIA, and had worked for both *The Daily Worker* and *Left Review*, this attack on bullshit might seem odd. Surely there were other and more deserving targets?

Perhaps. But like many others who fought, Boswell was a conscript. (He was called up in 1941.) It is one of the more obvious paradoxes of the two world wars that in August 1914 thousands immediately volunteered to fight in a war of questionable worth, whereas in September 1939, at the outset of one of the few just wars in history, the queues outside recruitment offices were far shorter. Leave aside the especial problem of members of the CPGB, who wanted to fight but were told by Harry Pollit, acting on orders from Moscow, that this was not their war, the fact is that many others were uncertain what they should do.

Some years earlier, Ernie Bevin, one of the few Labour leaders to understand the threat Hitler posed, had publicly attacked poor George Lansbury for hawking his pacifist conscience from party meeting to party to party meeting, but pacifism on the left was by no means confined to the Independent Labour Party (ILP), although significantly it was the ILP which George Orwell joined after his return from Spain. In September 1938 Orwell was signatory to a party manifesto printed in the *New Leader* under the title 'If War Comes We Shall Resist It', and when a year later Chamberlain committed the country to war against Germany, Orwell, according to D. J. Taylor, could detect no great enthusiasm among the London crowd with whom he had been mingling.[14]

Well, to adapt a famous phrase, there wouldn't be, would there? As has often enough been pointed out, virtually every family in Britain had been affected by the previous war: by deaths of fathers, brothers, husbands, sons, or other relatives, or by having to deal with war's aftermath such as incurable injuries, mental breakdown, impoverishment. Why go through that again? I am not sure what the evidence is on which Taylor bases his claim that 'the Left Book Club agitation about a war in defence of democracy had gone some way towards losing the Labour Party the anticipated general election'[15] but it is certainly true that, in C. L. Mowat's words, 'until after Munich there was no question that appeasement was popular, despite its many critics. . . . The alternative to appeasement was war . . . and no one advocated that. Certainly not the Labour party. . . . In retrospect everyone was against appeasement; at the time not so many.'[16]

As soon as war was declared Orwell offered himself for military service, but he did so as an English patriot, not because he greatly cared about the cause. And he had fought in Spain! For the vast majority, who hadn't, I suspect that war seemed to guarantee nothing so much as immiseration. And mass evacuation of children from the cities was the first sign of this. (It began on 1 September, even before the announcement of war.) In the space I have available I can't possibly go into this, nor the emotional impact it must have had on families, especially when news arrived of the torpedoing by U boat of the *Athenia*, the first ship to leave for Canada from Liverpool on the very day war was announced, with the loss of 120 people, including children. Boswell's contempt for Bullshit has therefore to be seen in the context of a disenchantment directed against those in power who had let this war happen. The lesson of history was that there was no lesson. At all events, no lesson had been learnt. Or not the right lesson.

For evidence of this, Boswell could have pointed to a cartoon by Will Dyson. In 1919, Dyson, like Boswell a New Zealander and cartoonist, had made a drawing for the *Daily Herald* which showed the statesmen who cobbled together the Versailles Peace Treaty coming down the stairs of the railway carriage where the treaty was signed. Smugness prevails. But one of them, cocking an ear, tells the others, 'Somewhere I hear a child crying.' At the bottom left of the cartoon is a baby bawling its eyes out, with a sash round its naked body which reads *Class of 1939*. Brilliant, cannily prescient. And now it had to be gone through again, this time with the dread near-certainty of invasion, and, horror of horrors, with more or less the same lot in charge. Hence, Bullshit. Hence, too, the wry exasperation of Keith Douglas's 'Aristocrats', for whom war is still great sport: 'The plains were their cricket pitch / and in the mountains the tremendous drop fences / brought down some of the runners. Here then / under the stones and earth they dispose themselves, / 1 think with their famous unconcern. / It is not gunfire I hear but a hunting horn.' The word 'dispose', with its hint of aristocratic drawl – the long *o* of the second syllable echoing the long *o* of 'stones', exactly catches what is at once admirable and insufferable about the professional officer class. 'Dispose': to arrange suitably; to put in its proper place. 'Disposed': to be available, to be inclined. Douglas half admires what he anathematizes.

Not so Boswell, for whom no doubt some trace memory of Gallipoli outlaws tolerance of bullshitting generals. Not so, either, for Gavin Ewart, whose 'Officers' Mess' is about bullshitters who toddle home not so much to safely die in bed as to collapse on it, dead drunk:

> It's going to be a thick night tonight (and the night before was a thick one);
> I've just seen the Padre disappearing into the 'Cock and Bull' for a quick one.
> I don't mind telling you this old boy, we got the Major drinking –
> You probably know the amount of gin he's in the habit of sinking –
> And then this new M. O. came in, the Jewish one, awful fellow,
> And his wife, a nice little bit of stuff, dressed in a flaming yellow.
> Looked a pretty warmish piece, old boy, – no, have this one with me –
> They were both so blind (and so was the Major) that they could hardly see.[17]

Ewart's contempt for brass hats, comic, dismissive, brings to mind a story told by Peter Ustinov. As a would-be recruit, the young Ustinov presented himself for active service and was greeted by a brandy colonel, glass at elbow and puffing on a cigarette, who took his name and then, leaning towards him, said confidentially, 'One thing this war's taught me, Ustinov. Never go south of Dover.'

* * *

We are here not so much dealing with general truths as with perceptions. Reading poets of the Second World War, I am struck by how, especially in the early days, they not only lack enthusiasm for the war, but by the way in which their stance of indifference to their superiors, no matter how varyingly expressed, suggests both a sense of sardonic disbelief in the wisdom of those in control, as well as a determination to enjoy themselves while they can – or at least to refuse any conventional idea of stiff-upper lip heroism. The great, and scandalously ignored Scottish poet, Hamish Henderson, for example, who was later in the war to write a song to be sung to the tune of 'Lily Marlene', called 'The D Day Dodgers', in 1940 produced 'X Still = 0', which ends: 'And we've had it, and all, this poor bloody generation. / Still, / for "history" the verdict is easy. Poor mugs, they bought / a pig in the same old poke. X still equals nought./ Still'. That apparently insignificant word, given a line to itself, is poised between two meanings: 'Always', and the acrid, laconic throwaway reflection that 'history' will give 'this poor bloody generation' short shrift. In his *Elegy for the Dead in Cyrenaica* Henderson more than makes amends for the shortcomings of 'history'. The poem knocks away the quotation marks that stockade any partial telling of truths. Like his fellow-Scottish-Marxist poets, Robert Garioch and Sorley Maclean, Henderson saw himself as fighting not for the cause of the British empire but for an emergent socialist democracy. In this sense, history was in the making.

English poets by and large lacked this conviction. In fact, you could say that at war's outset they lacked *any* conviction, *any* sense of a grand future to be fought for. I don't know exactly when Frances Scarfe's 'The Conscript' was written, but it can't have been later than mid-1941 because his two collections were published in 1940 and 1941. Its first stanza is utterly bleak, even defeatist, in its assessment of war:

Delicate ingenuous his quivering blue eye
Miniatures the horizon of the condemned sky
Where burns all history in the bones of children
And fall the tears of remorse and breaks the heart of heaven.

And the same holds true for the fourth and final stanza:

Tranquil the thrush sings on the twisted pylon
Its song unwinding the unbearable pattern
Of loss, fear, blood, night's aching empty arms,
Back to the heat of love and smell of home.[18]

Scarfe may intend a glance at Hardy's Darkling Thrush, which, despite its blast beruffled plume, nevertheless sings of 'some blessed hope', but the song of Scarfe's thrush is very different. The unwinding of a pattern from the twisted pylon (has the pylon been hit by a bomb?) leading back from loss, fear, blood, to love and home, is at best a forlorn gesture. I quote Scarfe's poem not because it is much good but because of its certainty of feeling that history now points towards universal conflagration.

And even among those for whom history had to be read more affirmatively, reassurance was hard to come by, and had to be asserted against the apparent implacable forces of present disaster. Geoffrey Mathews' fine 'Snow Piece', written in November 1940, begins in dejection. Soldiers:

Shiver, smokeless, for we have no hope, no
Hunger, but the spring may clothe despair
In flowers and vengeance. But it is vain . . .

At the end of the poem, Matthews exhorts his readers to

> Be ready. Out of this whiteness life will grow,
> And even if you wished, you could not spy on the spring.
> You would bruise your eyes against the unflinching snow.[19]

Matthews' spring is unlike Gascoyne's in that it promises not so much renewal as change: the life that will thrust itself out of the snow will be a radically new life. Life from new roots. But this confidence, diffidently expressed though it has to be, is unusual, and is predicated on Matthews' Marxist reading of history. For those who had no such comfort, that is, for most, you hunkered down to avoid bruising your eyes, and snatched at happiness while you could. The rest was bullshit.

Bullshit wasn't how Louis MacNeice would have put it. But his poem 'The Conscript', explores what is owing to history and what to individual in a way that will not distort the claims of either:

> Being so young he feels the weight of history
> Like clay around his boots: he would, if he could, fly
> In search of a future like a sycamore seed
> But is prevented by his own Necessity,
> His own yet alien, which, whatever he may plead,
> To every question gives the same reply.
> Choiceless, therefore, driven from pillar to post,
> Expiating his pedigree . . .

He becomes a divided consciousness: at once killer, by 'Necessity' (MacNeice's cap.), and 'aware, at times, of life's largesse'. The poem ends with MacNeice suggesting that 'by feeling down and upward' the conscript

>   can divine
> That dignity which far above him burns
> In stars that yet are his and which below
> Stand rooted like a dolmen in his spine.[20]

My feeling is that this poem, which was published in MacNeice's 1944 collection, *Springboard*, was probably written some years earlier. In her monograph on MacNeice, Edna Longley comments that '"conscription" is an apt metaphor for historical necessity. . . . Yet the two-dimensional "groove" of history can be counter-acted by a three-dimensional humanity: by "life's largesse."' And she quotes MacNeice himself as saying in 'Broken Windows', an essay of 1941, that 'Today we are all being dragooned by outside conditions, we all look like the shuttlecocks of War. It is therefore all the more necessary to think of ourselves as free agents.'[21] On this reading, MacNeice's is the classic liberal position, one memorably voiced by Dr Rieux in Camus's *The Plague*, when he chooses to go for a swim on the grounds that 'it's too damned silly, living only for the plague'. And though for all those called up conscription was no mere metaphor, a number of poems argue or intimate a wish for men to act as free agents, even if this amounts to nothing more glorious than a snatching of chances, of 'having a good time while we can', as Forster had put it in 'What I Believe' (1938/9).

This relishing of small pleasures and contempt for larger purposes, those windy militancies, is perfectly caught by Alan Ross in 'Angel of Harwich'. Ross, who served in the navy, wrote some of the best poems to have come out of the war. His long narrative 'J. W. 51 B *A Convoy*', is inexcusably overlooked in anthologies and literary histories of the period. As for 'Angel of Harwich', its title wittily and sardonically harks back to the Angel of Mons, whom soldiers of the First World War claimed to have seen hovering over them, saving them from death. (The Imperial War Museum has many picture postcards and illustrations that testify to this belief.) Here is the opening of Ross's poem:

She was usually good for a fuck
If she liked you, or just felt
Like a change from long hours
At the bar at the mercy of bores

Bores like the bar-leeches of Ewart's officers' mess, perhaps. The poem's closing lines run:

Better than to scorn is to bless
Such promiscuity, the 'angel of Harwich'
Who made love as a nurse
Might minister to the suffering, eyes
And legs wide, but with so rich,
So tender a compassion only fools would despise.
At sea, it was her you'd most miss.[22]

The awkward syntax of the penultimate line apart, this is an effective one-in-the-eye for conventional pieties. Those in peril on the sea didn't so much miss England as bless the miss who was good for a fuck. And who both gave and took pleasure: she 'knelt / As she liked and bucked as you felt / She was starting to come. She'd wail / Gently, straighten and then tuck / Her blouse back into her skirt, kiss, / And, slightly unsteadily, trot her way back, / Humming.'

The First World War had, of course, produced unanticipated benefits for many women. The same can be said of the second. And it wasn't merely sexual liberation. (That, too, had been a feature of women's experience in 1914–18.) For the first time women artists were officially commissioned to depict war scenes. Not that women artists did as well as their male counterparts. As Pauline Lucas remarks in her monograph on Evelyn Gibbs:

> Whilst many male artists received full commissions as war artists, the records of the Imperial War Museum show great disparity when it comes to women artists. There were around twenty-seven commissioned by the [War Artists' Advisory Committee], but in the main these were short term and for speci-fied work. The museum has pictures by fifty-eight women, but the majority of these had been work submitted independently to the WAAC, or had been purchased later by the museum. . . . Even artists as distinguished as Laura Knight were only in the B category.[23]

Category B was for artists issued with short term contracts only. Category A, contracts issued for the duration of the war, went exclusively to men. But Gibbs's major oil painting of 1942 'WVS Clothing Exchange', now in the Imperial War Museum, as well as her numerous drawings of, for example, women at work in a blood transfusion unit or a gun factory (Nottingham's Raleigh works converted to munitions-making) not only show women in wartime occupations, they inevitably depict lives changed by war, active in it. These arts or anyway crafts of war had been considered too inglorious for treatment in 1914–18, but not now. And as other drawings by Gibbs powerfully reveal, especially perhaps her studies of Nottingham streets shattered by bombs, *this* war was a total one. Nobody was safe. 'The record of the long safe centuries' for whose safeguarding Henry James had in an essay of 1915 voiced his fears, had finally been smashed. Now we were all 'Within the Rim'. This being the case, women became poets of the presence of war, rather than goaders on to glory or observers from afar. 'History', as Eliot said in 1942, although in a way he didn't mean, 'is now and England'.

E. J. Scovell had anticipated the coming of the terrible rain in her poem 'Child Waking'. This must, I think, have been written shortly after the infamous bombing of Guernica by Goering's Condor Legion, which took place on 26 April 1937, a day-long raid during which 1,600 people were killed and over 900 more injured, many seriously. In the second and third stanzas of Scovell's poem a mother, leaning over her child's cot, sees him as

> Relaxed in sleep and light,
> Face upwards, never so clear a prey to eyes;
> Like a walled town surprised out of the air –
> All life called in, yet all laid bare
>
> To the enemies above . . ..[24]

A mother's tender care becomes frighteningly transformed into threat, her fearful imagination sensing her child as defenceless against the coming bombs, and she herself powerless to protect him. And in 'Daylight Alert', Scovell deftly evokes the strange sense of having 'stepped across / A line in time, like a low wall that nettles guard, / Into a place marked off, an orchard or unkept grave-yard' which the siren's wail induces. I can still recall that sound and the truly weird impression it always made on me, a small boy: a sudden note that seemed to begin from inside the earth before it spiralled rapidly upwards to a high-pitched howl. I imagined it as climbing into air to greet the incoming bombers, as though its intention was to direct them to their target. There was also the prickle of fear, no doubt derived from the reactions of surrounding adults, but sharp though this was, it was far less keen than the shiver of wonder that came every time the siren began to uncoil itself.

For an adult the sound would have meant something very different. The siren's throb erupting into the familiar, daily world, must have brought with it an appalling threat of devastation, even if that was not quite believable, not fully graspable:

> we stand in grass and look, the low wall is crossed over.
> This is another realm where silence is so loud,
> The sky shines so, the grass springs thicker, the fruits rush and thud.
>
> Bombs have not fallen on our town; the shoppers scarcely
> Lift eyes to the clear sky and fighters crossing straight and sparsely.[25]

For this occasion, England the orchard survives, all that falls are fruit, the grave-yard is still unkept. (The town is Oxford.) Nevertheless, out of this clear sky death will surely come. 'In a Safe Area' begins, 'Life is changed, death is nearer; more will die younger / And suddenly'.[26] For in truth there is no safe area, and this sense of vulnerability to forces from above and without was bound to weigh particularly on women. Throughout the first three years of the war, the bomb-ing raids, by day and night, once started rarely let up, and for a while, and no matter how the BBC monitored the news, the entire world, including Britain, seemed to be there for Germany and Japan's taking. There was a widespread rumour that Hitler's High Command had settled on 25 May 1942 as the date when the British mainland would finally be invaded.

It is only *after* this invasion failed to materialize, *after* Rommel was forced out of North Africa, and, most important of all, *after* Russia withstood and then began to push back and pursue Hitler's forces, that history was widely seen to be doing its duty by anti-fascist democracies. The loathing of bullshit, the deter-mination not to be seen as willing conscripts, the angry contempt for those who had by their inaction or indecision allowed the war to happen, now found channels to run in that might, after all, lead to the fields of change where snow would give way to that new life which in 1940 Geoffrey Matthews hardly dared to envisage. Kingsley Amis's early short story, 'I Spy Strangers', brilliantly catches the sense of a new world opening up for soldiers who, in the closing months of the war, weren't going to be told by brass hats and bullshitters who to vote for, and who suddenly realized that together they could make change happen. This sighting of change, of a new world opening up, is also caught by the Marxist poet, Arnold Rattenbury, in his 'Calendar Song', written in 1944/5:

> The apples I ate in Bedforshire
> mocked me with red from Alamein
> and yellow from sand and the sun that's there
> and green from the wounds of Englishmen . . ..

So the poem begins, in near despair at the prospect of defeat. But it ends in triumph:

> But O, when they woke me up in June
>   and told all thumbs to touch the news
> I heard my boats grind into France
>   and the prisoning seasons let me loose.[27]

The D Day landings and the eventual victory in Europe seemed to bring the new season, whether one of change or renewal, or perhaps both. But all too soon the cold clamped weightily down. This, too, is history.

Notes

[1] Paul Nash, *Catalogue to an Exhibition at the Tate* (1975), 94.
[2] Ibid., 95.
[3] John Lucas, *The Long and the Short of It* (Bradford: Redbeck Press, 2004), 14.
[4] David Gascoyne, *Collected Poems* (London: Oxford University Press, 1978), 90.
[5] Owen Sheers, *Resistance* (London: Faber, 2007).
[6] See for this John Lucas, *The Good That We Do* (London: Greenwich Exchange, 2000), 158–62.
[7] Alan Powers, *Eric Ravilious: Imagined Realities* (London: Imperial War Museum/ Philip Wilson Publishers, n.d. but in fact 2003), 45.
[8] Ian Carter, *Railways and Culture in Britain: The Epitome of Modernity* (Manchester: Manchester University Press, 2001).
[9] Powers, *Eric Ravilious*, 45.
[10] 'The English War' in *The Terrible Rain: The War Poets 1939–1945*, ed. Brian Gardner (London: Methuen, 1977), 46.
[11] Louis MacNeice, *Autumn Journal*, XXIII (London: Faber, 1939), 90.
[12] Geoffrey Matthews, *War Poems* (Reading: Reading University Press, 1989), 8.
[13] *James Boswell, 1906–1971*: the catalogue to an exhibition of 1976 curated at Nottingham University by John Lucas and Ronald Pickvance.
[14] See D. J. Taylor, *Orwell: The Life* (London: Cape, 2003), 263–71.
[15] Ibid., 262.
[16] C. L. Mowat, *Britain between the Wars, 1918–1940* (London: Methuen, 1968), 591.

[17] Ewart, *The Terrible Rain*, 129.

[18] See *Components of the Scene: An Anthology of Prose and Poetry of the Second World War*, ed. Ronald Blythe (London: Penguin, 1966), 230.

[19] Matthews, *War Poems*, 32–4.

[20] Louis MacNeice, *Collected Poems*, ed. Peter Macdonald (London: Faber, 2007), 224–5.

[21] Edna Longley, *Louis MacNeice: A Study* (London: Faber, 1988), 90–1.

[22] Alan Ross, *Poems*, selected by David Hughes (London: Flarvill Press, 2005), 36.

[23] Pauline Lucas, *Evelyn Gibbs: Artist & Traveller* (Nottingham: Five Leaves Publications, 2001), 64–5.

[24] E. J. Scovell, *Collected Poems* (Manchester: Carcanet, 1988), 74.

[25] Ibid., 86.

[26] Ibid., 83.

[27] Arnold Rattenbury, *Several Forms of Speech: New, Early, Escaped and Last Poems* (Middlesbrough: Smokestack Books, 2008), 24.

Chapter 7

The Plains of War: Byron, Turner and the Bodies of Waterloo

Philip W. Martin

It is known that the British responses to the battle of Waterloo were many and various. While Simon Bainbridge has convincingly identified an orthodox mode in the generally triumphalist literary renditions of Waterloo, he also notes the presence of counter-cultural voices, particularly Byron's.[1] More recently, Philip Shaw's full-length study of Waterloo has revealed the battle and its moment as a highly complex and ramifying cultural cipher, capable of being mobilized as a claim for the validation of existing authority and national harmony, or as an indicator of the eternal instability of politics, power and human relations, as an anxious evocation of hubris, or indeed as an emblem of the sublime inconceivability of one epoch ending and another beginning. Despite all this, Shaw also tellingly proposes at the outset how Waterloo has been represented through two centuries as 'a resounding British triumph, symbolic not only of the defeat of French tyranny but also of the inevitable rise to power of an non-aggressive, anti-expansionist and, most dazzlingly of all, anti-Imperial mode of Empire'.[2] Shaw's landmark study unveils the inherent paradoxes of Waterloo as an enduring cultural symbol, and I wish to develop alongside this an argument for a related paradox by considering those contemporary responses to Waterloo that dwelt upon, or were perhaps fixated by, the dreadful extent and trauma of its carnage.

The writings that proliferated after Waterloo may have been predominantly celebratory in seeing the restoration of order in monarchical rights, or the reassertion of a providential universe, however desperately achieved, but even while the British status quo celebrated a victory which seemingly changed the fate of nations and decided the future shape of Europe, the shock of the extensive slaughter can be heard reverberating through accounts of the battle. In the Romantic writers, the variety of response ranges across the public celebratory poems of Southey and Wordsworth, through Byron's poetry of blood, to Hazlitt's idiosyncratic personal protest of walking the streets of London unshaven wearing a black armband. Romantic scholars and historians have provided analyses of these different reactions, and my purpose here is to explore further the kinds of vocabulary and rhetoric that Waterloo inaugurated by considering the dual response of Byron and Turner, a response which, I shall argue, requires us to concentrate on that which is frequently absent in most contemporary accounts: the dead body of the soldier, and more generally, the slaughtered dead in unimaginable numbers.

Our own awareness of the competing rhetoric of warfare has of course been sharpened recently by the urgency of the debates surrounding the wars in Iraq and Afghanistan. A single, but important, element of those arguments is the exhibition of bodies in television or newspaper accounts, reminding us that the documentary coverage of war, mediated through our advanced technologies, still takes place in a strongly contested iconography. While the casualties of war – if it is in any way possible to say this – are a diminished feature of its consequences in comparison to the debate surrounding its political effects (the notion of 'smart' weaponry having produced an illusion of reduced human suffering, and a calibration whose main currency is military casualties while civilian casualties go largely unreported) these contemporary controversies testify that the suffering and mutilated body remains the most volatile and potent symbolic representation of war's effects.

Both Mary Favret and Philip Shaw have investigated the place of this body in the discourse of war in the Romantic period. In her 1994 essay, Favret argues that the public imagination of the dead soldier's body was displaced in Britain by the fact that the war was fought overseas, and that one of the most powerful mechanisms for this displacement was the trope of the destitute war widow. She investigates the place of this figure in the dominant public sphere whose representational acts tended to exclude the primary site of suffering (the male body), but she also posits the existence of a counter-public sphere in which such violence might be realized.[3] Philip Shaw has drawn our attention to the elements through which such a counter-public sphere might be constituted, in particular through examples drawn from some little known poems of the 1790s included in Betty Bennett's anthology of 1976.[4] In one of these, 'The Field of Battle', Shaw suggests that the anonymous author opens up the workings of the trope by having the figure of the bereaved widow search for the corpse of her husband on the battlefield: the moment of discovery, and the literal nature of the journey it embodies (back from grief to its source in the fatally wounded body) places the widow and the corpse in the same frame.[5] Shaw's analysis requires us to concentrate on a compelling question he raised in an earlier essay, 'Leigh Hunt and the Aesthetics of post-war Liberalism'. In this piece, which considers how the sheer sublimity of Waterloo led to a patriotic rhetoric relying heavily on the trope of transcendence, on the idea that the battle was a 'peerless event, beyond the reach of public representation', Shaw notes how the counter-rhetoric generally struggles to find a way through. He then asks – 'Could it be that Hunt, alone among his contemporaries – with the possible exception of Lord Byron – comes closest to understanding what is really at stake in the representation of war: that the corporeal alteration demanded by conflict is exacted on the bodies of private individuals, not on the abstract or immortal body of the state?'[6]

The 'possible exception of Lord Byron' to this general rule is what I wish to propose here, while also following up Shaw's astute identification of 'The Field of Battle', with widow and corpse simultaneously framed, as a vital and highly specific iconography which forces attention on the body and domestic crisis all at once, an iconography which, in other words, bridges the conventional divide between domestic circumstances and the plains of war in which the tragedy of neither is fully realized. Turner's academy painting, *The Field of Waterloo* (1818) presents us with precisely this scene: a pile of corpses being searched for lost loved ones by bereaved women.

J. M. W. Turner, *The Field of Waterloo* **(1818) © Tate, London 2008**

The painting was the first of Turner's works to be accompanied by an epigraph from Byron (lines modified from *Childe Harold's Pilgrimage*, III, stanza 28, 'Last noon beheld them full of lusty life . . .'). Further, we know that the painting was based on sketches Turner made when, or subsequent to, his visit to the battlefield in 1817, a visit in which he used a guidebook: Charles Campbell's *The Traveller's Complete Guide through Belgium and Holland*, the second edition of which had been published that same year to include a newly inserted guide to the battlefield which quoted these same lines from Byron's poem. Byron, Campbell and Turner therefore present a nexus of works concerned with what I argue to be the aesthetic 'exception' in the responses to Waterloo: each acknowledges the representational crisis that Philip Shaw describes; each confronts, rather than displaces or denies, the spectacle of the battlefield's bodies. *Childe Harold's Pilgrimage*, Canto III, is the genesis here, but Byron's understanding of the carnage of modern warfare, and his condemnation of the price of its victories, begins – perhaps even more powerfully – with his lines on the battles of the Peninsular wars in *Childe Harold's Pilgrimage*, Canto I.

Byron: New Wars, New Rhetoric

The shock of Waterloo was not without precedent in the public imagination. Those following Napoleon's campaigns in the Iberian Peninsular (1807–14) would have witnessed two connected developments in modern warfare: first, the evidence that Napoleon's armies were not invincible now that British tactics, partly through Wellington, had been reformed, and secondly, that the casualties of warfare were escalating dramatically. Despite the events and atrocities of the French and American revolutions, it was unlikely that many people living in Europe in the late eighteenth century could conceive of the way warfare itself (and subsequently, the modes of its representation in the arts) were to change with the advent of the Napoleonic wars. This transformation was not so much to do with the technology of warfare itself (although it is true that the increasing use of artillery shells, and even rockets, on the battlefield made their mark) as it was to do with the new military acceptance of extremely high casualties. To the military in this period, the expendability of human life apparently had no limit, and so it seems that a new era in the conception of warfare's scale begins here, extends through the nineteenth century, reaches an apotheosis in the First World War, and does not end until the technological revolution of warfare in the late twentieth century (with its absurd notion of 'clean' or 'intelligent' weaponry).[7]

No one, probably, would have been prepared for the casualties of the Peninsular Wars, and the huge armies utilized by Napoleon in the imperial campaigns conducted through field warfare. In order to supply troops for the invasion of Russia, French armies in the Peninsula in 1812 were *reduced* to just under a quarter of a million. At the two-day Battle of Talavera in 1809, the mutual stubbornness of the French attacking in columns and the British standing firm led to the French losing over 7,000 men. The victorious British, having lost 5,000, and with more than 4,000 injured, scarcely had the capacity to bury the dead or carry the wounded to the makeshift hospitals.[8] Byron, writing to his mother while in Spain the following month, had this to say:

> You have heard of the battle near Madrid, and in England they would call it a victory – a pretty victory! Two hundred officers and five thousand men killed, all English, and the French in as great force as ever . . . .[9]

At Albuera (16 May 1811), the combined losses were calculated at 15,000. Wellington wrote in his dispatches from the battle of Talavera that it 'was certainly the hardest fought of modern days', and of Albuera that 'another such battle would ruin us'.[10]

The events of the Peninsular Wars began the transformation of war's representation in art to include corporeal suffering. The most famous artistic response was that of Goya, whose series, *The Disasters of War* (begun in 1810), catalogues not the new sublime scale of battlefield actions, but the individual cruelties and atrocities which might possibly be regarded as their emblematic representation. Goya's iconography turns sharply away from the rendition of war as the deeds of heroes to focus precisely on the mutilation of the body. Byron does not make such a complete break with the past in the first canto of *Childe Harold*, but his shift is analogous to Goya's. Byron's landscape of war is epic, in that it is scaled panoramically to take in the vastness of the events, but the scale does not magnify heroism; rather, the expanse of the frame is used to emphasize the enormous waste and carnage at the battles of Talavera and Albuera. Stanza 42 famously characterizes the dead of Talavera as 'Ambition's honour'd fools' and asks the reader to regard the bodies as instruments of tyrannical power ('. . . in these behold the tools, / The broken tools, that tyrants cast away / By myriads'). Albuera is described as a 'glorious field of grief' (43) which so quickly did away with so many lives ('a space so brief, / A scene where mingling foes should boast and bleed') that it leads to the pointed devaluation of commemorative verse, in the savagely ironic reference to the 'shining' of 'worthless lays', an allusion which almost certainly would have caused the contemporary reader to be reminded of Scott's *The Vision of Don Roderick*, published in July 1811.[11]

In contrast to Scott's poem, the first canto of *Childe Harold* is evacuated of the quality of heroism, and this is particularly evident in the absence of the tradition of naming heroes, or cataloguing their deeds. Indeed, in earlier versions the repudiation of the tradition of heroic or commemorative poetry was even more aggressive, originally opening in stanza 42 with the lines, 'There shall they rot – while rhymers tell the fools / How honour decks the turf that wraps their clay! / Liars avaunt!'[12] The alteration of these lines, in which the denomination of foolishness is transferred from the readers of eulogy to the dead of the battlefield might be revealing for what it tells us about Byron's typically perceptive understanding that the poetry of warfare was realized only in the parlours and drawing rooms of British society. There are, in this understanding, two sets of 'fools' or innocents: those whom consume the cant of eulogy, and those whose bodies are cut to pieces. The delusion of the former, in orthodox eulogy, displaces the reality of the latter, largely by way of the looming presence of the apostrophized hero whose domination of the poetry diminishes the stark and unpalatable truth that war's triumphs are grounded in the death and mutilation of countless anonymous people. For Byron, in the first canto, the antidote was to extend anonymity across all who fight in battle, so that they become 'battle's minions'. Here delusion is endemic: it inheres not only in the readers of poetry, but also in all those who fight in warfare.

Malcolm Kelsall has pointed out that 'Wellington – the liberator – is never mentioned in *Childe Harold*', arguing that Byron will look outside Europe for his models of freedom.[13] It is also the case, however, that Byron excluded Wellington's name from the original draft of the first two cantos when the manuscript was being revised.[14] While some of the alterations were doubtless at the behest of Murray and Dallas, who were anxious about the poem's heterodoxy, the erasure of Wellington (or Wellesley as he then was) is entirely consistent with *Childe Harold*'s refusal to capitulate to the conventional naming of leaders, which nomenclature automatically generates responses which discriminate between tyrants and liberators, and responses that discriminate between privates and generals. In *Childe Harold I* there are only the nameless, countless dead of the Peninsular, and the status of the unnamed in relation to the named (a relation examined again in the battle scenes in Canto VII of *Don Juan*) is precisely the point that is being avoided:

> Enough of Battle's minions! let them play
> Their game of lives, and barter breath for fame:
> Fame that will scarce reanimate their clay,
> Though thousands fall to deck some single name.

> (I, 44)

The 'single name' which is not named allows the reference to range across Napoleon, Wellington, Beresford, or even the Bourbons. This very deliberate conversion of eminence into anonymity has a converse effect of implying particularity and potential identity to the nameless, aggregated, dead; those thousands of privates whose commemoration, in the bulletins, always comes last in catalogues that begin with the officers (as in the case, indeed, of the Byron letter quoted above). At the end of the first Canto, Byron again returns to contemplate the sheer numbers of bodies being moved in to the battlefields of the Peninsular:

> Nor yet, alas! The dreadful work is done,
> Fresh legions pour adown the Pyrenees;
> It deepens still, the work is scarce begun,
> Nor mortal eye the distant end foresees.

> (I, 89)

Ironically, the 'distant end' was not so far away in the form of Waterloo; an event which replaced the dreadful sublimity of the Peninsular with the unimaginable carnage of Armageddon.

In the first canto of *Childe Harold*, Byron develops a distinctive rhetoric for the representation of war, one that is primarily concerned to visualize the vast impersonality of the new warfare while using a vocabulary capable of alluding to heroic virtue and simultaneously undermining it. By the time of Waterloo therefore, he had a poetic language to hand that was redoubtably immune to the patriotic strain. Furthermore, this language was underpinned by a post-revolutionary modernism that had lost faith in the notion of progressive history, or indeed, history made and changed by the deeds of great men.[15] This, I take it, was what the first two cantos of *Childe Harold* amounted to, and this historical revision was resistant to an interpretation of Waterloo as the moment of a great man who had turned the course of history. Equally, it was resistant to the notion that wholesale slaughter can be seen as a passage in civilization's improvement.[16]

Even so, the poetry of *Childe Harold III* is markedly less radical than that of the first canto. There is some capitulation here to conventional notions of heroism in war, and to the apostrophizing of individuals (chiefly through the references to the deaths of Brunswick and Howard). Similarly the stanzas dealing with the interruption of the Duchess's ball (III, 21–5) dramatize the moment of the battle's inauguration through its effects on the ball's participants, who are thereby realized as feeling, sensible beings, and not simply as an anonymous mass. Yet if Byron concedes here to the powerful draw of the romance of the brave, such an effect magnifies the traumatic contrast between the body full of life and that which, emptied of blood, decomposes in the earth:

> Last noon beheld them full of lusty life,
> Last eve in Beauty's circle proudly gay,
> The midnight brought the signal-sound of strife,
> The morn the marshalling in arms, – the day
> Battle's magnificently-stern array!
> The thunder-clouds close o'er it, which when rent
> The earth is covered thick with other clay,
> Which her own clay shall cover, heaped and pent,
> Rider and horse, – friend, foe, – in one red burial blent!
>
> (III, 28)

This indifferent amalgam of bodies and earth is Byron's realization of the field of Waterloo: it is a 'place of skulls' (III, 18), of bodies which 'moulder cold and low' (III, 27), a realization that many who toured the battlefield, with its stench of bodies, or later its bleached bones, shared.[17] It is with much the same sense of contrast that Byron seemingly concedes to the cliché of spring's fertile return (III, 30), for this also serves to magnify those who cannot return, the dead thousands:[18]

> I turn'd from all she brought [the spring] to those she could not bring.
>
> I turn'd to thee, to thousands, of whom each
> And one as all a ghastly gap did make

In his own kind and kindred, whom to teach
Forgetfulness were mercy for their sake;

(III, 30–1)

The reference is significantly precise in the context of Favret's argument about displacement, for Byron's poetry reverses what she represents as the standard tropic order, starting with the battlefield's corpses and implying from there the gaps and absences in the domestic lives back home. *Childe Harold III* not only requires its readership to imagine the terrible slaughter of Waterloo, its poetry carries the consequence of that slaughter back into the British populace: the theatre of victory celebration is also the theatre of war, and more specifically, the 'ghastly gaps' are both domestically localized and the abysses of humankind as a whole ('kind and kindred').

Campbell's *The Traveller's Guide*

Charles Campbell's guidebook gives an account of Waterloo which draws mainly on eye-witness accounts. This section of the *Guide* begins with an acknowledgement of the necessity of the battlefield visit:

> As it cannot be expected that any Briton will now visit Brussels without proceeding to Waterloo, strangers are generally solicited to take a guide, but this is unnecessary, as a peasant on the spot will answer every purpose. Waterloo has become a kind of pilgrimage . . ..[19]

And a pilgrimage complete with relics it had indeed become. While the battlefield had been cleared of all objects of value quickly, debris remained for some time after, particularly scraps of clothing, and oddly, paper.[20] Scott, visiting Waterloo later that summer, took as his relic a *livret* or booklet that belonged to a soldier who had been in the French armies since 1791; more to the point of my argument here, he noted how parts of the field still carried the strong scent of the decaying bodies; unsurprisingly so, since he suggests that recent ploughing was disturbing the shallow graves.[21] After a brief description of the battle, Campbell goes on to document, in solemn tone, and hierarchical order, the extent of the casualties:

> Never were laurels gained at such an expense of blood as in the battle of Waterloo. . . . Eleven British staff officers out of twenty-four were killed or wounded. Of inferior officers, not including subalterns, a dreadful list also appeared of 920 killed, wounded and missing; that of the privates was rated at 10 or 12,000.[22]

It is questionable whether the anonymity of the dead privates diminishes or
indeed emphasizes the death toll, but Campbell's guide does not shy away from
the representation of carnage. Far from it: this is, in some respects, the central
and obsessive theme of his writing. For while there is an account of the battle
itself, there is a continuous return to imagining scenes of desolation:

> Detachments from various regiments, and numerous Belgian peasants, were
> directed to assist the wounded, and to inter the dead of both armies. During
> the night, tribes of unfeeling wretches had assembled for the purposes of
> plunder; the soldier, while breathing his last, was inhumanly stripped, and his
> agonies were terminated by the chill of night; or if he resisted, he perished by
> the hand of a brutal depredator. . . . But, when the sun rose on the morning
> of the 19th, the dreadful scenes affrighted every beholder. The crops of corn
> were trodden to the earth: arms, accoutrements, tumbrels, cannon, horses
> and human bodies, were strewed in every direction . . ..[23]

After further descriptions of the military details of the engagement, and a quotation from Southey's 'The Poet's Pilgrimage to Waterloo', Campbell returns
again to the spectacle of death, and in particular, the sheer number of dead
bodies:

> The account of the field of battle, by one of the first persons who saw it, was
> dreadful. The first thing that struck him at a distance was, the quantity of caps
> and hats strewn on the ground. At first, there was a great preponderance of
> British dead, but more in advance, vengeance was dreadfully marked, for ten
> French lay dead for one British. The field was so much covered in blood that
> it appeared to be completely flooded with it . . . those who died in the wagons
> or on the way to Brussels, being thrown out, were hastily interred here. Thus
> the road between Waterloo and Brussels resembled one long uninterrupted
> charnel-house; the smell the whole way being extremely offensive, and in
> some places, scarcely tolerable . . ..[24]

Campbell's account of the battlefield, and indeed of the battle, is marked by
this continuous regression to the traumatic spectacle of the dead. Although his
description formally defers to the conventions of heroism and patriotism in his
conclusion (where he notes that despite these feelings of shock and sympathy,
'the glow of satisfaction at the results must be acknowledged; and we cannot but
appreciate the value of our heroes in the enthusiasm their deeds inspire')[25] the
burden of his narrative is to relate a history in which the trauma of mass human
slaughter is given primacy. His drawing on the oral history of the eye-witness
accounts leads us first to the widest and perhaps most innocent view of a battlefield filled with hats, through finally to that of stinking corpses being thrown
from carts, and the ignominy of makeshift burials.

Turner's *The Field of Waterloo*

This then, is the guidebook that Turner took with him when he toured the battlefield in 1817, made sketches, 17 pages of notes, and produced the oil painting, *The Field of Waterloo*, which was exhibited at the Royal Academy in 1818, accompanied by the lines that Campbell had also quoted from the Waterloo passage in *Childe Harold's Pilgrimage*.[26] Turner's painting had a mixed but generally hostile reception, but on the whole was not well-received by the critics, who objected to the Rembrandtesque darkness, its obscurity, and its execution. The painting takes what might be regarded as a conventional field of view, in that it centres on the farm of Hougoumont, the symbolic centre of the British repulsion of the French attacks, but apart from that, its composition and content make no deferential gestures to the conventional aesthetics governing history painting. Instead, Turner covers the battlefield in a pall of smoke and darkness, pierced only by the lamps of the women, and the dying falling flare illuminating the central sky, offering a shaft of light through which the spectacle of the battlefield's bodies is revealed, a feature that probably derives from Byron's torn thunder-clouds. Like Turner's famous painting, *The Slave Ship*, the viewer is required to peer into the foreground (ironically enough) to gather the full significance of the bodies that are there depicted. For indeed, the painting depicts a startling and traumatic scene – women searching the battlefield for their spouses and relations among the piles of dead French and Scottish soldiers. In this, if in nothing else, it produces a remarkable recasting of Waterloo as an anthem to doomed youth, the antipathy of glorious victory, by placing an emphasis, like Campbell, on the extent of the casualties, the grief, and the pathos.

Turner's representation of Waterloo, as commentators have noted, is a breach of painterly decorum. David Blayney Brown, for example, states that 'Turner's "Waterloo" ran absolutely counter to the established tradition of the victorious battle picture; it was, for example, the last thing the British Institution had in mind when in 1816 it offered a premium of one thousand guineas for a large sketch of the recent triumph.'[27] But this breach of decorum has another dimension: the picture's power comes not simply from its clearly antithetical stance, its refusal – for example – to show the death of Brunswick (as even Byron had done), or the staunch defiance of Wellington. For in the place of the military hero, centre canvas, are four women. Possibly the only living forms on the canvas, their presence denotes the displacement of a heroic and specifically male agency with one that is very specifically female. Before going on to explore this further, I want to refer to a contemporary account of the painting, in the *Annals of the Fine Arts*, which refuses to recognize these women's quest, and indeed, refuses to see the dead bodies which they are inspecting.

Before we referred to the catalogue we really thought this was the representation of a drunken hubbub on illumination night, and the host as far gone as his scuffling and scrambling guests was, with his dame and kitchen wenches looking with torches for a lodger, and wondering what was the matter.[28]

Even so, this critical blindness is not devoid of insight. The identification of the women as women largely of the lower orders might alert us to the derivation of this feature. For after the battle, women did indeed range across the field, searching for their spouses, but almost certainly, these were not the wives of officers. David Howarth offers this account:

> Officers, for the most part, who had their wives or lovers with them in Belgium, had left them in their billets or sent them to safety in Brussels or Antwerp. But private soldiers, with less money and possibly less sense, kept their wives with them on the march and in the bivouacs. A good many of these women had been there all through the battle, anxiously hovering on the edges of it. Some, hearing their husbands had been hurt, had dashed onto the field to try to help them and been wounded or killed themselves. Sad stories were told of corpses of married couples found lying together. But most, of course, failed to find their men, and had no way of telling whether they were still lying there or had been carted back to Brussels; and these distraught creatures could be seen, when dawn broke again, hunting among the corpses and begging for news from any of the wounded who could speak.[29]

Almost certainly, Turner is drawing on oral sources, also recorded in the diaries and journals which inform Howarth's account, in order to place women on the battlefield and allude to such oral histories, which no doubt, included some apocrypha too. But in doing so, he is considering his academy audience. The women of Waterloo are painted as class-hybrids. They are clearly dressed as the wives of officers: their clothes look like ball-gowns covered with fine shawls; their hair is dressed, and they are wearing jewellery. The tacit allusion, of course, is to Byron's dramatizing of the interruption of the Duchess of Richmond's ball in Brussels with which the battle began, and the suggestion is, that like those men who allegedly rushed out to fight in evening dress, these women clad in ball-gowns have followed them. At the same time, they are clearly not officer's wives, for they are carrying children with them, and this marks them out as the wives of the ordinary soldiers. We could conclude that Turner was confused, or that his rendering of the women is resonantly metaphorical of the war widow rather than literally allusive. Alternatively, we could suggest that he most deliberately constructed the women in this way to persuade his academy audience, and in particular the women among them, to recognize themselves in the scene – in other words, not to perform the misreading that the critic of the Annals perversely and aggressively adopts.

Whatever the class-identity of the women and our interpretation of it, the painting's placing of the women and their children centre foreground against the pile of bodies effectively breaches the divide between domesticity and foreign fields which Favret and Shaw have identified as the key element which excludes the body from warfare's representations. Here the domestic and the bounded worlds of the battlefield are strongly engaged: it is no longer possible to preserve the aesthetics of warfare from the intrusion of a domestic critique. Turner, Campbell and Byron break down these boundaries in their different ways, but there is also a powerful material fact about Waterloo that, regardless of the interventions of artists and writers, was likely to breach the divide between the battlefield and its domestic or polite realization: its proximity to Brussels. The slaughter of Waterloo was widely witnessed. Fanny Burney, in recording her own hazardous journey from Brussels through the chaos of Waterloo in search of her injured husband (who was at Treves on the French border) provides accounts of the devastation in a series of letters. There are numerous examples, and I draw on just two here. On the 19 June 1815 she writes:

> NEVER yet, all agree, has there been so bloody a battle fought! We have had as yet no consistent details – but the continued sight of the maimed, wounded mutilated and tortured victims of this exterminating warfare is shocking and affecting beyond description.[30]

And then on the 24th:

> The wretched prisoners are now brought in every hour, in a condition so horrible, the streets seem pestilential as the Carriages pass with them. Even all the shopkeepers bathe their faces with Eau de Cologne to support the effluvia! There were so many English & Belgians wounded and maimed to remove, that the carriages for the prisoners were not at liberty – though ALWAYS in motion, till the blood, *drying* upon them, & their garments, caused, I imagine, this nearly putrid effect. The Dead! – the Piles of Dead, are now burying, by 3000 peasants – to prevent a pestilence so many are employed at a time![31]

The dead – the piles of dead – their blood and their burial are the predominant features of the Romantic accounts of Waterloo that I have discussed here. The 'exterminating warfare' of Waterloo was not confined to the battlefield itself, any more than the stench of the dead and the impossibility of their disposal could be kept out of the polite quarters of Brussels, out of the noses of those visitors who trod the fields as tourists or pilgrims months later, or indeed, out of the imaginations of those who read Byron or study Turner in the twenty-first century.

These representations of Waterloo deliberately set themselves against the sanitization of military conflict by a dogged insistence on its realization as corporeal destruction, an insistence that has startling resonance for us at the start of this century, as we witness the denial of the plains of war through political representations that rendered invisible the civilian corpses sprawled across Baghdad. Turner perhaps, is the most tenacious in his refusal to allow the passing of time to temper the trauma of Waterloo. For him, the bodies of Waterloo had a kind of spectral omnipresence. His adaptation of the academy painting in the watercolour he produced for the engravings to illustrate the 1832 edition of Byron's works draws the eye through the painting *via* countless corpses, scattering bodies through the foreground and the middle-ground, and possibly beyond. His later watercolour of 1833, a revisiting of the battleground when all is supposedly at peace, rearranges the scene completely, but makes strong gestures towards the battle itself by depicting a gathering storm, riders galloping for shelter, and the rows of rude stones marking the interred bodies. Those stones might be taken as a sign that the dead are, at last, buried, but Turner effectively cuts off this reading by placing a skeleton in the left foreground as a potent reminder of the 'piles of dead' and the impossibility of their permanent interment.[32]

Notes

I would like to acknowledge here the literary-historicist influence of Peter Widdowson, and in particular his important essay, '"Literary Value" and the Reconstruction of Criticism', *Literature and History* 6.2 (1980), 138–50, where a strong defence of literary value is made in the context of a pragmatic and materialist approach to literary texts. My method here derives from such a realization of literature, which recognizes how texts are produced within history, how their historical significance might be recovered, and then revitalized in a contemporary context. My nomination of this essay for this volume also derives from my sense of its complementary relation to Peter's early work in his Ph.D., which was titled 'Illusion to Disillusion: The Poetry and Painting of the First World War'.

The figure, Joseph Mallord William Turner's *The Field of Waterloo* (exhibited 1818), is reproduced here by kind permission of Tate Britain, London, where it is held in the Turner Bequest collection.

[1] See Simon Bainbridge, *Napoleon and English Romanticism* (Cambridge: Cambridge University Press, 1995), 153–82. Bainbridge describes a rapid establishment of readerly expectations that attended the numerous poetic and literary renditions of Waterloo, which he calls 'the matter of Waterloo'. He discusses Byron's lines in *Childe Harold's Pilgrimage* (Canto III) in the context of their shocking disruption of these expectations. See also Bainbridge, 'To "Sing it Rather Better": Byron, the Bards, and Waterloo', *Romanticism* 1.1 (1995), 68–81.

[2] Philip Shaw, *Waterloo and the Romantic Imagination* (Basingstoke: Palgrave, 2002), 2–4. I am greatly indebted to Shaw's study, to which my work here has a supplementary relation, picking up on what I understand to be an important coalescence and relation between three works noted individually by Shaw (Turner's painting, Byron and Campbell's guide book).

[3] Mary A. Favret, 'Coming Home: The Public Spaces of Romantic War', *Studies in Romanticism* 33:4 (1994), 539–48.

[4] Betty Bennett, *British War Poetry in the Age of Romanticism: 1793–1815* (New York and London: Garland, 1976). See 112.

[5] *Romantic Wars: Studies in Culture and Conflict, 1793–1822*, ed. Philip Shaw (Aldershot and Burlington: Ashgate, 2000), 3–4.

[6] Shaw, *Romantic Wars*, 190.

[7] The death toll at Waterloo is estimated to have been around 47,000, comprising 15,000 allies, 7,000 Prussians and 25,000 French. The battle was fought over 24 hours. To provide some sense of the scale of the slaughter, it is worth noting that on the first day of the Somme (1916), commonly understood as the most devastating battle of the First World War, the British lost 20,000 men; total casualties (dead and wounded) were around 57,000.

[8] See Michael Glover, *Wellington's Peninsular Victories* (Gloucester: Windrush Press, 1996). For details of the numbers of men in the French armies in Spain, see 50–2; for details of the casualties at Talavera, 7.

[9] *Byron's Letters and Journals*, ed. Leslie A. Marchand, 12 vols (London: John Murray, 1973–81), I, 221.

[10] Cited in *The Works of Lord Byron*, ed. E. H. Coleridge, 13 vols (London: John Murray, 1899), II, 51.

[11] For ease of reference, all quotations from Byron's poetry are taken from *Byron*, ed. Jerome J. Mcgann, *The Oxford Authors* (Oxford and New York: Oxford University Press, 1986). Canto and stanza numbers follow in brackets. Byron's condemnation of commemorative poetry may have been partially responsible for Walter Scott's later hostility towards *Childe Harold's Pilgrimage*, since it is strongly attached to the bloodshed of Albuera, the battle so triumphantly celebrated at the end of Scott's *The Vision of Don Roderick* (iii, xiii–xiv) in which Lord Beresford, the commander, is given pride of place. Scott clearly rebukes those 'who should grudge him Albuera's bays'. Scott's poem was published in July, 1811, thereby predating Byron's. While most of the first Canto of *Childe Harold* was already written by the summer of 1811, it is possible that Byron would have known of Scott's celebration of Beresford when he was working at the revisions to *Childe Harold I and II* at Newstead in the autumn of 1811, prior to its publication in April of the following year. For an excellent reading of *Childe Harold* and the Peninsular Wars, including discussion of *Don Roderick*, and the ways in which Byron alludes to and undercuts other poets, see Simon Bainbridge, *British Poetry and the Revolutionary and Napoleonic Wars: Visions of Conflict* (Oxford: Oxford University Press, 2003), 148–89.

[12] Coleridge, *The Works of Lord Byron*, II, 50.

[13] Malcolm Kelsall, *Byron's Politics* (Brighton: Harvester Press, 1987), 67.

[14] See Coleridge, *The Works of Lord Byron*, II, xi. For a thorough-going investigation of Wellington in *Don Juan*, see Jane Stabler, 'Pit-Bull Poetics: One Battle in Byron's "War in Words"', *Romanticism* 1.1 (1995), 82–9.

[15] For further elucidation see my 'Heroism and History: *Childe Harold I and II* and the Tales' in *The Cambridge Companion to Byron*, ed. Drummond Bone (Cambridge: Cambridge University Press, 2004), 77–98.

[16] Simon Bainbridge demonstrates the clear distinction between Byron and Scott, Southey and Wordsworth in this respect. See Bainbridge, *Napoleon and English Romanticism*, 178–9.

[17] See Shaw, *Waterloo and the Romantic Imagination*, 67.

[18] For the cliché of fertility, see Shaw, *Waterloo and the Romantic Imagination*, 57–8, 203–4. See also Bainbridge, *Napoleon and English Romanticism*, 178, for an argument that proposes a tactical awareness in the use of the cliché.

[19] Charles Campbell, *The Traveller's Complete Guide through Belgium and Holland*, Second Edition (London, 1817), 62.

[20] A number of visitors to the field of Waterloo commented on the amount of paper which still littered the battlefield months after the conflict. See Shaw, *Waterloo and the Romantic Imagination*, pp. 45–6. See also Walter Scott, *France and Belgium, Originally Published as 'Paul's Letters to His Kinsfolk*, 2 vols (Edinburgh: Adam and Charles Black (London: Houlston and Stoneman, 1855), I, 150.

[21] Ibid., I, 152, 155. Scott's tour of the battlefield in 1815, of which this letter is an account, makes it clear that the Waterloo pilgrimage was a tourist attraction, and he notes in some detail, the 'trinkets' and the relics which could be obtained there for relatively small amounts of money. Along with the *livret*, for example, Scott acquired (as a gift) a collection of old French songs (which he conjectured to have been carried by a French soldier as a form of solace), a cross of the Legion of Honour, a plain cuirass, and 'a handsome inlaid one' (I, 158). Scott frankly admits that his enthusiasm for collecting such pieces was frowned upon by his guide, who had taken part in the battle. Despite all this, Scott's letter takes pains to note – in some detail – the immensity of the slaughter and the 'stench in several places of the field' (I, 155).

[22] Campbell, *The Traveller's Complete Guide*, 62.

[23] Ibid., 67.

[24] Ibid., 71–2.

[25] Ibid., 72–3.

[26] See figure. See David Blayney Brown, *Turner and Byron* (London: Tate Gallery, 1992), 92, for details of Turner's preparations for the painting.

[27] Brown, *Turner and Byron*, 30. Brown goes on to emphasize the radical nature of Turner's picture, noting that 'to a London audience, few of whom had actually seen a battle, it must have been an extraordinary revelation, hardly to be matched before Roger Fenton's photographs arrived from the Crimea.'

[28] Cited in Martin Butlin and Evelyn Joll, *The Paintings of J. M. W. Turner*, 2 vols (New Haven and London: Yale University Press, 1977), II, 93.

[29] David Howarth, *Waterloo: A Near Run Thing* (Gloucester: Windrush Press, 1997), 148.

[30] Fanny Burney, *The Journals and Letters of Fanny Burney*, 12 vols (Oxford: Clarendon Press, 1975–1984), VIII, 215 (Letter to M. D'Arblay, 15–19 June 1815).

[31] Burney, *Journals and Letters*, VIII, 248–9. (Letter to M. D'Arblay, 24 June 1815).

[32] For reproductions of these, see Eric Shanes, *Turner's Human Landscape* (London: Heinemann, 1990), 116–17.

Chapter 8

'Giving Them Back Their History': Peter Widdowson and Literature

Martin Randall

In Peter Widdowson's characteristically precise introduction to his study *Literature* (1999), he delineates three categories – Literature, Literary Value, the Canon – and describes 'one procedural strategy in their emancipatory deconstruction [that] has been common to all'. He continues:

> In the process of denaturalising and defamiliarising such categories – so that they may, if required, be reconstituted and recuperated – it is the business of giving them back their history which is of primary and fundamental importance. Dehistoricised, the marks and meanings of their manufacture are erased, so that they do indeed appear 'natural', 'given' and impervious to challenge; *re*historicised, their partiality – in both senses – is restored to view; and their invulnerability as mythic monoliths is countered.[1]

Aside from being typically lucid and illuminating, these thoughts capture much of what has made Peter Widdowson a presiding influence over this author's academic and intellectual progress. Of particular importance have been these processes of 'denaturalising and defamiliarising . . . categories' and of 'rehistoricising' them such that hegemonies can be challenged and deconstructed. As an undergraduate student, these underpinning ideas informed my own initial readings of modernist and contemporary fiction and poetry. Professor Widdowson's commitment to this rehistoricizing of theories and texts helped to unlock the complexities of works ranging from *Howards End* to *Beloved*, from *The Waste Land* to *Midnight's Children*. This essay will explore the influence of Widdowson's radical ideas on my own academic progress as a starting point for a larger exploration of his key insights – about the necessity of opening out the text by careful reading, and about the centrality of history.[2]

Salman Rushdie's *Midnight's Children* (1982) exemplifies the arguments that Widdowson made in lectures. Saleem Sinai strives to tell the history of India in the twentieth century. This is a pressing obligation for the narrator – he sees himself as a 'prophet in the wilderness', cursed with the burden of his life having been, from the moment of his birth, a mirror of the emerging nation itself.[3] Saleem uncovers connections and repetitions everywhere, between the past and the present, between major political upheaval and familial relationships, between the local and the national. Throughout the vast story, there is an all-consuming sense of a teeming chorus of voices straining to be released and of a world of endless possibilities and permutations. The voices that Saleem hears – he has telepathic powers; a metaphor for the novelist's omniscient presence – proliferate and he realizes that he must describe everything, much to the chagrin of his muse and fickle audience, Padma, who constantly berates him for not sticking to the point. Saleem assumes the role of 'All-India Radio' (166) allowing him to tune in to the various 'inner monologues' (168) of the otherwise anonymous and unheard millions. These are, so to speak, a multitude of 'his-*stories*' rather than History and the novel argues for these to be heard.

Widdowson stressed the importance of the novel's attempt to reposition Indian experience in an entirely new context, away from the realms of singularity and unequivocal meaning towards a view of redescribing history where, as Bill Ashcroft puts it, 'excess performs the function of shouldering a space for oneself in the world'.[4] Rushdie's narrative sweeps across vast territories, darting back and forth in time in an almost intuitive, improvised manner. The novel encompasses the pre-independence India of Saleem's grandfather, Aadam Aziz, the burgeoning optimism of post-colonial Bombay, right up to the State of Emergency instigated by Indira Gandhi in 1975. And as these seismic shifts in the political structures occur, Saleem recounts the comparatively small but equally significant upheavals in his own family; from the moment he spies his mother's posterior from the secrecy of the washing-chest – 'black as night, rounded and curved, resembling nothing on earth so much as a gigantic, black Alfonso mango!' (161–2) – to the revelation of Mary Pereira's 'revolutionary act' (117), a decision that alters both Saleem's and his nemesis, Shiva's, destinies forever: 'And when she was alone . . . she changed name-tags on the two huge infants, giving the poor baby a life of privilege and condemning the rich-born child to accordions and poverty' (5). Saleem threads the personal and the social together seamlessly so that family life and the political machinations of the period are inseparable.

But, as Widdowson often argued, these attempts at retelling the entirety of history are doomed to failure. While the novel acknowledges this ultimate futility it also emphasizes how such an urge is crucial in piecing together the myriad 'shards of memory' (426) and give them shape and coherence. Similarly, in Graham Swift's *Waterland* (1983), Tom Crick, a history teacher whose entire department is under threat, yearns for the 'Grand Narrative'.[5] He wants to 'disentangle history from fairy-tale' and 'idle gossip' (86) and to explain the past that eludes fixed meanings. Under such auspices Crick tries, like Saleem, to retell the world and even if this task ends as ultimately a doomed exercise, there is a profound sense that every individual must accept this in order to come to terms with one's life. It is this affirmative curiosity, an 'ingredient of love', a 'vital force' (51), this urge to ask 'why?' that drives Crick on to a deeper archaeology of the past.

Ostensibly, Swift tells the histories of the Atkinsons and the Cricks, two families whose lives circle and collide over 200 years of living in and off the Fens. The novel also deals with the pull of the geographical, describing how the 'fairy-tale' (3) land affects and influences the characters, so much so that it becomes a central motif, a place of shifting meaning and secrets buried in its depths. They form digressive strands trailing off in many directions that Crick seeks to control and define: 'How it repeats itself, how it goes back on itself, no matter how we try to straighten it out. How it twists and turns. How it goes in circles and brings us back to the same place'(142). Such reflections capture the arduous nature of Crick's (and Saleem's) relationship to the complexities of history and as Crick reaches out for his memories his career, marriage and identity are jeopardized. And as Crick is all too aware, there never can be any one final 'version' of history. Events are just 'accidents' (264), Crick concedes. There is the mystery of Dick Crick's heritage; he is told that 'he's a bungle', a 'mix up' (323), a casualty of an incestuous relationship. And there is the fact of Freddie Parr's drowned body discovered by Crick and his father. Even though the coroner records an official verdict of accidental death, clues still point to another version of events. And perhaps most beguilingly there is the controversy surrounding the eel, that 'phallically suggestive creature' (196), whose sex life remains obscure, something that leads Crick to muse that the 'world is so arranged that when all things are learnt . . . the world shall have come to its end' (204).

Crick retells the story of Sarah Atkinson who, after having been beaten by her husband one night, suffers permanent brain damage and becomes a 'prophet'. Her husband, so racked with remorse, turns to religion: 'History has stopped for him. He has entered the realms of superstition' (80). Two hundred years later Crick speculates whether Mary, his wife, has 'seen' Sarah's ghost. Later still, Mary also turns to religion and explains her abduction of a child by saying that God ordered her to do it. Crick is shocked: 'Maybe this is where history dissolves, chronology goes backwards. That's your wife over there; you know. Mary, the one you thought you knew. But maybe this is unknown country' (265). These unsettling echoes continue as Crick immerses himself in a 'reality-obscuring drama' (40). Consequently, Crick questions not only the validity of history but also traditional notions of identity and belonging. As in *Midnight's Children*, the narrator's sense of self is a mutable thing, dependent on the circling voices and experiences of the past. Saleem refers to this as a 'process of revision' that should be 'constant and endless' (460).

Widdowson pointed out that both *Waterland* and *Midnight's Children* reach similar conclusions about history (and its relation to the future). Crick's rebellious student, Price, proclaims: 'But – I want a future. . . . We all do. And you – you can stuff your past!' (141). Crick 'swallows' the world in order to achieve something of Price's optimism, hoping to achieve mastery over his feelings that 'all is nothing' (270) and to finally 'assuage emptiness' (177) by claiming a future. Saleem also ends his narrative with hesitant optimism. He knows that 'for every ladder there is a snake' (*Midnight's* 143) and that he has experienced all the 'confusion and ruin' (333) of his country and yet he bids farewell still believing in the future. One last talismanic pickle jar remains empty ready to be filled with 'what cannot be pickled, because it has not taken place' (462). Both characters recognize that these stories are necessarily fictions but that they also 'possess the authentic taste of truth' (461). The structure and form of the two novels embodies this sense of the interconnectedness between history and fiction: the reliance of one discipline on the other and the production of what might be termed 'true fictions'.

Widdowson's exploration of such ideas influenced my undergraduate – and later doctoral – studies. My choice of subject matter arose directly from his supervision and mentoring and from often-lengthy discussions (all of them intensely textual, of course, but also increasingly concerned with politics and history). My initial research was on the influence of Thatcherism on the British novel of the 1980s. Evidently there was a focus in my own work on political ideas and concepts and their articulation in fictional tropes, narratives and motifs. Martin Amis's *Money* (1984), for example, reflected and anticipated the impact of free market economics upon individuals and upon society overall. In this regard Widdowson's notion of 'literature as history' was extremely useful in unpicking Amis's playfully post-modern novel. More than simply reflecting *laissez-faire* politics, *Money* delineates the ways in which excessive consumerism and rapacious profiteering deracinate the individual – in this case the novel's narrator John Self. Indeed, Amis's text is useful in that it fictionalizes – through satiric exaggeration – many fundamental tenets of Thatcherism.

Through discussions with Widdowson it became evident that despite the efficacy of this approach, the novels of the 1980s had been critiqued extensively in the subsequent years. Indeed, perhaps there was a sense that because of the pervasiveness of Thatcherite policies and ideas there was an all-too-clear relationship between the literary text and history. Gradually discussions led to the possibility of investigating British novels of the 1990s, settling on the historical 'book-ends' of 1989 (the end of the Cold War) and 2001 (the World Trade Centre terrorist attacks) as a framing device. And again it seemed natural to analyse what fiction of the 1990s was saying about the social and political realities of the decade. It became apparent that one of the most dominant genres of 1990s' prose was that of the historical novel. Certainly, as Widdowson pointed out, there was a sense of profound nostalgia in many of these novels for certain parts of British history. But there was also a concomitant sense of melancholy and conflict, of articulating regretful, even mournful narratives that consistently problematized the conventions of the part history plays in the contemporary world.

My own research into the novels of the 1990s and the Holocaust took me to Michèle Roberts' *Daughters of the House* (1993). My reading of this text was heavily informed by Widdowson's teaching of it.[6] Roberts' novel deals with the persistence of the Holocaust, and in this respect it shares a 'haunted' narrative with other fiction of the 1990s. Nick Rennison has written that *Daughters of the House* is concerned with 'marrying past and present' and 'creating intricate webs of connections between characters' current circumstances and the histories which have led them there'.[7] Evidently such a novel held great interest for Widdowson and, through discussions, the importance of the Holocaust's role in representing a 'guilty past' that is made up of 'collaboration and murder' became clearer.[8] This 'guilty past' haunts the daughters, Thérèse and Léonie, but on a wider scale Roberts shows how it haunts the villagers who have 'buried' the knowledge of their collaboration with the Nazis and their role in the deaths of a Jewish family. The novel portrays a haunted present in relation to a traumatized past – a trope that could be found in a number of novels from the decade. Widdowson pointed out, this arguably had much to do with a cultural 'millennial angst': writers both looking forward, with trepidation, to the end of the century and also looking back at the century and in particular its wars and conflicts.

This trend in 1990s' fiction seems in part to be a fictional response to the broader *fin de siècle* sense of the Holocaust representing the 'dark heart' of a violent and often catastrophic century. Apocalyptic and genocidal images that came from Rwanda and the Serbo-Croatia conflict added to this belated reappraisal of the Holocaust.[9] In light of this, the 1990s seemed a more apposite decade in which to analyse the relationship between fiction and history. Roberts' novel exemplifies much of this literary genre: novels such as Zadie Smith's *White Teeth* (2000), Martin Amis' *Time's Arrow* (1991), Caryl Phillips' *The Nature of Blood* (1997), Justin Cartwright's *Masai Dreaming* (1993) and Rachel Seiffert's *The Dark Room* (2001) are each 'haunted', in markedly different ways, by the traumatic memory of the Holocaust and the resonance of its impact some 50 years later. The 'sinister echo'[10] of the Holocaust is also an aspect of Roberts' narrative in which the two cousins (who may or may not be sisters), who have been estranged for over 20 years, are reunited in the Normandy house where they used to spend summers as children. Thérèse has been a nun living in convent while her cousin has married a local man and has had children. Thérèse's return to the house – she intends to write her autobiography – precipitates a 'return' to the women's shared past in the immediate postwar years. The novel explores the secrets, lies and suppressions that at first unite and then undermine the young girls' friendship.

Léonie and Thérèse, following the death of Thérèse's mother, 'see' visions of a Virgin Mary figure in the woods near the house. This is one of the first secrets that bind the girls together but also precipitates the beginning of their estrangement. Linked to these visions is the prevailing sense of other secrets that reside 'beneath' the surface of the house, the village, and, by extension, France. Roberts gradually reveals them and in doing so emphasizes the novel's 'archaeological' view of history. *Daughters of the House* exposes the levels of collusion and collaboration that signify the guilty secrets the villagers have kept hidden. The girls discover that a Jewish family on the run from the Nazis arrived at the village to hide only to be betrayed and recaptured. They were then taken out into the woods and killed. It is subsequently discovered – following the orders of the local priest who has demanded that a stone shrine be taken down – that the bones of the Jewish victims are, in Léonie's words, 'mixed up more than ever before' (137). Thérèse discovers that her mother helped to hide the remnants of a statue in the cellar and Léonie reveals that she knew the priest had informed the Germans about the location of the Jewish family but that she had kept the information to herself.

These revelations encompass private and public concerns, a trope that Widdowson returned to in his readings of other novels including Isabel Allende's *The House of the Spirits* (1982) and Toni Morrison's *Beloved* (1987). The private secrets include the possibility that the girls may be twin sisters: their mothers, themselves sisters, appear to have lied about Léonie's father who was believed to have been English but may have been Louis, Thérèse's father. After the new grave was built to accommodate the Jewish family's remains it has been desecrated with swastikas, Léonie muses upon this 'return of the repressed':

> The grave in the cemetery had been forced open, made to give up its dead. At the same moment mouths had opened to shout words that Léonie had tried not to hear, tried to believe that no one still spoke, would ever utter again. . . . Murderous red signs painted on the headstone of the grave. Leonie had to look steadily at what was rising up in her village, out of the grave of war, the unburied and the undead arriving to lay hands upon them all, claim them for its own. (52)

Daughters of the House shows that the more traumatic the past the more likely it is to be resurrected. The mixed public and private histories that are at stake are necessarily incomplete and often ambiguous narratives that require acts of interpretation and articulation, narrativization and fictionalization – tropes that were a constant throughout Widdowson's lectures and supervisory discussions.

The final chapter of the novel is titled 'The Words' and these words are the necessary utterances that must be attached to events to give them meaning. Léonie sees that 'history was voices that came alive and shouted' (171). These ghostly voices belong to the Jewish family that the young girl hears praying in her old bedroom (in a language she does not understand), but they are also figuratively the buried voices of history. Until this occurs, the Jewish family remains outside of history, without names or narrative. The last words of the novel are the returning of identity and history – of language – to people otherwise guiltily forgotten and hidden. Léonie has also found the words so she can speak and subsequently write her history. Widdowson clarified for me the ways in which the 'trace' of the Holocaust is linked with other smaller but still profound hidden histories that the girls found themselves involved in.

The desecrated graves indicate that anti-Semitism continues to exist in a country struggling to confront the issue of some of its residents' collaboration with the Nazis. The novel looks at the ways in which the victims of the Nazis are 'heard' in the subsequent years.

These voices represent the history that underlies all the competing authorized and unauthorized interpretations of the past. Léonie is especially antagonistic towards Thérèse's plans for going back to their childhood. She threatens that 'if you tell any more lies about the past I'll kill you', (23) and accuses Thérèse of being a 'ghoul' who is 'picking over what's dead and gone, what's best left undisturbed' (24). This phrase – 'what's best left undisturbed' – captures perhaps the essence of the tension not only in Roberts' novel but also in many of the texts Widdowson explored. There exists, these novels argue, an opposition between the need to 'speak' of conflicting, often troubling histories and the concomitant impulse to 'look away' and to 'bury' such experiences in comforting mythologies and nostalgia. In *Daughters of the House, Beloved, Midnight's Children, Waterland* and others, hitherto untold histories threaten to profoundly unsettle the hegemony of History. These translate into fictional characters – caught in the stasis between the private and the public realms – debating the merits of remembering and forgetting.

Victorine, the household's maid, is the individual whose version of events initially dominates the girls' view of the past. She tells them that 'everything was topsy-turvy then' (42) and that they will only fully understand when they are older (43). Léonie likens Victorine's casual allusions to the war to a 'sort of bookmark which divided the pages of history', (44) a phrase suggesting the 'textuality' of the past. Victorine's speaking of the war, though, is as characterized by silences and ellipses, as it is by disclosure and detail. This reluctance to fully return to the past means that Victorine has apportioned blame to the wrong collaborator – she tells the girls one of the local women in a bakery was the informer. She has 'misread' history because there are so many crucial aspects of the past that have not been spoken, or for that matter, written down. Thérèse recognizes the gaps and omissions in her memories when she tells Léonie her reasons for writing her memoir: 'I thought if I wrote down what happened to me when we were children it would help me to decide what it is I've got to do. But there's so much I've forgotten. You'll have to help me remember' (23).

The sense of the history of their childhood being a collaborative effort, at best, and at worst a site of competing versions of truth, is matched by the villages' responses to the girls' differing visions and also in the complex 'mixing' of their respective parents. Initially, Léonie believes that the past is a comparatively simple narrative to understand. She has been inculcated with a particular version in which the 'war was terrible for everybody', and that everyone knew who the collaborators were (54). Naturally, the more she pieces together the strands of the narrative of the past, the more 'mixed up' the truth becomes. Roberts stresses the complexities of the telling and retelling of history throughout the novel – from the differing views of the visions through to what was or was not hidden in the house's cellar (49). But the shallow grave that is discovered underneath the shrine that the priest orders to be destroyed is the truth that cannot remain hidden. Léonie persists in asking questions about this discovery of the bones, but she is constantly confused and unable to comprehend the political and cultural practices of what is only relatively recent history.

An important conversation occurs after the bones are found when Léonie asks Victorine about their identity. Victorine tells her that they are Jewish bones. The young girl is confused and Victorine wonders why she has not learned any of this in school. Leonie replies, 'the war's too modern for us to do in history' (54). *Daughters of the House* dramatizes a transitional period in which the war and by extension the Holocaust, is in an aporetic state. In other words, it is 'too modern' for history and too recent and traumatic to be appropriated into memory. The novel discusses the ways in which different individuals and groups seek to impose narrative structure and meaning upon the past in order to justify both those events and those of the present day. This sense of belatedness echoes Freud's concept of *Nachtraglichkeit* (deferment, 'afterwardness'), which, as Nicola King observes, offers a productive model for memory that is akin to theories surrounding narrative structure.[11] The theory suggests an active reworking of memory, and also acknowledges the 'rewriting' and 're-evaluating' of a memory. *Nachtraglichkeit* disrupts the 'truth' of the first event. In traumatic memory the experiences of that first event may not have been fully assimilated and thus will 'return' in the present, awaiting narrative structuring and the coherency of form. But this form must constantly acknowledge its own incomplete nature.

Jay Winter and Emmanuel Sivan write that collective remembrance is a 'quixotic act' which is both painful and subject to inevitable 'decomposition' over time.[12] *Daughters of the House* is concerned with this 'quixotic act' of remembering. It is the figure of Rose Taillé who offers Léonie the fullest account of the history that is 'too modern' for her to learn at school. Rose's husband, Henri, was killed along with the Jewish family. Rose comes to the house occasionally to work and to look after Léonie. She tells the young girl about how the Nazis rounded up Jews in France:

> They kept the Jews in a sports stadium outside Paris. Packed in with hardly any food or water. Of course lots of them died. Then they were sent to the camp at Drancy, and from there they were put on trains and sent to Auschwitz to be gassed. (126)

Rose speaks further of these train journeys and stresses that knowledge of such events was available 'afterwards' but only for 'those who wanted to know' (126). She goes on to describe the arrival of the Jewish family and how Rose and her husband sheltered them. She tells Léonie that the identity of the informer remained unknown. Rose speaks of the collective desire to 'move on': 'And then once the war was over people wanted to forget. I can't' (127).

People, she says, 'wanted' to forget, but the evidence of the murders and the knowledge that someone informed upon the family rises up to the surface against their collective wishes. Rose's conviction that the memories will not leave her, even if she wanted them to disappear, confirms the novel's sense that the traumatic past simply will not die. In other words, the villagers want to forget because of their guilt, and Rose may wish to forget, but what is repressed will return because of its incomplete and traumatic nature. The priest's desire to build a plain headstone, for example, and the fact that the Jewish family's bones and those of Rose's husband are 'mixed up', signifies the ways in which events have been hurriedly repressed. Added to this is the sense that any monument or shrine cannot stand in for memory. Léonie denies Thérèse's assertions about her confused lineage and accuses her of not caring about 'those dead Jews' (158). Léonie argues that the past should be forgotten: 'We can't live in the past. We've got to get on with our lives' (159).

Daughters of the House treats the Holocaust as a metaphor for the difficulties in remembering and forgetting. What is at stake in the text is history – or rather disputes over who tells history. In this regard, Roberts' fiction highlights a number of key points in the vexed relationship between the present and the past – points which Widdowson's work has addressed. These include the following: the persistence of the past – its 'presence' in the present; the different and sometimes competing examples of historical 'evidence' that are needed to bring the past back to life; the sense that there is always 'excess' within history that remains unrepresentable; the implication that traumatic history will always return, however buried it might be, and the tensions between articulating (remembering) and silence (forgetting). Widdowson's lectures on this novel showed, with forensic attention to Roberts' narrative, how it fictionalizes these issues. It is here that his theories surrounding the relationship between literature and history had their most marked influence.

The secrets that the villagers have conspired to keep hidden cannot be contained and return in various guises. This is connected with the theme of the 'competing evidence' that one has to inevitably rely on to piece together the fragments of the past. The past 'haunts' the present and its truths can be found in texts, documents, voices and objects that embody history. The Jewish family's bones are the indisputable evidence of the atrocity that was committed, but there are other examples of the evidence of the past. For instance, as a 10-year-old, Léonie discovers that Madeleine kept a 'baby book' of photographs: the young girl 'discovered that she had a past' (34). Similarly Thérèse reads the letters that Antoinette wrote to the Sœur Dosithée at the convent (123) that fill in the gaps inherent in memory. The third aspect of historical representation – that of an 'excess' which always remains unrepresented – is intimately linked with the novel's treatment of the effects of the Holocaust on subsequent generations.

This aspect of historical representation is linked to the fourth issue, namely that of the traumatic history that belatedly returns. The shallow grave that holds the bones of those murdered by the Nazis is a signifier of the hidden, unexpressed but still profoundly 'felt', trauma that rises to the surface. Connected to this is the last issue, that of the tensions between remembering and forgetting. *Daughters of the House* dramatizes the attitudes and points of view that represent these responses to the speaking and 'not speaking' of the past. The traumatic nature of the past bypasses such considerations given the involuntary nature of it. But the characters all have investments in whether the past is spoken or not spoken. Léonie, for example, recalls how she listened to the Jewish family in the room in the house where they hid:

> They had chanted prayers in a language she could not understand. They had called out their own names and the name of the informer who had betrayed them. Léonie knew the names of the three members of the Jewish family, and she knew the name of the person who had led them to their deaths. She had heard them, night after night when she was ten years old. She had put the words away in here and left them because she was afraid. (57)

She wants to forget the evidence of what she has heard, and hence it remains unspoken and unwritten and therefore is not able to be included in history. The names of the Jewish family are similarly not spoken, as if their identities remain forever mysterious and unavailable for representation.

Roberts' decision not to include the name of the Jewish family has a dual effect. First, it evokes the absence of Jews from the postwar world – without names in the text, they are not properly accommodated into the historical account of what happened. Second, the anonymity of the family implies a limit to what can and cannot be sufficiently represented. The novel articulates belatedness in the ways in which that past is recuperated into the present and also highlights the limits of how such a history can be 'redeemed'. Widdowson argued that many contemporary British novels were intimately concerned with these problematics, suggesting that there was an 'end of the century' malaise evident in many of these texts. These novels looked back at the major events of the century, most pointedly the two world wars and the Holocaust, and articulated many of the existing (some might suggest post-modern) anxieties surrounding the telling and representation of histories. There was an evident sense that the Holocaust represented a profound 'rupture' in the flow of history and that theories surrounding the complexities of memory have had an enormous impact on novelists and historians. For Widdowson such issues were of immense significance and his contribution to this – and other critics' – thinking in this area has been immeasurable.

Notes

1. Peter Widdowson, *Literature* (London: Routledge, 1999), 25.
2. See, for example, Peter Widdowson, *Graham Swift* (Tavistock: Northcote House, 2006) and 'Newstories: Fiction, History and the Modern World', *Critical Survey* 7.1 (1995), 3–17; Martin Randall, *Appointments to Keep in the Past.* Ph.D. thesis. University of Gloucestershire, 2005.
3. Salman Rushdie, *Midnight's Children* (London: Jonathan Cape, 1981; repr. Pan, 1982), 394. Hereinafter cited parenthetically within the text.
4. Bill Ashcroft, 'Excess Post-Colonialism and the Verandums of Meaning', *Describing Empire: Post-Colonialism and Textuality,* ed. Chris Tiffin and Alan Lawson (London: Routledge, 1994), 34.
5. Graham Swift, *Waterland* (London: William Heinemann, 1983; repr. Picador, 1992), 62. Hereinafter cited parenthetically within the text.
6. Michèle Roberts, *Daughters of the House* (London: Virago, 1992; repr. 1995). Hereinafter cited parenthetically within the text.
7. Nick Rennison, *Contemporary British Novelists* (Abingdon: Routledge, 2005), 139.
8. Ibid., 139.
9. Steven Spielberg's *Schindler's List* was released in 1993. This was also the year that the United States Holocaust Memorial Museum in Washington, DC, was opened.
10. This phrase is taken from W. G. Sebald's *Austerlitz,* trans. Anthea Bell (Berlin [Ger]: Carl Hanser Verlag, 2001; repr. Penguin, 2002), 240.
11. Nicola King, *Memory, Narrative, Identity* (Edinburgh: Edinburgh University Press, 2000), 11–32.
12. Jay Winter and Emmanuel Sivan, eds, *War and Remembrance in the Twentieth Century* (London: Routledge, 2003), 10.

Chapter 9

The 'Servant Problem', Social Class and Literary Representation in Eighteenth-Century England

R. C. Richardson

In the late 1970s and 1980s Peter Widdowson, alongside whom (as a historian) I once taught in London, was very notably in the vanguard of those who were fundamentally redefining 'English' as a subject. He was the prime engine behind the launching of the journal *Literature and History* in 1975 and a key figure in the CNAA, which validated and encouraged the non-university sector and promoted interdisciplinarity. In a succession of publications Widdowson challenged existing orthodoxies about literary value and the canon of literature, and about the politics of studying it. Issues relating to class, ideology, gender issues, materialism, reader response, objectivity/subjectivity were all foregrounded in his edited collection *Re-Reading English* (1982) to which he supplied a provocative introduction. His books and essays on E. M. Forster, Thomas Hardy and Patrick Hamilton showed what could be done when writers' work, reputations and associated critiographies were deconstructed and vigorously re-examined.

Widdowson's authors – Hardy, Forster, Hamilton and others – are all drawn from the late nineteenth and twentieth centuries. This chapter takes up some of his recurring themes – class, ideology, gender relations – and his interdisciplinary strategies for expanding the literary canon and exploring the dialectical interactions between text and context and applies them to a different period (the eighteenth century) and a topic (the servant problem) which loomed large within it.[1] Whereas Widdowson's authors all tended to consign servants to the background – even the self-fashioning Hardy whose own family included servant members – while others occupied centre stage, in the eighteenth century, things were often very different. In this period the employing classes' perceptions of a serious, widespread and socially damaging 'servant problem' were placed high on the agenda and became a frequent and major topic for writers to address, usually very trenchantly and sometimes experimentally, in a variety of literary genres. In these literary representations servants became more alarmingly visible than ever before and all manner of social engineering was projected to bring them more firmly under control to safeguard the best interests of the social and moral order their labours were intended to serve. Tract writers Defoe (much admired by Widdowson's Hardy), Mandeville and Swift come under review here as does the now largely forgotten playwright James Townley. The distinctive, if oblique, contribution to the debate on master–servant relations made by Samuel Richardson's novel *Pamela* is also noted. This was a subject that was insistently present in the eighteenth century.[2]

That said, the identification of a 'servant problem' was not an intrinsically new development of the decades after 1700. Complaints about servants' failings and vices had been heard since the Elizabethan age and underpinned the great tide of godly literature calling for the reform of households and the recognition of their respective duties by both men and masters.[3] The 'servant problem' also figured as a staple ingredient of Restoration comedies of manners, as Congreve's *The Way of the World* (1700) amply demonstrates. But complaints about servants reached new heights in the Augustan age as the practice of servant-keeping and competition for servants both spread, as London continued its staggeringly relentless growth, as the economy boomed, and as new sensibilities developed. Court records and family papers abound with individual case histories of dysfunctional households and the apparently unstoppable exercise of servant 'power'. For example, a litany of complaints about the wrongs inflicted by servants fills countless pages in the diaries of the long-suffering wife and then widow Elizabeth Freke (1671–1714) and the insecure and neurotic spinster Gertrude Savile (1697–1758).[4] These are just two instances among many. Not surprisingly, since the 'servant problem' was constantly discussed and complained of by eighteenth-century employers, literature – always alert to its context and market – joined in the chorus, actively contributing to the ongoing debate. New vehicles of satire and farce placed themselves alongside conventional prose and verse as vehicles of denunciation. The result, as Widdowson would have immediately recognized, was literature *in* history and literature *as* history.

Daniel Defoe (c.1661–1731), economic conservative, inveterate moralist, and one of the most prolific of Augustan writers, turned frequently to the subject of the 'servant problem' in a succession of books and tracts on society and the economy in the second and third decades of the eighteenth century; after his novel *Roxana* (1724), which had a criminal mistress and maid at its heart, he turned his back on writing fiction.[5]

The Family Instructor (1715, 1727), clearly echoing a long-standing tradition of books on household religion and distinctly clerical in its tone, was his first venture into the field. The five dialogues which comprised the second part, dealing with masters and servants, put this subject in the centre of the stage. Here godly and ungodly masters and men and their relationships with, and effects on, each other are constantly contrasted. Unsurprisingly, since Defoe had a fixed moralizing agenda, the ungodly are made to see the errors of their ways and recognize their respective responsibilities. In one of these stories a reformed apprentice becomes a blessing to others. A godly servantmaid in the first dialogue of volume 2 is depicted as a shining example and prompts the predictable moral conclusion: 'If all servants in such places did their duty like her it would spread religion through the world.'[6]

Religious Courtship (1722, 10th edn, 1796) addressed a number of the same topics in a lengthy appendix devoted to servants and servant-keeping. The conviction that 'irreligious servants are the plague of families' was Defoe's starting point. To prevent contagion it was crucial that such social and moral misfits should not be recommended to other employers in glibly dispensed testimonials.[7] Masters and mistresses, however, were most at fault when family religion was not upheld in the households over which they presided.[8] Part, at least, of the notorious 'servant problem' lay squarely at their own door.

Defoe returned to some of the same themes, but at greater length and with even greater vehemence, in his book *The Great Law of Subordination Considered* (1724), 'a black history of the degeneracy of English servants', written not in dialogue form but in hard-hitting continuous prose.[9] Household servants, he thundered, were now so out of control and idle that they constituted a national problem crying out for immediate remedy. 'If it goes on the poor will be rulers over the rich and the servants be governors of their masters. . . . The *canaille* of this nation impose laws upon their superiors'.[10] Although in general Defoe was an advocate of higher wages as a stimulus to the economy, in this case servants' wages, he believed, had simply got out of control, due an imbalance of supply and demand. London servants in particular, many bad ones included, he argued, were arrogantly dictating their own terms. Even good servants, he claimed, easily became corrupted by being overrewarded and by their unchecked, false pride. The 'servant problem' in London, not surprisingly, was in a class of its own and Defoe, a Londoner himself (the son of a dissenting tallow chandler) was well placed to observe it. Masters were no less responsible than men for this deplorable state of affairs by allowing household religion to decline and only the sternest of remedies, Defoe concluded, would halt the downward spiral. Fines should be imposed on masters giving misleading character references to their household staff. A servant who threatened his master should be transported for a 21-year term.[11] 'Now is the time for the people of England to rescue themselves out of the hands of the worst slavery they were ever yet in. . . . I mean a bondage to their own servants.'[12]

Given the fact that his subject was so closely in line with the preoccupations of his own times Defoe must surely have thought that *The Great Law of Subordination* would become a runaway success. But it was not to be. His characteristically forthright style notwithstanding, this book – by his own standards – was a commercial failure. The reasons, perhaps, are not hard to find. The book was too long and expensive. The chosen persona of the author – a Frenchman writing to his brother at home – was a strategic error; Englishmen, Defoe ought to have known, did not take lightly to being reprimanded by an opinionated foreigner. There was also too much pointed criticism of masters. The 'servant problem' was widely recognized by the employing classes but they would have approved much more readily of an analysis which exonerated them from any share of the blame.

Undaunted and indefatigable Defoe attempted to put things right almost immediately by bringing out in the following year *Everybody's Business is Nobody's Business*, a tract this time, not a book, and on sale for only 6d. Moreover the new author persona was this time unmistakably the grumpy archetypical and misogynist old Englishman who saw servants themselves, especially maidservants, as the sole creators of the 'servant problem'. Maidservants' wages, Defoe lamented, had trebled or quadrupled 'of late', often putting them beyond the reach of hard-pressed tradesmen. Well-paid maidservants now scorned dirty, exhausting labour.[13] Maidservants' high wages naturally encouraged menservants to agitate for more. Compulsory wage reductions were urgently needed as well as strict regulation of servant dress.[14]

All this was welcome music to the ears of the employing classes. Unlike *The Great Law of Subordination* which had failed to find a market, *Everybody's Business* went through four printings with relative ease in the space of a few months in 1725. It unashamedly cashed in, too, on the backlash provoked by Bernard Mandeville's allegory *The Fable of the Bees*, originally a pamphlet titled 'The Grumbling Hive' brought out in 1705. Going through successive enlargements it culminated in a book-length offering first published in 1714 and was substantially expanded again in later editions.

Mandeville (1670–1733), a Dutch doctor of medicine who settled in London, turned conventional morality on its head.[15] Fraud, he argued, was endemic among the professions not just the criminal element of his own day, and luxury and pride had been embraced by the whole nation. The latter trend was in fact to be welcomed since conspicuous consumption helped generate full employment and national prosperity. Frugality, a virtue long praised by churchmen, had no economic benefits whatever. Luxury, by contrast, was socially beneficial.[16] Poverty and ignorance, Mandeville insisted, were two of the necessary foundations of the nation's well-being and for this reason, to the horror of conventional moralists, he lambasted charity schools and their promoters both for their mistaken attempts to eradicate what they considered social evils and for facilitating, or at least raising hopes of, social mobility. Removing poverty and promoting popular education made no sense, in Mandeville's view.[17] The 'servant problem', as Mandeville saw it, was the inevitable consequence of their overeducation which made them discontented, insolent, avaricious and ambitious. 'People of the meanest rank know too much to be serviceable to us.'[18] Education all too easily weakened the bond between men and their masters. 'A servant can have no unfeigned respect for his master', Mandeville declared in a cynical aside, 'as soon as he has sense enough to find out that he serves a fool'.[19]

Servants had exploited their scarcity value to push up wages to punishingly high levels for employers and tips (vails), now claimed as a right, were an added infliction. 'A [householder] who cannot afford to make many entertainments and does not often invite people to his table can have no creditable man servant.'[20] A writer in the *Gentleman's Magazine* in 1734 denounced the practice of vails as a national disgrace. Partial eradication of vails had been achieved by the end of the century but extinction lay well into the future. For vails-seeking footmen in particular Mandeville had an undisguised contempt and he was alarmed to see those in London forming an 'association' or proto-trade union to 'protect' themselves and keep both wages and vails high. 'The greatest part of [footmen] are rogues and not to be trusted [he went on]; and if they are honest half of them are sots. . . . Many of them are guilty of all these vices, whoring, drinking and quarrelling.'[21] Compulsory attendance at church, where servants could be made to learn their duty, and the general, enforced abolition of vails were Mandeville's prescriptions for improvement.[22] Workers of all kinds, servants included, should work uncomplainingly for the wages offered to them, said Mandeville; that was their lot in life. It was a conclusion not out of line with Defoe's even though Mandeville had reached it by a different route.

The 'servant problem' was no less a preoccupation of Defoe's and Mandeville's contemporary Jonathan Swift (1667–1745), though he wrote on the subject rather later than the other two and in a very different way.[23] Swift's own house-hold in Dublin, where he was a high-ranking churchman, was run according to strict routines. Laws drawn up in December 1733 prescribed penalties for various servant transgressions and acts of negligence. By contrast, his own long-serving, faithful manservant was celebrated on a memorial tablet in Dublin cathedral. Swift's views on the servant class at large were every bit as pessimistic, however, as those of Defoe and Mandeville. But his highly distinctive approach to servants' failings and vices was not simply to straightforwardly denounce them. Instead he pilloried them in biting satire. It was a strategy which obvi-ously relied on the recognition that what was being treated with black humour was at bottom a depressing reality all too familiar to his readers. Swift's *Directions to Servants*, written in the late 1730s and published in 1745, deservedly ranks as a minor classic.[24]

The opening general section rehearsed the characteristic failings of all ser-vants and covered a variety of topics relating to conduct and decorum, the receiving of visitors, and to interactions with other servants and with tradesmen in the outside community. Tardiness in obeying a command, it was stressed, ought to be standard practice. 'Never come until you have been called three or four times, for none but dogs will come at the first whistle.'[25] Internal doors were best left constantly open to improve air circulation and to avoid the unnec-essary effort of opening and closing them. However, if closing doors was insisted upon 'give the door such a clap as you go out and make everything rattle in it to put your master and mistress in mind that you observe their directions'.[26]

Taking a mental note of the names of callers to the master's house was a prac-tice best avoided 'for indeed you have too many other things to remember'.[27] Other helpful tips followed about welcoming servants' own guests to the house without the master's knowledge and about general cleanliness. 'Wipe your shoes for want of a clout with the bottom of a curtain or damask napkin. . . . If the butler wants a jordan in case of need he may use the great silver cup.'[28] Accidents, breakages, and acts of negligence, of course, should never be confessed. In good households the best diet ought to be expected as a right. 'Don't stint what you spend on provision at [your master's] expense.'[29] Going on errands, naturally, should be taken as an opportunity for leisure and hard bargaining with shopkeepers should be avoided at all costs.[30] The master's guests should also be intimidated to pay the highest vails on departure and if, unwisely, they did not oblige then the advice was that revenge should fall on them on them when they next entered, or attempted to enter, the house.[31]

Eighteen separate sets of detailed advice followed for particular servants in the household hierarchy to ensure that the overall ethos and *modus vivendi* of the domestic establishment were properly understood. A few examples of Swift's fertile satire must suffice to illustrate the general drift. The butler, for instance, was advised to lock up a cat in the china cupboard to deter mice from breaking the fine plates. Bottling wine with tobacco-flavoured corks was recommended 'which will give the wine the true taste of the weed, so delightful to all good judges in drinking'.[32] Another good practice was when making tea to use water from the pot 'where cabbage or fish have been boiling which will make it much wholesomer by curing the acid corroding qualities of the tea'.[33] Not surprisingly in this sustained satire lots of advice went to the cook. 'To give the soup a high French taste', for example, soot falling down the chimney into the pan should, naturally, be stirred in thoroughly.[34] Footmen were advised to make light work of moving plates from the dinner table to the scullery by simply tipping them all downstairs. 'There is not a more agreeable sight or sound, especially if they be silver.'[35] To cut heating bills fires in dining rooms should be lit only two minutes before serving the meal.[36] Dress code for footmen was no less important. 'Never wear socks when you wait at meals on account of your own health as well of them that sit at table, because most ladies like the smell of young men's toes as it is a sovereign remedy against the vapours.'[37] And what better way to end the advice to footmen could have been thought of than some helpful tips on facing the inevitable grand finale of death by hanging!

Chambermaids were advised to have a good stock of excuses ready when anything got broken; breaking a mirror, for example, could easily be blamed on a flash of lightning coming through the window. Fastidiousness was needed with the preparation of bread and butter so that only one thumb-print per slice was visible.[38] Similar niceties should be observed when clearing chamber pots from bedrooms.[39] Throwing pails of water out on to the street, especially in winter on frosty nights, was good practice and additionally provided much needed entertainment since 'a hundred people [would fall down] on their noses and backsides before your door when the water is frozen'.[40] To maidservants Swift gave helpful detailed advice on what to do when their sexual favours were sought by the master. A predatory elder son, however, should be avoided at all costs since 'you will get nothing from him but a big belly or a clap and probably both together'.[41]

In Swift's hands satire became a cutting-edge instrument to deconstruct the 'servant problem'. Its tone lightly concealed its serious purpose and a reforming impulse that in reality was as strong as Defoe's. Swift was clearly addressing and warning the employing classes even though the *persona* assumed by the writer in this text seemingly is that of an insider, a fellow servant, fully and approvingly acquainted with the artful ways of life below stairs. The text proceeds throughout at two levels: advice to servants on how to get away with anything and by bringing all this into the open a pointed exhortation to employers to implement the unexercised power they already possessed to prevent all this from taking place.

Satire was also the preference of James Townley (1714–78), clergyman, schoolmaster, and friend of the actor-manager David Garrick, though this time drama was the vehicle chosen for its presentation. 'The author thought the stage, where the bad might be disgraced and the good rewarded the most ready and effectual method for this purpose'. 'High Life below Stairs', Townley's farce, first performed at Drury Lane in 1759, was all the rage for a time though elite and plebeian audience reactions were understandably at odds.[42] The published version was reprinted at least eight times in the year of its first performance and though it inevitably became a period piece its enduringly relevant message ensured that it went on being presented on stage and reissued in print well into the second half of the nineteenth century. Apart from its particular applications of satire the play's main novelty lies in its setting and *dramatis personae*. It lives up to its title by being set chiefly in the service quarters of a London house and with two exceptions – Lovel, a young gentleman with a fortune gained from a West Indies plantation, and Freeman, his friend – all the other characters are servants belonging to Freeman's and other households. They include two blacks, perhaps brought over from Lovel's plantation, and servants from other gentry and aristocratic households who haughtily adopt the identity and airs of their employers.[43] The Duke's servant, his own low origins notwithstanding, looks down condescendingly on ordinary, vulgar servants while Lady Bab's maid arrogantly disdains the Vauxhall pleasure gardens since 'there is nobody there but filthy citizens'.[44]

The plot is simple and predicable enough. Lovel, alerted by his friend Freeman's faithful servant to the misrule prevailing in his own household, decides to discover the truth for himself by taking leave of his London home and promptly returning in disguise as a countryman in search of employment. Once readmitted to his own house as a would-be employee he sees for himself that he has only one honest servant – Tom – the man he had previously trusted least. Philip, the man Lovel had up to that point especially valued, turns out to be the worst of the whole domestic staff, a man determined to make the most of his master's absence by helping himself to provisions and clothing and throwing a party for invited guests from other London households. 'The cellar shall bleed', he boasts. 'I have some burgundy that is fit for an emperor.'[45]

The disguised Lovel, invited to the servants' party, is instructed by Philip in the ways of the world, particularly those enshrined in his favourite handbook *The Servants' Guide to Wealth*.

Let it for ever be your plan
To be the master not the man
And do as little as you can.[46]

With a sumptuous supper spread before them, with the best wine flowing freely, and with the party in full swing the guests are regaled with a favourite song.[47] Only the previously disparaged Tom stands up for his master. 'His honour is a prince; gives noble wages and keeps noble company, and you two are never contented but cheat him wherever you can lay your fingers. Shame on you.'[48]

But virtue, inevitably, triumphs. Lovel reveals his true identity and firmly dispenses justice. Philip, the hypocrite, is sent packing, the honest, plain-speaking Tom is promoted, and Freeman's faithful servant who first alerted Lovel to the deceits practised in his own house is rewarded for his pains. Lovel, suitably chastened by his recent experience, acquires a clearer sense of a master's responsibilities.

If persons of rank would act up to their standard it would be impossible that their servants could ape them. But when they affect everything that is ridiculous it will be in the power of any low creature to follow their example.[49]

Townley's moral, it seems, is essentially the same as Swift's. Servants, the endnote to the 1759 published text states, were made in the play 'the instruments of conveying the satire and therefore it is not unnatural for them to mistake the object of it. . . . [Those placed] in a superior station in life, by acting improperly in it, afford much juster matter for censure and ridicule.' In the last analysis masters were to blame for negligently allowing a 'servant problem' to develop.[50]

Pamela (1741) by Samuel Richardson (1689–1761) seems in some ways a misfit in this 'Servant Problem' gallery though most of the novel in one way or another is set in hierarchical elite households and it is concerned throughout with the subject of domestic management and with the ideals and realities of employer/servant and gender relations. Its author, the son of a joiner, served an apprenticeship to a printer, was largely self-taught, and was familiar with the workings of the lower, though not the lowest, sections of society. He had close links, as publisher and printer, with Defoe. Unlike Defoe, however, there is a case for seeing Richardson as a closet radical, even – possibly – a proto-feminist or subversive. Certainly not a satire – its heavy- and slow-moving moralizing had no room for that quick instrument – *Pamela* was not, on the face of it, a direct contribution to the debate on the 'Servant Problem'. Very clearly, however, it was an innovating text and, obliquely, it made its own distinctive input to the ongoing discussion. It solicited reader response which was utilized in successive editions. It pioneered the epistolary novel – the author's early experience as an unofficial letter writer in his Midlands village served him well here – and allowed Richardson to present himself as editor of real letters and journals not author of fiction. It was the first work of its kind to have a maidservant as its central character. Pamela indeed is present in the novel both as an individual and as a representative case. 'You see by my sad story and narrow escapes', she declares, 'what hardships poor maidens go through whose lot is to go out to service'.[51] Once she becomes Mr B's wife and mistress of his house she vows to profit from her experience as a servant; indeed it is clear that Pamela views the new combined roles which await her as an extension of service.[52]

Pamela herself, a lady's maid and not a common servant from whose ranks and work routines she always distances herself, is virtue personified and her virtue is 'rewarded' by her eventual marriage to her would-be seducer, Mr B her master. The only 'problem' she represents to her gentleman admirer is her stubborn and high principled resistance to his advances. She insists on her personal freedom, her right to freedom of speech. She is no man's property until – cruellest of ironies – she marries! There are other servant characters in the novel, it is true, who emerge in an unflattering light – the vile, immoral housekeeper Mrs Jewkes and John the footman who slyly betrays Pamela's confidences – are the prime examples. Even these, however, were not enacting the 'servant problem' as it was commonly understood in the eighteenth century since in both cases they were simply carrying out their master's selfish instructions and they themselves, though led astray, are not presented as irredeemable. Other servant characters – the good-hearted and caring housekeeper Mrs Jervis (prepared to stand up for Pamela and speak her mind to her master when he overstepped the mark), Mr Longman, and 'honest old Jonathan' – are aligned on the side of virtue with Pamela herself.

Pamela's eye-catching record and presence as a model servant serve as her means to social advancement and it was no doubt this feature of the novel as much as anything which attracted hopeful readers from the servant community as well as from the employing classes when the book was first published. 'Pray have you read Mrs Pamela? (an entry in Fanny Robinson's correspondence for 20 July 1741 enquires, shortly after the novel's first appearance.) My maids got it and one of them cried for hours together.' Reading novels, however, was by no means always an approved recreation either for young mistresses or maids. 'Though many of them contain some few good morals', opined Lady Sarah Pennington, 'they are not worth picking out of the rubbish intermixed'.[53]

Double standards of morality figure prominently in Richardson's novel. Men like Mr B in the upper ranks of society claimed sexual licence as a right and weighed lower-class females and their virginity as theirs for the taking.

That Pamela successfully defends herself with armour-plated rhetoric, survives her abduction and confinement, and becomes Mr B's wife and not his whore combine to give the novel some of its distinctive, if improbable, character. The narrative line no doubt helped ensure *Pamela*'s considerable success. Within a year of its original publication a revised edition and a two-volume sequel had been called for. Other new editions followed in 1746, 1754 and (finally) in 1801; the printer in him predisposed Richardson to be always making revisions. The novelty of its epistolary form, its challengingly different depiction of master–servant relations, and its highly respectable and 'safe' conclusion, all heightened its literary profile and linked it firmly with current debates on a ubiquitous topic: the proper conduct, responsibilities and duties of employers and their household staff.[54]

The texts by Defoe, Mandeville, Swift, Townley and Richardson considered here all belong to the four decades after 1720 and share obvious common denominators in subject matter. (Such was the perceived importance of the topic that not long after the appearance of *Pamela* William Blackstone in his *Commentaries on the Laws of England* (1765–9) provided an authoritative digest of the law as it impinged on the master–servant relationship.) In addition, all these texts were in some way innovatory in their literary or dramatic strategies – in their use of authorial persona, satire, stage setting and dramatic characters, and in the development of the epistolary novel form. All made their mark in their day even if, *Pamela* excepted, like Hardy's *Hand of Ethelberta* carefully exhumed by Widdowson, they subsequently faded from view. They all foreground issues (urgent at the time) relating to gender and class relations and all are profoundly ideological in the ways in which they introduce and handle their agendas. They could scarcely have failed to do all this, of course, since as one of the largest occupational categories of its day household service more clearly than any other visibly proclaimed the class divide. The dialectical exchange between materialism and culture is vividly expressed in all these works. All these texts are profoundly historical, anchored in history, products of a particular moment in time and its convictions, anxieties and vulnerabilities, and active constituents of, and contributions to, the making of social, economic, political and cultural history in their own period. Unmistakably all these writings manifestly exhibit the complex, multilayered interface between literature as history and literature in history to which Peter Widdowson's own work has always alerted us.

Notes

[1] This article is an offshoot of my new book on *Household Servants in Early Modern England* (Manchester: Manchester University Press, forthcoming). My thanks go to Dr Elisabeth Arbuckle of the English Department at the University of Puerto Rico for reading an earlier draft.

² There is a growing literature on servants and servant-keeping in this period. For a survey see Richardson, *Household Servants*, chapter 1.

³ See Richardson, *Household Servants*, chapter 6.

⁴ *Remembrances of Elizabeth Freke 1671–1714*, ed. R. A. Anselment (Camden Society, 5th ser., 18, 2001) and *Secret Comment. The Diaries of Gertrude Savile 1721–57*, ed. A. Saville (Thoroton Society, 41, 1997).

⁵ There is a considerable body of literature on Defoe as a literary figure and social commentator. See especially P. Earle, *The World of Defoe* (London: Weidenfeld & Nicolson, 1977) and M. Shinagel, *Daniel Defoe and Middle Class Gentility* (Cambridge, MA: Harvard University Press, 1968).

⁶ D. Defoe, *Family Instructor* (1715, 1722), II, 252.

⁷ D. Defoe, *Religious Courtship* (1722, 10th edn, 1796), 288, v.

⁸ Ibid., 250–1.

⁹ D. Defoe, *The Great Law of Subordination Considered* (1724), 13.

¹⁰ Ibid., 17.

¹¹ Ibid., 295–6.

¹² Ibid., 302.

¹³ D. Defoe, *Everybody's Business is Nobody's Business* (1725), 7, 13.

¹⁴ Ibid., 16.

¹⁵ On Mandeville see, for example, M. M. Goldsmith, *Private Vices Public Benefits. Bernard Mandeville's Social and Political Thought* (Cambridge: Cambridge University Press, 1985).

¹⁶ The title page of Erasmus Jones' *Luxury, Pride and Vanity. The Bane of the British Nation* (London, 1735) proclaimed a very different view. Increasing attention has been devoted recently to eighteenth-century views on luxury and its effects. See, for example, *Luxury in the Eighteenth Century. Debates, Desires and Delectable Goods*, ed. Maxine Berg and Elizabeth Eger (Basingstoke: Palgrave Macmillan, 2003). Mandeville's central place in the debate on the subject is generally agreed.

¹⁷ B. Mandeville, *Fable of the Bees* (1714, 1723), ed. P. Harth (Harmondsworth: Penguin, 1970), 294.

¹⁸ Ibid., 307. Others, of course, sprang to the defence of charity schools, a favourite social investment of the times, claiming that by inculcating obedience and humility as well as imparting some basic knowledge, they made the children of the poor more, not less, serviceable to society. See, for example, W. Hendley, *A Defence of the Charity Schools* (London, 1725).

¹⁹ Ibid., 296.

²⁰ Ibid., 308.

²¹ Quoted in Pamela Horn, *Flunkies and Scullions. Life below Stairs in Georgian England* (Stroud: Sutton, 2004), 207; Mandeville, *Fable of the Bees*, 307.

²² Mandeville, *Fable of the Bees*, 315.

²³ On Swift see, for example, J. G. Gilbert, *Jonathan Swift, Romantic and Cynic Moralist* (New York: Haskell House, 1973).

²⁴ 'Directions to Servants' in *Jonathan Swift*, ed. H. Davis (Oxford: Oxford University Press, 1964), publisher's preface.

²⁵ Ibid., 10.

²⁶ Ibid., 9.

²⁷ Ibid., 12.

28 Ibid., 14.

29 Ibid., 7.

30 Ibid., 9.

31 Ibid., 12–13.

32 Ibid., 27, 22.

33 Ibid., 23.

34 Ibid., 30.

35 Ibid., 36.

36 Ibid., 42.

37 Ibid., 41.

38 Ibid., 56.

39 Ibid., 53.

40 Ibid., 62.

41 Ibid., 56–8.

42 Noisy opposition from footmen in the gallery at the first performances led David Garrick, the actor-manager in charge, to prohibit free entry to the theatre. (John O'Keeffe, *Recollections*, 2 vols, 1826, I, 161–2.)

43 The black servants, Kingston and Cloe, were apparently cut in an Edinburgh staging of 1782. See Gretchen Gerzina, *Black England. Life before Emancipation* (London: John Murray, 1995), 38. John O'Keeffe's play 'Tony Lumpkin in Town' (1776) similarly holds forth on servant hierarchies and the snobbery associated with them. (O'Keeffe, *Dramatic Works*, 4 vols, 1798, I, 228.)

44 J. Townley, *High Life below Stairs* (3rd edn, 1759), 7 and 9.

45 Ibid., 12.

46 Ibid., 18.

47 Ibid., 28, 29.

48 Ibid., 21.

49 Ibid., 35.

50 Ingeniously, Townley, under the pseudonym of Oliver Grey, directly advanced the servants' case in his *An Apology for Servants* (1760). David Garrick moved in the other direction by bringing out a sequel to Townley's play called 'Bon Ton or High Life above Stairs' in 1776.

51 *Pamela, or Virtue Rewarded*, ed. P. Sabor, intro. Margaret A. Doody (Harmondsworth: Penguin, 1980, 1985), 371.

52 Ibid., 364. On Richardson see Margaret Anne Doody, *A Natural Passion. A Study of the Novels of Samuel Richardson* (Oxford: Oxford University Press, 1974), 14–98 and C. Flint, *Family Fictions. Narrative and Domestic Relations in Britain 1688–1798* (Stanford, CA: Stanford University Press, 1998).

53 Quoted in Bridget Hill, *Servants. English Domestics in the Eighteenth Century* (Oxford: Clarendon Press, 1996), 212–13. The Robinson quotation is cited in Jane Holmes, *Domestic Service in Yorkshire, 1650–1780*, D.Phil. thesis, University of York (1989), 269; *An Unfortunate Mother's Advice to Her Absent Daughters* (London, 1761), 39.

54 Richardson's moral stance in Pamela was quickly parodied by Henry Fielding in *Shamela* (1742) with its heroine opportunistically exploiting her 'virtue' simply as a bargaining counter in the sexual politics in which she finds herself. Richardson, for his part, in due course registered his dislike of *Tom Jones* (1749) as a thoroughly immoral novel. (Doody, *A Natural Passion*, 6, 14–15.)

Chapter 10

'Sway between a Dance and a Fight':
Black Religions in Toni Morrison's *Paradise*

Shelley Saguaro

In an interview in 1998, at the time of the publication of *Paradise*, Toni Morrison noted those critical responses that claimed: '*Paradise* will not be well studied, because it's about this unimportant intellectual topic, which is religion.'[1] It is clear, however, that Morrison's own view is that religion is central to the history of African-American defiance and compliance and therefore a serious matter, for representation and its reception. There are various religious groupings and theological premises outlined in this novel set in the 1970s, which also harks back to the post-bellum diasporas of the 1860s. Survival, identity and legitimacy are the post-slavery and post-World War contexts for each of the religious – and political – positions represented. In the novel's present there are three distinctively different Christian churches in the all-black town of Ruby, Oklahoma. There is also the Convent; once a school run by nuns for Native American girls, it is now a refuge where the Afro-Brazilian refugee, Consolata, develops a ritualized community of outcast women. This exploration will focus on the representation of two main characters: the Reverend Misner, 'struggling mightily with the tenets of his religion, the pressures of the civil rights, the dissolution of the civil rights' in the light of James Cones' liberationist Black Theology,[2] and Consolata, whose ceremonies bear the traits of the Afro-Brazilian religion of *Candomblé*, developed by slaves to retain a separate African identity while dissembling a conforming Catholic one. As the history of race and religion in America takes another turn, seen, for instance, in Barack Obama's necessarily public disowning of his home church, the present status of this 'unimportant intellectual topic' will be evaluated.

I

In the early part of the new century, my colleague Peter Widdowson and I found ourselves to be at work on the same text: Toni Morrison's *Paradise*. Not surprisingly, perhaps, we placed our emphases a little differently. At that time, I was at work on a book about the politics and poetics of gardens in twentieth- and twenty-first-century fiction, in which *Paradise* would be a key text. Peter, who also had long experience of teaching Morrison's earlier novel, *Beloved*, was intrigued by this new novel's 'timelines': its complex structure, its 'connecting narrative filaments' and its engagement with the politics of post-Reconstruction and 'Second Reconstruction' America. In 2001 he published his article in *The Journal of American Studies*: 'The American Dream Refashioned: History, Politics and Gender in Toni Morrison's *Paradise*'. As always, Peter was a helpful reader of my work and I am indebted to him for his advice and support in advance of the publication of *Garden Plots: The Politics and Poetics of Gardens*.[3] Of my own reading of *Paradise* and, in particular, what he calls 'the supernatural coda' of the novel, he simply stated that he 'did not read it like that'. Peter's view that the resurrection of the murdered women 'ends the novel on a note of upbeat fantasy and beguiling mystery' is one that few, if any, would contest. However, his view that 'the true message is that it is in the hands of young women . . . just emerging from their constraining chrysalis, that the possibility of true change resides' is, from my perspective, arguable. It is, I suggest, an 'upbeat' projection rooted less in gender, and more in religious, politics.

Since our first discussions and the completion of our respective projects, I have continued to work on and think further about the novel, and this *Festschrift* gives me the opportunity to carry on my conversation with Peter. It is not my aim simply to defend my earlier approach, but, rather, to attempt to clarify the position religion holds within the novel and should hold in critical assessments of it. My focus is fuelled by the apparent general reluctance of literary critics to engage with religion, even though it may be seen to be crucial, if not central, to the novel. This is a reluctance of which Morrison is well aware:

> I think that literary people don't realise the number of people who are really, really faithful. . . . And that number may be larger than the number of people who *don't* believe. What's interesting, too, is that in the larger mainstream discourse, it's always suggested that belief is a form of delusion. If I approached the people in this book with that notion, I wouldn't be worthy of them as an author. In any case, all of the subjects . . . have their roots in some form of moral structure and religion . . . . I wanted to tackle these things head-on, not pretending that there was no such thing as belief.[4]

Critics prefer, instead, reference to 'magic realism' (a label which, for her own work, Morrison refutes), or the vague categories 'supernatural', 'spiritual' and 'mystical'. The tendency to make light of religion in texts, or to feel that the discussion of religion is only for the religious, is to distort those texts, and to belie their range and complexity. It also engenders readers who are ignorant of religions and blind to their presence in literary texts, as in other discourses. To read a novel such as Toni Morrison's *Paradise* with due attention to religion is to find an important statement about the diversity of black theological belief and further, its profoundly integral relation to Black American history – including literary history. Several critics have noted Morrison's allusions to the Brazilian syncretic religion, *Candomblé* and its relation to the rituals developed by the community of women in 'the Convent'.[5] Further, Morrison's inclusion of part of the Gnostic, Nag Hammadi scripture known as 'Thunder, Perfect Mind' as an epigraph – in *Paradise* and in the earlier *Jazz*, has also been noted severally.[6] However, this is still largely at the level of identifying and explaining sources rather than attending to Morrison's own deployment of Black religiosity, in content and in form. Other specifically Christian aspects, which are far more pervasive and sustained in the novel, and particularly relevant to its historical framing, appear to have been consistently overlooked.

In her well-known essay, written in 1984, 'Rootedness: The Ancestor as Foundation', Morrison outlined what, for her, were the major characteristics of Black art, among them, a method and mode with its roots in religion:

> It should try deliberately to make you stand up and make you feel something profoundly in the same way that a Black preacher requires his congregation to speak, to join him in the sermon, to behave in a certain way, to stand up and to weep and to cry and to accede or to change and to modify – to expand on the sermon that is being delivered.[7]

Morrison may be metaphorical in this regard, but in *Paradise*, black preachers and their congregations are not merely formally analogous but are also its subject matter. The story of the establishment of two, all-black and devout communities, each aiming to be a paradise (Haven, in the late 1890s and early 1900s, and Ruby in the mid-twentieth century), is thoroughly inflected by the prevailing Black religious practices of their respective eras: African origins, diasporic developments, survival strategies and the more strident, liberationist coming of age. Included in these are to be found strands of ancient Gnosticism, colonial *Candomblé*, African-American Christianity and Black Theology.

The founders of the town of Haven, the 'newly freed led by the Old Fathers', established their community in Oklahoma in the face of dire persecution and adversity, some of it at the hands of other black communities. On their long journey from Mississippi, through Louisiana to their eventual destination, God-given signs prompted and protected the seekers. Their sanctified, communal Oven, with its prayerful (though later contested) inscription on its lip, inspired them as a chosen community with a dynamic, non-denominational faith at its centre: 'In 1910 there were two churches in Haven and the All-Citizens Bank . . . but the traffic to and from the Oven was greater than to all of those.'[8] There is much about religion to be explored in this situation alone, including the influence of and assimilation to European Christianity and the continuation, in the Oven, of the more African-oriented 'village values' mode of congregation and 'communion'.[9] As James H. Evans, Jr explains, in *We Have Been Believers: An African-American Systematic Theology*:

African slaves who embraced Christianity also modified it and shaped it to meet their existential needs and saw, even in the contorted presentations of the Gospel by some white people, a continuity between what they knew of God in Africa and the God of the Bible.[10]

However, it is the later town of Ruby and its context of the 1960s and 1970s which is the novel's main focus. Another all-black Oklahoma town established by the successors of the founding families, it comprises three churches – the Methodists, the Baptists and the Pentecostals (83), with their respective messages: New Zion – Evil Times; Holy Redeemer – Last Days; Calvary – Good News (102/3).

It is a town at odds over many matters, including the Oven, formerly the communities' symbol of cohesion – albeit 'a utility [that] became a shrine (cautioned against not only in scary Deuteronomy but in lovely Corinthians II as well)' (103) – but now a feature of dissension and a meeting place for loitering youth. No one is able to agree on the exact wording of the original inscription: 'Beware the Furrow of His Brow' or 'Be the Furrow of His Brow'? Patricia conjectures, why not make it 'Be the Furrow of Her Brow'? – but it is the 'young people' who hang around the Oven who are deemed responsible for the new militant graffiti on its hood 'We are the Furrow of His Brow'. When a painted fist, 'jet-black with red fingernails', and raised like a Black Panther salute, appears on the Oven, divisive, controlling fear prevails. The community itself is as protectionist as ever, (predicated on the 'intact' purity of the nine founding families, known as '8-rocks' for their deep-seam-coal colour and on their exclusivity: 'neither the founders of Haven nor their descendents could tolerate anybody but themselves') (13), but now the threats are also coming from within. Although the three churches differ, members from each of the congregations unite to destroy the Convent women.

The Reverend Misner is seen as part of the problem. One of the other ministers, the Reverend Pulliam, preaches chastising sermons, ('You have to earn God . . . . Love is not a gift. It is a diploma') (141) which are designed to widen 'the war he had declared on Misner's activities: tempting the young to step outside the wall . . . to think of themselves as civil warriors' (145). Misner is a newcomer, and he brings with him a new Theology: Black.

By 'Black Theology' I refer particularly to the seminal text by James H. Cone, *Black Theology and Black Power*, first published in 1969, the year after the assassination of Martin Luther King, four years after the assassination of Malcolm X, during the height of the Civil Rights movement, and coincident with the war in Vietnam. In Cone's own estimation, in a Preface to the 1989 edition:

> *Black Theology and Black Power* was a product of the Civil Rights and Black Power movements in America during the 1960s, reflecting both their strengths and weaknesses. As an example of their strengths, this book was an initial attempt to identify *liberation* as the heart of the Christian gospel and *blackness*

as the primary mode of God's presence. I wanted to speak on behalf of the voiceless black masses in the name of Jesus whose gospel I believed had been distorted by the preaching and theology of white churches.[11]

The Reverend Richard Misner brings to Ruby the liberationist views outlined by Cone. For him, Christianity remembers 'the execution of this one solitary black man propped up on these two intersecting lines . . . his woolly head alternately rising on his neck and falling on his chest' (146). Misner's politics, while progressive, also promote 'returning to roots' and pride in African origins:

> He had thought any place to be fine as long as there were young people to be taught, to be told, that Christ was judge and warrior too. That whites not only had no patent on Christianity; they were often its obstacle. That Jesus had been freed from white religion, and he wanted these kids to know that they did not have to beg for respect; it was already in them, and they needed only to display it. . . . 'If you cut yourself off from the roots, you'll wither.' (209)

Misner's colleagues and most of the members of all three congregations are much more conservative (Cone would say 'distorted' by white theology), alienated from Africa and resistant to the 'consciousness raising' he encourages as a proponent of the Civil Rights movement and an advocate of King's great Dream:

> Now, seven years after the murder of the man in whose stead he would happily have taken the sword, he was herding a flock which believed not only that it had created the pasture it grazed but that grass from any other meadow was toxic. . . . No matter who they are, he thought, or how special they think they are, a community with no politics is doomed. (212–13)

This community, preoccupied as many of its members are with purity, safety and self-segregation, believe they are endorsing a paradise, where politics is irrelevant – or rather, too dangerous to countenance, articulate or to leave open to possible dissent. However, when the community of 'wayward women', and the contemporary emphasis on political radicalization intrude and unsettle the hard-won status quo, extreme violence ensues.

Originally, the title chosen for this novel was *War*, but Morrison's publishers encouraged her to change it to something more appealing. The conventional opposite of war is peace, synonymous with and integral to Paradise, and yet Morrison points to the fact that wars are fought and continue to be fought in the establishment of Paradise, according to different visions and versions of it.

> I was interested in the kind of violent conflict that could happen as a result of efforts to establish a paradise. Our view of Paradise is so limited: it

requires you to think of yourself as the chosen people – chosen by God, that is. Which means that your job is to isolate yourself from other people. That's the nature of Paradise: it's really defined by who is *not* there as well as who is.[12]

The energy and anxious vigilance required to sustain such a paradise, according to one or other precept, means that it is invariably a place set apart, gated, monitored, frozen in time, and static in its precepts. 'The isolation, the separateness, is always part of any utopia' noted Morrison in one interview, but isolation 'carries the seeds of its own destruction because as times change, other things seep in'.[13] In this novel, what seeps into one 'paradise' is another: two paradises with different priorities. Hence, a 'war' ensues in which nine 'pure' and vigilant protectors of one paradise, 'the New Fathers', take reprisal on the other, the Convent, entering it and murdering five 'harmless' women, only one of whom is white. With 'God at their side, the men take aim. For Ruby' (18).

The women reside, in their intermittent fashion, in a mansion known as the Convent. First built by a wealthy embezzler, it became the venue for an 'asylum/boarding school for Indian girls in some desolate part of the American West' (223–4) established by a Catholic Order, the Sisters Devoted to Indians and Colored People.[14] By the late 1950s only two remain: Mother Mary Magna, the elderly white nun, and the mixed-race Brazilian, Consolata, whom Mary Magna had 'kidnapped' from the 'shit-strewn' streets of a city in Brazil where she was a street orphan. Eventually the Convent functions as a refuge for abused and distressed women, some of them from Ruby. In time Consolata, a pious Catholic under the tutelage of her adopted mother, assumes the mantle of a 'new and revised Reverend Mother', whose practices are seen as 'irregular'. At first fearful of the ritual modifications which she sees as 'forbidden' and at odds with her Christian faith, she eventually says a regretful goodbye to Him, and instructs her motley household: 'if you have a place . . . that you should be in and somebody who loves you waiting there, then go. If not, stay here and follow me. Someone could want to meet you' (263). What follows are the 'lost days' of singing and storytelling and dreaming and painting and healing. Who – or rather what – they meet is unexpected: violent death at the hands of a posse of black men who are their neighbours.

The women are killed on the basis that they are conducting obscene acts using unhallowed arts. A *New York Times* review of *Paradise* noted that, like the earlier *Beloved*, a 'real-life' account had given rise to a work of fiction:

On a trip to Brazil in the 1980s, Ms. Morrison heard about a convent of black nuns who took in abandoned children and practiced candomblé, an Afro-Brazilian religion; the local populace considered them an outrage, and they were murdered by a posse of men. 'I've since learned it never happened', Ms. Morrison said. 'But for me it was irrelevant. And it said much about institutional religion and uninstitutional religion, how close they are'.[15]

The 'ceremonies' developed by the Convent women are undoubtedly similar
to those practised in *Candomblé*. *Candomblé* is a religion which brings together
tribal beliefs from West Africa with Brazilian Indian spiritual practices. There is
also a strong measure of Catholic imagery combined in it, which, when first
adopted by the African slaves, was a way of enveloping their practices in the
guise of something more acceptable to their Portuguese slave-masters. Perhaps,
too, *Candomblé*'s veil of Catholicism afforded a good number of Catholic women
more scope than the patriarchal European religion would allow. *Candomblé* also
incorporates religious and medicinal rituals involving all aspects of the natural
world and, in particular, 'the sacred leaves' of certain plant species, adapted
from knowledge of African to Brazilian flora.[16] Further, the residual 'discredited' knowledge found in *Candomblé* and in other black folk-religious elements
reveal how 'African cosmologies held the interrelationships between the divine
world, nature, and the human community in an intimate balance.'[17] Consolata
is not, however, simply remembering and faithfully following the practices she
may have encountered in Brazil. Her 'ministry' is more intuitive, incidental and
fluid. She develops a friendship with Lone DuPres; a former midwife (until
women began to choose hospitals for their birthing) and a healer. Lone is a
venerable though outsider figure, who encourages Consolata's gift of 'stepping
in' and recalling the dying to life. When Consolata at first refuses, on the basis
that 'the church and everything holy forbade it', Lone responds: 'Don't separate God from His elements. He created it all. You stuck on dividing Him from
His works. Don't unbalance His world' (245). It is not that Lone is irreligious,
but rather that hers is a non-institutionalized religion. When she herself has
tried not to heed signs, visions and portents, trouble ensues:

> Playing blind was to avoid the language God spoke in. He did not thunder
> instructions or whisper messages into ears. Oh no. He was a liberating God.
> A teacher who taught you how to learn, to see for yourself. His signs were
> clear, abundantly so, if you stopped steeping in vanity's sour juice and paid
> attention to His world . . . she whispered, 'Thy will, Thy will'. (273)

Lone is not the only person to apprehend the world in ways that go beyond
the post-enlightenment five senses. There are several women who are able to
perceive 'visitors': Soane's Lady (102); Dovey's Friend (90 ff) and Consolata's
male 'alter-ego' (251–2). However, it is not only the women who have this facility. In fact, the original town of Haven was founded on the basis of the 'supernatural guidance' given to one of the Founding Fathers, Big Papa or Zechariah,
by 'the walking man' (98).

Morrison's propensity for including the supernatural in her work has led her
to be identified as a 'magical realist', a term she herself repudiates: 'just as long
as they don't call me a magical realist, as though I don't have a culture to write
out of. As though that culture has no intellect.'[18] One of the best keys to understanding the culture Toni Morrison writes from and to is to be found in her
essay, 'Rootedness: The Ancestor as Foundation'.

There are things that I try to incorporate into my fiction that are directly and deliberately related to what I regard as the major characteristics of Black art . . . the acceptance of the supernatural and a profound rootedness in the real world at the same time with neither taking precedence over the other. It is indicative of the cosmology, the way in which Black people looked at the world. We are very practical people, very down-to-earth, even shrewd people. But within that practicality we also accepted what I suppose could be called superstition and magic, which is another way of knowing things. But to blend those two worlds together at the same time was enhancing, not limiting. And some of those things were 'discredited knowledge' that Black people had; discredited only because Black people were discredited therefore what they *knew* was 'discredited'.[19]

Morrison goes on to note the importance of evaluating Black literature on the basis of 'what the writer does with the presence of an ancestor'. 'These ancestors are not just parents, they are sort of timeless people . . . benevolent, instructive, and protective, and they provide a certain kind of wisdom.'[20] There is no doubt that Morrison's supernatural figures in *Paradise* – the Friend, the Lady, the Walking Man – are ancestor figures and the various people who perceive them are still connected to a 'knowledge' that has been 'discredited' by Western institutions – and not only religious ones.

The mysterious disappearance of the murdered women's bodies and their apparent resurrection can thus be seen as part of a 'discredited' wisdom tradition that Morrison depicts and defends. For Peter Widdowson this, albeit supernatural, coda contains, at the very least, the promise that the women will win 'the war'. He finds that the novel fulfils the definition of 'womanist' outlined by Alice Walker: 'Appreciates and prefers women's culture, and women's emotional flexibility . . . and women's strength'.[21] For Kelly Reames the 'mystical ending' 'suggests reincarnation and that [the wish] for the women to return will be fulfilled'.[22] Both readings maintain that this novel is primarily about the power of women regained. In many respects this can also be seen as an engagement with, or response to, the original tenets of 'Black Theology'. In his 1989 Preface to *Black Theology and Black Power*, Cone admits that his and other works coming out of the 'black freedom movement' of the 1960s had as a major weakness, 'its complete blindness to the problem of sexism, especially in the black church community':

When I read my book today, I am embarrassed by its sexist language and patriarchal perspective. There is not even one reference to a woman in the whole book! With black women playing such a dominant role in the African American liberation struggle, past and present, how could I have been so blind?[23]

With her emphasis on a community of wounded and martyred women, who rise again, and in the imagination of Billie Delia, will return, it could be seen that

Morrison is providing something of a feminist or, more pertinently, 'womanist' riposte to Cone and his contemporaries. Many African-American woman writers, notably Alice Walker and Maya Angelou, did just this, but Morrison has always tried to distance herself from a strictly 'feminist' perspective; 'I don't subscribe to patriarchy, and I don't think it should be substituted with matriarchy' she noted in one interview; 'I don't write "ist" novels'.[24] And yet, the novel is about a controlling patriarchy and, in the face of damage, a community of women who try to live outside patriarchy and without men, and who are thus blamed for imagined atrocities, and held responsible for the atrocities they incite.

If the novel's beginning is shocking with the murder of the Convent women and the stark but unrevealing opening line: 'They shoot the white girl first', then the end is bewildering. The bodies of the five women have disappeared – as has a baby who was still unharmed in a cot – and cannot be found by the citizens of Ruby even though some of them have witnessed the murders and previously seen the corpses. These women are then depicted as visiting their earthly estranged loved ones in places both identifiable and alien. Consolata's reunion is the most enigmatic to behold: it is a strange pietà, with Connie rocked in the arms of a Black Madonna named Piedade, her 'black face framed in cerulean blue' (318). My conjecture in a fuller discussion in *Garden Plots* is that Piedade is a figure akin to the divine, female speaker in the Gnostic text 'Thunder: Perfect Mind', in a tradition that incorporates a Black Goddess, variously, Isis, Sophia, Sheba and Mary Magdalene , as 'the Woman who Knows All'. Or perhaps she is to be aligned with the *Candomblé orixa* figure, Iemanja, the predominant mother figure and the national Orixa of Brazil, associated with the sea, and the colours white and blue. Consolata used to tell the Convent women about Piedade, 'who sang but never said a word' (264) in mesmerizing stories about a seemingly fantastical place, perhaps Brazil, 'where white sidewalks met the sea and fish the color of plums swam . . . of scented cathedrals made of gold where gods and goddesses sat in the pews with the congregation' (263–4). The place Consolata now finds herself after death is more Brazil than Heaven, for there is mundane detritus everywhere. It is, as the novel's last words emphasize, 'down here', 'down here in [p]aradise'.[25] Morrison explains:

> The very last lines about the ships and passengers should suggest that an earthly paradise is the only one we know. . . . I wanted this book to move toward the possibility of reimagining paradise. . . . If we understood the *planet* to be that place, then this is all there is. So why not make it that way?[26]

The insistence on reimagining an earthly, rather than heavenly, paradise can also be seen to have its roots in the development of black churches, which witnessed conflicts in relation to 'otherworldliness'. As Dale P. Andrews explains in *Practical Theology for Black Churches*: 'Black eschatology does not separate "otherworldly" and "this-worldly" hope.' Many black churches in the period were criticized by adherents of Black Theology for their acquiescent emphasis on a future transcendent glory rather than on present liberation:

> Black theology places black churches of the post-Civil Rights era under the same general indictment of the post-Reconstruction churches. In the spirit of black power, black theology contends that black churches 'shrank behind walls of religious otherworldliness and distracted themselves with institutional maintenance and ecclesiastical politics'.[27]

Morrison is dramatizing these conflicts and hence the attention to the locus of paradise, in this novel, is deliberately not 'otherworldly', but 'down here'.

Morrison's personal religious beliefs are not generally well known. James Marcus's question about whether she herself was 'a churchgoing woman' had a brief and oblique response: 'I am a religious person. As you might guess, I have arguments with institutionalized religion.'[28] About her Catholicism she also seems reticent. She noted it briefly in conversation with Cornel West in 2004 and similarly, cursory reference was made to it in a 2008 profile in *The Observer*: 'At 12, Morrison converted to Catholicism and took Anthony as her middle name.'[29] In terms of the novel, it is Richard Misner with whom Morrison's sympathies would be most closely aligned. However, the novel goes beyond both Misner's and Morrison's institutionalized religion. Instead, the novel suggests not just the reconciliation of diverse denominations and the integration of traditions but – with the mysterious disappearance and lively reappearance of the murdered women – something much less doctrinaire.

Richard and Anna, looking together in the Convent garden for the bodies, find none but, rather, perceive an elusive door – or a window. It is a passage which deliberately combines Christian Paschal imagery with African 'heat and spice' (not to mention the sexual symbolism of the eggs and pepper pods):

> It was when he returned, as they stood near the chair, her hands balancing brown eggs and white cloth, his fingers looking doubled with long pepper pods – green, red and plum black – that they saw it. Or sensed it, rather, for there was nothing to see. A door, she said later. 'No, a window', he said laughing. . . . Whether through a door needing to be opened or a beckoning window already raised, what would happen if you entered? What would be on the other side? What *on earth* would it be? What *on earth*? (305)

Later, gazing at the coffin of a dead child, Richard again sees the window beckoning 'toward another place – neither life nor death – but there, just yonder, shaping thoughts he did not know he had' (307). Preaching at the funeral of this child, (ironically, the citizens of Ruby only really begin to live when they accept death and funerals *in* their community), he cites 1 Corinthians 15.36: 'What is sown is not alive until it dies' and then continues with his own elaboration: 'although life in life is terminal and life after life is everlasting, He is with us. Always, in life, after it and especially *in between*, . . . there never was a time when you were not saved . . . (307) [my emphasis]. 'Another place – neither life nor death' is here the enigmatic alternative to a range of segregations, including eschatological ones. Thus, the disappeared women are not *not here*, but simply in the 'in between' of common apprehension. It may be that in this 'in between' they join the Ancestor figures, the beings that come and go in individual visitations, generally unseen. In this regard, there may be an African theological or cosmological premise that escapes many a reader's – and, indeed, Richard's – understanding. 'The ending requires', stated Morrison in response to frustrated readers on the Oprah Winfrey Show's Book Club, who were most preoccupied with knowing whether the women were living or dead, embodied or not, 'being open to all these paths and connections and interstices in between'.[30]

Presiding over the funeral of a child, engaged to be married to Anna, newly committed to the flawed beauty and misguided imagination of the citizens of Ruby and spiritually *open*, Richard fulfils the combination, outlined in 'Rootedness': 'profound rootedness in the real world' with an 'acceptance of the supernatural' in ways that will not be limiting, but enhancing.[31] 'Diminished expectations' and lack of 'confidence in an enduring future', notes Morrison in a lecture delivered in 1996, are most prevalent in the modern West:

> One reason has to do with the secularization of culture. Where there will be no Messiah, where afterlife is understood to be medically absurd, where the concept of an 'indestructible soul' is not only unbelievable but increasingly unintelligible in intellectual and literate realms, where passionate, deeply held religious belief is associated with ignorance at best, violent intolerance at its worst, in times as suspicious of eternal life as these are, when 'life in history supplants life in eternity', the eye, in the absence of resurrected or reincarnated life, becomes trained on the biological span of one human being.[32]

For Morrison, a dynamic understanding must encompass more than 'biological span' and 'time that only has a past', being rather, one where 'an informed vision based on harrowing experience . . . gestures toward a redemptive future'.[33] Accordingly, in *Paradise*, Misner is a man prepared to fight a future frozen, and to facilitate the arrival of something redemptive and relevant: 'the future [that] panted at the gate', 'down here', 'on earth' (306).

II

At the time of writing, Barack Obama is America's president elect; a black man in the White House is for many, black and white, an improbable feat. Although Barack Obama's aim in his campaign was not to make race a divisive issue (not least because, as 'the son of a black man from Kenya and a white woman from

Kansas', he himself was deemed either 'too black' or 'not black enough'),[34] the media focus on the rhetoric of his pastor, the Reverend Dr Jeremiah Wright, forced it into the spotlight. Jeremiah Wright's theology is predicated on Cone's Black Theology and his Church, Trinity United Church of Christ on Chicago's Southside with its motto: 'Unashamedly Black and Unapologetically Christian', espouses the Black Values System derived from the Nicaraguan Liberation Theology Movement. Before Obama was forced to resign from the church that had been his place of worship since the 1980s, and to disassociate himself from his Pastor's more radical 'anti-American' views ('not God Bless America: God Damn America'), Wright tried in a television interview,[35] to make clear that his ministry's emphasis on being African-centred and on Black values, traditions and religious experiences, *had* to be evaluated in the context of Cone's Black Theology in order to be properly understood. Accused of being 'separatist', Wright demurred, saying that the emphasis on Black values and experience did not assume separation, but rather, self-determination. Obama's resignation speech, 'A More Perfect Union', is long, eloquent and moving, but it rues Wright's anachronistic emphasis on past divisions:

> The profound mistake of Reverend Wright's sermons is not that he spoke about racism in our society. It's that he spoke about it as if it was static; as if no progress has been made; as if this country – a country that has made it possible for one of his own members to run for the highest office in the land and build a coalition of white and black; Latino and Asian, rich and poor; young and old – is still irrevocably bound to a tragic past.[36]

In January 2008, Toni Morrison wrote to Senator Obama in an open letter to *The New York Observer*, personally endorsing his candidacy for President, switching from her prior support for Hilary Clinton. She claimed that what compelled her vote was 'quality of mind' rather than gender or race: 'I would not support you if that was all you had to offer or because it might make me "proud"'.

> When, I wondered, was the last time this country was guided by such a leader? Someone whose moral centre was un-embargoed? Someone with courage instead of mere ambition? Someone who truly thinks of his country's citizens as 'we' instead of 'they'? Someone who understands what it will take to help America realize the virtues it fancies about itself.
>   Our future is ripe, outrageously rich in its possibilities. Yet unleashing the glory of that future will require a difficult labor, and some may be so frightened of its birth they will refuse to abandon their nostalgia for the womb.[37]

Richard Misner is a fictional character with a job to do in the 1970s; Barack Obama is about to be tested from January 2009 in a position that many thought inconceivable. It should not be seen as unexpected that the very same issues of religion are common both to the fictional tale of a historical past and the next chapter in America's complex racial history. What is adventitious, perhaps, is that Toni Morrison has engaged so specifically with both.

Of her art, Morrison describes the opposite of the sealed 'womb' of nostalgia or the enclosed space of prescriptive paradise: 'I can't take positions that are closed. Everything I've ever done . . . has been to . . . open doors.'[38] The extreme vigilance and the lack of imagination in a place like Ruby (or a church like Chicago's Trinity United, perhaps) have their reasons and roots. As Rachel Harding explained in her study of *Candomblé* and other related 'alternative spaces of blackness':

> This heightened awareness was necessitated by their marginality to the struc-
> tures of power and was the means by which they attempted to 'sway between
> a dance and a fight', to situate themselves alternately in alliance, resistance,
> and restraint vis-à-vis the separate spheres and the often hazardous terrain
> between.[39]

Morrison's *Paradise* explores what happens when separate spheres, 'paradises', are at war with each other but, also, what internal damage ensues with stasis, control and not letting go of a tragic past. In *Paradise* one community dances, literally, to destruction while the other fights to the same end. The 'sway between' these two defensive modes is still a gesture of stasis and entrapment. Morrison shows that religion – in various configurations – was integral to the dance, the fight and the terrain between, and is now implicated in an openness to the delivery of something new.

Notes

1 Zia Jaffrey, 'The Salon Interview: Toni Morrison' (2008). http://www.salon.com/
   books/int/1998/02/cov_si_02int.html
2 Ibid.
3 Shelley Saguaro, *Garden Plots: The Politics and Poetics of Gardens* (Aldershot, Hants &
   Burlington, VT: Ashgate, 2006); Peter Widdowson, 'The American Dream Refashioned: History Politics and Gender in Toni Morrison's *Paradise*', *Journal of American
   Studies* 35.2 (2001), 313–35.
4 James Marcus, 'This Side of Paradise: Toni Morrison' (2008). http://www.amazon.
   com/exec/obidos/ts/feature/7651/103-2684994-5999054
5 See Kelly Reames, *Toni Morrison's* Paradise: *A Reader's Guide* (London and New York:
   Continuum, 2001); Channette Romero, 'Creating the Beloved Community: Religion, Race and Nation in Toni Morrison's *Paradise, African American Review* (2005).
   http://findarticles.com/p/articles/mi_m2838/is_3_39/ain15895660/print?tag
   =artBody; Maha Marouan, 'Candomblé, Christianity, and Gnosticism in Toni
   Morrison's *Paradise*', *The African Diaspora and the Study of Religion*, ed. Theodore
   Louis Trost (Basingstoke and New York: Palgrave Macmillan, 2007), 111–31.
6 M. Meryer, ed., *The Nag Hammadi Scriptures* (New York: Harper Collins, 2007).

7   Toni Morrison, 'Rootedness: The Ancestor as Foundation', *What Moves at the Margin: Selected Nonfiction*, ed. Carolyn C. Denard (Jackson: Mississippi University Press, 2008), 56–64, 59.

8   Toni Morrison, *Paradise* (London: Chatto & Windus, 1998), 15. Future references will be made parenthetically within the text.

9   Toni Morrison, 'City Limits, Village Values: Concepts of Neighborhood in Black Fiction', *Literature and the Urban American Experience*, ed. Michael C. Jaye and Ann Chalmers Watts (New Brunswick, NJ: Rutgers University Press, 1981), 35–43.

10 James H. Evans, Jr, *We Have Been Believers* (Minneapolis: Fortress, 1992), 3.

11 James H. Cone, *Black Theology and Black Power* (revd edn) (Maryknoll: New York, 1999), vii.

12 Marcus, 'This Side of Paradise'.

13 Elizabeth Farnsworth, 'Conversation: Toni Morrison' (1998). http://www.pbs. org/newshour/bb/entertainment/jan-june98/morrison_3-9.html

14 Based on the Sisters of the Blessed Sacrament for Indian and Colored People, the wealthy founder of which, Katherine Drexel (1858–1955), was canonized as America's first saint in 2000.

15 Dinita Smith, 'Toni Morrison's Mix of Tragedy, Domesticity, and Folklore'. *The New York Times*, 6 January 1998. http://www.nytimes.com/library/books/ 010898toni-morrison-interview.html

16 As in Robert Voeks, *The Sacred Leaves of Candomblé: African Magic, Medicine and Religion in Brazil* (Austin: University of Texas Press, 1997).

17 Dale P. Andrews, *Practical Theology for Black Churches: Bridging Black Theology and African American Folk Religion* (Louisville and London: Westminster John Knox Press, 2002), 13.

18 Paul Gilroy, 'Living Memory: A meeting with Toni Morrison', *Small Acts: Thoughts on the Politics of Black Cultures* (London and New York: Serpent's Tail, 1993), 181.

19 Morrison, 'Rootedness', 59–61.

20 Ibid., 62.

21 Widdowson, 'The American Dream Refashioned', 334.

22 Reames, *Toni Morrison's Paradise*, 61.

23 Cone, *Black Theology and Black Power*, x.

24 Jaffrey, 'The Salon Interview'.

25 Toni Morrison originally wanted this, the novel's final word to be presented in lower case ('paradise') although the first publication was erroneously printed as Paradise: 'The last word in the book, "paradise", should have a small "p", not a capital "P". The whole point is to get paradise off its pedestal, as a place for anyone' (Smith).

26 Marcus, 'This Side of Paradise'.

27 Andrews, *Practical Theology for Black Churches*, 47, 57.

28 Marcus, 'This Side of Paradise'.

29 Toni Morrison and Cornel West: In Conversation, The Nation Institute at the New York Society for Ethical Culture, 24 March 2004. http://www.freespeech. org/fscm2/contentviewer.php?content_id=802; H. Anderson, 'When She Speaks, America Listens; Profile: Toni Morrison'. *The Observer*, 12 October 2008, http:// www.guardian.co.uk/books/2008/oct/12/tonimorrison-fiction/print

30 Reames, *Toni Morrison's Paradise*, 74.

31 Morrison, 'Rootedness', 61.

[32] Toni Morrison, 'The Future of Time: Literature and Diminished Expectations', *What Moves at the Margin*, ed. Denard, 170–88, pp. 171, 172.

[33] Ibid., 185.

[34] Barack Obama, *Change We Can Believe In* (London: Canongate, 2008), 237.

[35] See YouTube: Jeremiah Wright on Fox News, http://www.youtube.com/watch-http://www.youtube.com/watch?v=aNTGRL0OJWQ

[36] Obama, *Change We Can Believe In*, 237.

[37] Tom McGeveran, 'Toni Morrison's Letter to Barack Obama', *The New York Observer* 28 January 2008, http://observer.com/2008/toni-morrisons-letter-barack-obama

[38] Jaffrey, 'The Salon Interview'.

[39] Rachel Harding, *A Refuge in Thunder: Candomblé and Alternative Spaces of Blackness* (Bloomington and Indianapolis: Indiana University Press, 2003), 146.

Chapter 11

Women, War and the University: Rosamond Lehmann's *Dusty Answer*

Judy Simons

In July 1920, having just completed her first year at Cambridge, 19-year-old Rosamond Lehmann, together with her elder sister, Helen, went on holiday to France. From their comfortable base at the Hotel Crillon in Paris, the two young women made an excursion to the battlefields of the Somme, a countryside disfigured by the carnage of war. The landscape was charred and littered with the remnants of conflict. For Rosamond, it was a stark encounter with the scale of military devastation. 'It was extremely interesting, but dreadfully sad to see all the villages razed to the ground', she wrote to her younger brother, John, then at Eton. 'We walked over a bit of the Hindenburg line that hasn't been restored. You never saw such a sight: shell-holes as big as the library; barbed-wire that you tripped over; old gas masks, tunics, unexploded shells, hand-grenades & debris.'

However naively, she began to gain a glimmer of understanding of the conditions endured by the troops, that lost and scarred generation who were her contemporaries. 'Helen & I went miles into the earth into a German dug-out, through a tunnel, & saw where the soldiers used to sleep. Ugh! They must have had frogs jumping all over them', she reported graphically.[1] Yet, 18 months earlier on Armistice Day, at her parents' tranquil home in the Thames Valley, her feelings had been all for herself. Out for a solitary walk across the Buckinghamshire countryside, she thought with typical teenage angst only of vanished romantic opportunities. 'Well, what do I do next?', she had mused silently. 'As *all* the young men have been killed, I shall never marry. There'll be nobody left to marry.'[2]

The way in which war impinges on the consciousness of women is an enduring theme in Rosamond Lehmann's fiction, whose heroines' futures are shaped by battles in which they took no part. Her novels of the interwar years are infused with the unseen presence of dead youth, and peopled by families who are silently mourning beloved sons, or by maimed survivors, whose attitude to life is unalterably impaired. The presence of the slain permeates Lehmann's first novel, *Dusty Answer* (1927), where the Fyfe family, a group of cousins whose lives are changed forever by the Great War, are shown in both their pre- and postwar incarnation. Peter Widdowson has commented that all fiction is history,

> not, of course, history as a more or less direct rendering of factual evidence, but as itself part of the historical process, which contains and reveals the pressures of social and cultural change. Fiction does not simply *reflect* its times. It expresses them, rather, in a complex synthesis which cannot be defined solely in terms of 'subject matter' or 'ideas', a synthesis in which all the given material is fused and transformed within its particular form.[3]

Dusty Answer, juvenile, episodic and subjective, perfectly expresses the fusion of nostalgic past and anxious present that characterizes its historic moment. In its focus upon an ingénue heroine and her 'entry into the world', it mimics the traditional nineteenth-century novel with which its author was so familiar. But it locates this heroine in a culture of modernity that creates both unprecedented opportunity and a concomitant uncertainty. This essay explores the tenor of that modernity in a work that was hailed by its contemporary readers as a consummate formulation of present-day sensibility. *Dusty Answer* was a best-seller when it was first published; today it has been banished to the critical margins. Yet it heralds the literary emergence of the new woman of the interwar phase, whose autonomy surfaces as an indirect and double-edged legacy of the war. Its heroine, progressive, educated and sexually adventurous, nonetheless remains confused, her consciousness shifting between past and present, and her identity forged by memory and loss.

As has been said about Virginia Woolf, in many ways Lehmann's literary mentor, her 'experience of loss as disruption characterized her vision of history, both political and literary'.[4] That same vision, transmuted through the fluctuating reminiscences of its youthful protagonist, gives substance and form to *Dusty Answer*. This highly autobiographical work features the earliest portrait of what was to become a recurrent theme in Rosamond Lehmann's fiction, the romanticized family. Critics have pointed out the tendency of writers in the 1920s and 1930s to visualize the immediate pre-war years as a golden Arcadian summer.[5] The early essays of *Dusty Answer* filter this nostalgia through a child's perspective, shot through with ironic longing for a delusory past. Judith Earle, the lonely daughter of wealthy parents, lives, as did her creator, in a house on the banks of the Thames, where the Fyfe children are occasional visitors to the house next door. Judith's exclusion from their camaraderie reflects the displaced consciousness that in one way or another defines all Lehmann heroines. Selina Hastings has noted that the roots of Lehmann's works 'lie bedded in definitive areas of emotional experience', in particular 'a perception of herself as permanent outsider, which was to shadow her all her life'.[6] The artistic preoccupation with alienation in works of this period has been reviewed extensively in studies of European and American modernism, with Eliot's *The Waste Land*

(1922) defining the literary landscape that moulded Lehmann and her contemporaries. The epigraph to *Dusty Answer,* taken from George Meredith's
Modern Love (1862) – 'Ah, what a dusty answer gets the soul / When hot for certainties in this our life!' – employed in a post-*Waste Land* era, evokes Eliot's 'fear
in a handful of dust' for a generation desperate for reassurance.

Judith's hold on joy is as intense and as tenuous as the age itself. She envies
the easy intimacy of the Fyfes with a longing that her adult perception subsequently invests with a cooler detachment. But in childhood, she is only aware of
her exclusion from Eden. The technique recalls Nick Carraway's first impressions of his neighbour's laughter-filled mansion in F. Scott Fitzgerald's *The Great
Gatsby* (1925), where dust is also a pervasive motif and which was published in
England the year before Lehmann embarked on her own novel. Many years
later, in a letter to her brother, Lehmann refers to Fitzgerald and his 'careless
people', who transmit the glamour of sophisticated metropolitan society.[7] So, at
first glance the five Fyfe children represent a carefree world, a self-sufficient
family unit from which Judith Earle is a permanent outsider. The cold intrusion
of adult reality signalled by the Great War is the novel's first warning of imper-
manence, and swiftly discharges others: premature widowhood, a fatherless and
unwanted child, casual sensuality, heartbreak, death by drowning and family
collapse, as one by one the natural bonds of which human society is woven are
shown as increasingly fragile.

'That a break must be made in every life when August 1914 is reached seems
inevitable. But the fracture differs, according to what is broken', wrote Virginia
Woolf in her biography of Roger Fry.[8] Rosamond Lehmann was 13-years-old at
the outbreak of war, 17 when it was over. It is hardly surprising that the war and
the anxieties of teenage experience are intimately connected in her work. In
her 1967 memoir, *The Swan in the Evening,* the first section of which forms a
wistful tribute to her early life, Lehmann describes growing up in a uniquely
advantaged family, 'quietly prospering in a temperate Edwardian climate'.[9] The
announcement of war interrupted the Lehmanns' annual summer holiday,
and was accompanied by small domestic discomforts that put an end to the
invulnerability of Rosamond's childhood. It 'cracked the whole structure of
our secure, privileged and very happy life. The bath water grew cold; the huge
lawn was dug up for potatoes, the sons of friends were killed. I became aware of
grief – other people's grief, world grief.'[10]

That same semi-awakened perception is the subject of Lehmann's third novel,
Invitation to the Waltz (1932). In this apparently slight account of a girl attending
her first ball, the protagonist, Olivia, is introduced to a young man whom at
first she does not realize has been blinded in battle. Impassively he tells her how
he joined up straight from school and three months later, in June 1918, was hit
by a sniper 'plunk between the eyes'. In the midst of the elation of the dance,
Olivia is stunned into silence.

War, a cloud on early adolescence, weighing not too darkly, long lifted. . . .
A cousin in the flying corps killed, the cook's nephew gone down at Jutland,

rumour of the deaths of neighbours' sons . . . and butter and sugar rations; and the lawn dug up for potatoes (the crop had failed); and Dad being a special constable and getting bronchitis from it; that was about all that war had meant. And during that safe, sheltered, unthinking time, he had gone out to fight, and had his eyes destroyed. She saw him reel backwards, his hands on his face, crying: I'm blind . . . or coming to in hospital, not realizing, thinking it was the middle of the night. . . . Imagination stretched shudderingly towards his experience. She had a moment's dizziness: a moment's wild new conscious indignation and revolt, thinking for the first time: This was war – never, never to be forgiven or forgotten, for his sake.[11]

For Lehmann, as the temperature of the bath water dropped, so the recognition dawned that many of the golden young men and boys, objects of her juvenile adoration, who had gone exultantly away to the front, were not coming back. The sons of the Lehmann's neighbours, Julian and Ivo Grenfell, whom she had worshipped from afar at parties as thrilling but distant figures, were both killed on the Somme within a few weeks of each another in 1915. Images of shattered promise dominate *Dusty Answer,* where the heroine's serene childhood is gradually overshadowed by the ruined lives of the young men who grew up alongside her. Although daily routine at the Lehmann family home, Fieldhead, went on more or less unchanged, and the visible signs of war could be treated as a source of excitement – light-heartedly Rosamond wrote to her schoolboy brother, 'Lucky boy to see 9 aeroplanes – I wish I had such luck. I'm sure you don't appreciate the dear little aviators inside them half so much as I should! (only don't tell Mummy I said that!)' – she knew that life could never be the same again.[12]

Rosamond Lehmann's writings eloquently chart the shifting society in which she lived, a society splintered by war, political change, class antagonism, and characterized by social turmoil. These are the vicissitudes that skulk beneath the veneer of the polite world her heroines inhabit. Her ostensible subjects are those that traditionally have been the business of the woman's novel: romance, marriage, family and the fabric of domestic existence. Yet her fiction turns these subjects upside down. Her love stories expose the anguish and bitterness of passion; her families are minefields of jealousy and resentment; her domestic scenes contain unspoken danger zones. In her books, well-brought-up young women are framed against a background of instability and social upheaval that mirrors all too clearly their own internal traumas. Her narratives, self-aware, often caustic and always experimental, tell a powerful story of anarchic modernity against the palimpsestic story of war.

In *A Room of One's Own*, published the year after *Dusty Answer*, Virginia Woolf wryly observed that 'This is an important book the critic assumes, because it deals with war. This is an insignificant book because it deals with the feelings of women in a drawing-room. A scene in a battlefield is more important than a scene in a shop.'[13] Like *Mrs Dalloway* (1925), Woolf's great war novel set at home, *Dusty Answer* 'deals with the feelings of women', feelings that are subject to the reverberations of a combat that profoundly affected female lives. It draws on Lehmann's own experience of coming of age, and registers an ambivalence about the present day that combines the optimism that followed the Armistice with the world-weariness of its battle-scarred survivors.

The novel opens in spring 1919 with the image of an empty house being prepared to receive its returning inhabitants after four years of absence. It establishes with startling immediacy the mood of postwar malaise; the death of Charlie Fyfe, killed just a few weeks after joining up, provides the vehicle for exploring its manifestations. Charlie's ghost haunts the memories of the remaining characters. Whole in body, they are psychologically damaged, unable to build satisfying mature relationships, either because they are thwarted in love or because they have become emotionally paralysed. Beautiful Mariella, who married Charlie on the eve of his departure for the Front, now finds herself adrift, widowed and with a baby son whom she is ill-equipped to mother, and whom eventually she gives away. Roddy, charming but feckless, avoids confronting the reality of Charlie's death. The object of Judith's girlish infatuation but sexually indeterminate, he exemplifies the volatility of the times, his future uncertain and his past too painful to recall. His homosexuality, especially disconcerting to Judith in the Cambridge episodes of the novel, also evokes the ethos of hostility to women that was integral to the society of the Cambridge Apostles, refuge of Rupert Brooke, Forster and others of Lehmann's contemporaries. The third cousin, Martin, is Roddy's antithesis. Anticipating Waugh's Tony Last in *A Handful of Dust* (1934), Martin longs to recover the imaginative idyll of an English rural existence, living with Judith as his wife in his ancestral home and farming the land as did his forefathers. His death in a boating accident illustrates the impossibility of realizing that fantasy in a casual and unforgiving world governed by unpredictability.

It is, however, Julian, the eldest of the Fyfes, whose eyes are transformed into 'pits of misery' when he speaks 'in epitaphs' about his younger brother, Charlie, who truly embodies the cynicism of the age. Of the three surviving Fyfe men, he is the one whose experience at the Front has most visibly fashioned his current mind-set. Before the war a brilliant career as a composer lay ahead of him; now his creative talent has been stifled. Still in his early twenties, but world-weary and listless, he dismisses his musical gift as 'a feeble spark; and the God of battle has seen fit to snuff it. The war made some chaps poets – of a sort; but I never heard of it making anyone a musician'.[14] Music has become a diversion, an escape from the nightmares that plague his consciousness. He suffers from sleeplessness and his days are spent chasing a bogus gaiety to offset the emptiness of his existence. As he tells Judith, 'Some chaps dance. They haven't stopped dancing since they've been back', whereas he plays the piano to stave off confrontation with a blank future.

In his account of the period between the wars, Roy Hattersley refers to Terence Rattigan's *After the Dance* (1939), where a young woman attributes the

casual hedonism of the postwar decades to the four years of carnage they
followed. 'You see, when you were eighteen, you didn't have anybody of twenty-
five or thirty-five to help you. They'd all been wiped out. . . . The spotlight
was on you and you alone. . . . You did what any child would do, you dance.'[15]
Dancing became a metaphor for the irresponsibility of the upper-class set in
the interwar years. The foxtrot in particular, a dance that features prominently
in *Dusty Answer*, summed up what their elders viewed as the new generation's
tendency towards moral laxity. Named after its inventor, the American vaude-
ville actor, Harry Fox, the foxtrot was introduced into his stage routine in 1914
and was subsequently adopted as a social dance, its combination of pace and
slow intimacy making it all the rage in the mid-1920s. At the same time classes
in modern dance became fashionable, together with the growing trend for
exhibition dancing, originally pioneered by the celebrated Vernon and Irene
Castle. The sensuous movement of the foxtrot licensed familiarity between
partners and was publicly denounced as a 'syncopated embrace'.[16] This is the
dance that Judith learns under the tutelage of the Fyfe boys, and when she and
Julian meet in the French spa resort of Vichy, where a leisured community idles
away its time, their proficiency becomes the focus of the room's admiring
gaze.

He put an arm closely round her and murmured:

'Come on now. Perform! Perform!' – and they went gliding, pausing and
turning round the empty floor, while everyone stared and the band smilingly
played up to them. The rhythm of their bodies responded together, without
an error, to the music's broken emotionalism.[17]

In contrast to early scenes in the novel, where dancing signifies pure delight in
physical movement, 'entire happiness, entire peace and harmony', it functions
here as a symbol of postwar decadence. Emulating the Castles' cabaret act, the
emphasis on the performative prioritizes style over substance. The accompany-
ing music conveys only a 'broken emotionalism', replicating its protagonists'
injured psyche. The apotheosis of this vacuity comes when Julian proposes to
Judith that she become his mistress 'for a season' and travel with him through
Europe. With this final blow to her dreams of amorous fulfilment, she accepts
his offer in a state of romantic inertia.

'Nothing's worth-while, Julian? It doesn't matter what one does? There's no
point, really, in being alive?'
    He laughed.
    'Poor Judy! Give it up! You'll have to in time. Resign yourself, and the com-
pensations won't seem so preposterously inadequate. There was a time. . . .
But that's past. So long as there's a balance of happiness, I'm content to be
alive. That it's all futile has ceased to trouble me.'[18]

In the wave of adulation that followed the publication of *Dusty Answer*, Julian was singled out as a particularly accurate construct. 'You can't think how I have enjoyed it', wrote the poet, Robert Nichols, to Rosamond's father, Rudolph Lehmann, himself a respected man of letters. 'The men are real – especially Charlie and Julian (great creation Julian and very much of our day) and that is by no means always the case in women's novels.'[19] Indeed *Dusty Answer* was generally acclaimed for its truthful picture of modernity. 'This is a remarkable book', wrote the critic, Alfred Noyes, reviewing the novel for *The Sunday Times*. 'It is not often that one can say with confidence of a first novel by a young writer that it reveals new possibilities for literature. But there are qualities in this book that mark it out as quite the most striking first novel of this generation. It is a study of modern youth and its outlook is entirely that of the present day.'[20]

It is difficult now to recapture the sense of excitement that greeted the novel's publication and equally tricky to explain just why it was received so rapturously. The author's own social standing may have had something to do with it. From a privileged background, Lehmann had the added advantages of youth and extreme prettiness, was newly married to the heir to a shipping fortune and feted as a society beauty, her photograph appearing in *The Tatler* and in *Vogue*. Her outspokenness touched the times. For *Dusty Answer*, while it gives what some readers felt was overblown attention to the passionate aspirations of its heroine, is in fact about a young woman who rejects the romantic destiny that completed the story of her literary predecessors, and that had formed the limits of Lehmann's own 17-year-old ambitions. Rather it records a voyage of self discovery set in a climate of intellectual and personal experiment, and that allowed Judith to test out the different dimensions of her own erotic leanings without any sense of resolution.

One of the more remarkable outcomes of the aftermath of the Great War was its impact on the rigid nature of the English establishment, and the ways in which it irredeemably altered relations between the sexes in the middle ranks of society. Rosamond Lehmann was among the first generation of young women to enact the effects of this change. In the years 1914–18, many bourgeois women had been able to cast off their status as the supposedly weaker sex, together with certain of their frustrations, and had replaced their male contemporaries in the work of keeping the country going. Whether as nurses or ambulance drivers on the Western Front, or whether at home in munitions factories, offices or on the land, women of all social classes joined in the war effort. As is well documented, the wartime contribution of so many women to the national welfare was a direct factor in the electoral reform of 1917 that resulted in female suffrage. In March that year, Asquith reported to the House of Commons on the vital role played by women in the war effort.

How could we have carried on the War without them? Short of actually bearing arms in the field, there is hardly a service which has contributed, or is contributing, to the maintenance of our cause, in which women have not been at least as active and as efficient as men, and wherever we turn we see them doing with zeal and success, and without any detriment to the prerogatives of their sex, work which three years ago would have been regarded as falling exclusively within the province of men. But what I confess moves me still more in this matter is the problem of reconstruction when this War is over . . . for, do not doubt it, the old order will be changed.[21]

Rosamond Lehmann, born into that old order, triumphantly embraced the new, with its promise of sexual equality and academic opportunity. While education for women had been on the increase from the latter years of the nineteenth century, the period that saw the founding of the great public schools for girls as well as women's entry into university, it was only in the years following the First World War that higher education became both reputable and realistic. Yet while women were allowed to study, sit examinations and have their results recorded, they were not eligible to receive full degrees. In 1919 Rosamond Lehmann, who had been educated privately at home, followed her sister, Helen, to Girton College, Cambridge, to read English, itself a relatively new subject in the academic curriculum and a distinctive signpost of the modern. Despite the egalitarian hopes for the College, it was during Rosamond's time at Girton that the move to admit women as full members of the university was defeated – it was only in 1947 that this was finally achieved – and the sense of being a second-class citizen was pronounced. Such anomalies reinforced the mixed messages about women's status that pervade not only Lehmann's writing but that of other contemporary female authors, including Elizabeth Bowen, Jean Rhys and Rebecca West.

Nonetheless Girton did provide opportunities for female advancement. Admittedly its population remained narrow, drawn mainly from the differing ranks of middle-class women, many of whom, denied marriage prospects because of the dearth of male partners, went on to a teaching career.[22] As Mabel Fuller, the ungainly undergraduate who shares a staircase with Judith, tells her, 'Most girls who come here have got to depend on their brains for a livelihood, so of course no one's got a right to come here just to amuse themselves, have they?'[23] The sentiment echoes the attitude of Lehmann's own tutor, who apparently marked her down in the Tripos when Rosamond, asked at the end of a viva if she intended to teach, replied instinctively and 'with horror, "Good God, no. I'm going to be a writer, write novels."'[24] Such self-interest, frowned on by university authorities as unwarranted frivolity, throws into sharp relief the fictional portrait of struggling lower middle-income women, treated with snobbish disdain by Lehmann's bright young things.

Dusty Answer is one of the first campus novels and certainly one of the very few that presents student life from the perspective of a female undergraduate. If the 'student experience' of sex, drugs and popular music as depicted in the novel seems strikingly similar to that of today's student population, we should not forget that it is also rooted in its precise historical moment. In a climate of equivocation about women's standing and in the hothouse atmosphere of an all-female environment that nurtured introspection, it was understandable that the cult of the self should triumph and that Cambridge should figure as a perfect locus for personal adventure rather than a career route, much to the disgust of some critics. Nor is it surprising that the heroine's interrogation of the self in the enlightened cadence of the mid-1920s, when Radclyffe Hall was already a celebrity, should feature sexual enlightenment as a natural element in the process of self-recognition. Yet the lesbian subtext in the novel, particularly explicit in the portrait of the sinister, controlling Geraldine Manners, undoubtedly contributed to the novel's shock value, partly because it came from the pen of a well-brought up young female author.

In 1983, invited to contribute to a series on 'My First Book' in *The Author*, the official publication of The Society of Authors, Rosamond Lehmann described somewhat ingenuously, her surprise at the scandal provoked by *Dusty Answer*. 'The first couple of reviews I saw gave the impression that I had gravely offended against standards of womanly decorum. I wished the earth to open and swallow me up. How could I have unwittingly overstepped the mark? Had I written too frankly on unhealthy subjects such as sexual love and passion? Was there not a hint somewhere of something ambiguous, unmentionable? My loyal mother was startled and distressed. There was talk among elderly relatives and neighbours. One wrote to say that there was alas! a lot of unpleasantness in the world, but why write about it?'[25]

The directness with which the book treats the female body and its desires reflects the challenge to past restrictions in a newly democratized society. As a modern young woman, Judith relishes the exhilaration of all forms of physical activity: skating, swimming, climbing, dancing all confirm her athletic prowess and sensuous confidence. Swimming in particular, drawing attention to the unclothed female form, signified female strength and empowerment. In 1926, the year of *Dusty Answer's* composition, the 18-year-old American, Gertrude Ederle, had become the first woman to swim the Channel, and immediately achieved international celebrity. Her photograph appeared in the *Illustrated London News* and she was lionized by the popular press, a public ovation to the marriage of endurance and beauty. Paul Fussell has noted how *al fresco* swimming scenes were a common feature of the First World War literature, a 'vignette of soldiers bathing under the affectionate eye of their young officer' so familiar as to seem almost a set piece. Such scenes occupied a symbolic textual space, incorporating suggestions of pastoral innocence, voyeurism and vulnerability against a backdrop of war, and frequently masking a homoerotic subtext.[26] In *Dusty Answer*, Judith's indulgence in solitary late night swims from her garden, watched from the bank while believing herself to be unseen, both draws on this tradition and gives it a distinctively gendered inflection. In the Cambridge section of the novel, nude bathing with fellow-undergraduate Jennifer Baird provides an opportunity for celebrating feminine beauty and intimacy without apparent pornographic intent.

'Off, off, you lendings!' cried Jennifer. 'Do you know, darling, that comes home to me more than anything else in all Shakespeare? I swear, Judith, it seems more natural to me to wear no clothes.'

She stood up, stretching white arms above her head. Her cloud of hair was vivid in the blue air. Her back was slender and strong and faultlessly moulded.

'Glorious, glorious pagan that I adore!' whispered the voice in Judith that could never speak out.

Beside Jennifer she felt herself too slim, too flexible, almost attenuated.

'You are so lovely', Jennifer said watching her.

They swam in cool water in a deep circular pool swept round with willow, and dried themselves in the sun.

. . . Judith crept closer, warming every sense at her, silent and entirely peaceful. She was the part of you which you had never been able to untie and set free, the part that wanted to dance and run and sing, taking strong draughts of wind and sunlight.[27]

Judith's reticence about her own erotic impulses is cloaked in rhetoric that foregrounds the pantheistic rather than the carnal dimension of the experience. Her insight into her own libido remains undeveloped, and in a subsequent bathing incident, this time with Julian, she is taken aback when he accuses her of deliberately parading her body to inflame male desire. The ambivalence of such episodes assimilates the sexual teasing and the guilelessness that capture the emotional confusions of the age. As Noyes noted, 'The modern young woman, with all her frankness and perplexities in the semi-pagan world of today, has never been depicted with more honesty, or with a more exquisite art.'[28]

In a polemical article in early volume of *Literature and History*, Peter Widdowson argued for the need for a materialist and historical criticism 'to develop the tools as well as the models to penetrate the special space occupied by literature in the social process'.[29] The intervening decades have witnessed a major shift in both the practice and the teaching of literary criticism. *Dusty Answer* is a work that responds peculiarly well to this shift, and at the same time illuminates the perspectives modern readers now have at their disposal. The change in the book's critical fortunes points up the vagaries of taste as a dimension of a specific cultural sensibility. Its contemporary success can be located as a phenomenon that occurs as part of the dialogue between other modes of cultural and material production, and its hesitant, episodic structure mirrors the confusions that beset women writers in the decades immediately following and registering the shock of the Great War.

Notes

1. Letter, Rosamond Lehmann to John Lehmann, 18 July 1920, Firestone Library, Princeton University.

2. Rosamond Lehmann in conversation with Selina Hastings, quoted in Selina Hastings, *Rosamond Lehmann* (London: Chatto & Windus, 2002), 38.

3. Peter Widdowson, *E. M. Forster's Howards End: Fiction as History* (London: Chatto & Windus for Sussex University Press, 1977), 7.

4. Julia Briggs, *Reading Virginia Woolf* (Edinburgh: Edinburgh University Press, 2006), 2–3.

5. See, for instance, Paul Fussell, *The Great War and Modern Memory* (Oxford: Oxford University Press, 1975).

6. Hastings, *Rosamond Lehmann*, 91.

7. Letter, Rosamond Lehmann to John Lehmann, 26 October 1981, Firestone Library, Princeton University.

8. Virginia Woolf, *Roger Fry* [1940], ed. Diane F. Gillespie (Oxford: Blackwell, Shakespeare Head Press, 1995), 160.

9. Rosamond Lehmann, *The Swan in the Evening: Fragments of an Inner Life* (London: Virago Press, 1983), 52.

10. Bel Mooney, 'Lost Loves of a Soul Survivor', The Times Profile: Rosamond Lehmann, *The Times* (9 February 1984), 8.

11. Rosamond Lehmann, *Invitation to the Waltz* (London: Chatto & Windus 1932; London: Virago 1981), 254–5.

12. Letter, Rosamond Lehmann to John Lehmann, dated 'May the Goodness knows what' [no year], Firestone Library, Princeton University.

13. Virginia Woolf, *A Room of One's Own* [1928] (Harmondsworth, Middlesex: Penguin, 1975), 74.

14. Rosamond Lehmann, *Dusty Answer* (London: Chatto & Windus 1927; Harmondsworth: Penguin Books, 1936), 56.

15. Roy Hattersley, *Borrowed Time: The Story of Britain between the Wars* (London: Little, Brown, 2007), 320.

16. Hobart College Herald. http://www.eijkhout.net/rad/dance_specific/ballroom.html

17. Lehmann, *Dusty Answer*, 261.

18. Ibid., 272.

19. This letter, in the Firestone Library, Princeton University, is unsigned and undated but can be almost certainly attributed to Robert Nichols, the author of *Aurelia and Other Poems* (London: Chatto & Windus, 1911).

20. Alfred Noyes, *The Sunday Times*, 22 May 1927.

21. Midge Mackenzie, *Shoulder to Shoulder* (Harmondsworth: Penguin, 1975), 326.

22. For more information on career destinations of Girton graduates see Pat Thane, 'Girton Graduates: Earning and Learning, 1920s–1980s', *Women's History Review* 13.3 (2004), 347–61, 150.

23. Lehmann, *Dusty Answer*, 114.

24. Rosamond Lehmann in conversation with Selina Hastings, quoted in Hastings, *Rosamond Lehmann*, 55.

25. Rosamond Lehmann, 'My First Book', *The Author* (1983), 42.

26 Fussell, *The Great War*, 299–309.
27 Lehmann, *Dusty Answer*, 137.
28 Noyes, *The Sunday Times*.
29 Peter Widdowson, '"Literary Value" and the Reconstruction of Criticism', *Literature and History* 6.2 (1980), 147.

Chapter 12

Mythological Presents: Modernity, Edward Thomas and the Poetics of Experience

Stan Smith

I speak in the present tense, it is so easy to speak in the present tense, when speaking of the past. It is the mythological present, don't mind it.

(Samuel Beckett, *Molloy*)

A Changed Style for a Changed World

Reviewing D. H. Lawrence's *Love Poems and Others* in the *Daily Chronicle* in February 1913, Edward Thomas discerned a direct correspondence between what he called the 'apparent arbitrariness' of the volume's rhymes and free verse form and the modernity of the self it expressed. 'But it is obvious at once that the poems would be impossible in "In Memoriam" stanzas', he wrote: 'Their metrical changes, like their broken or hesitating rhythms, are part of a personality that will sink nothing of itself in what is common', achieving an 'effect which Whitman only got now and then'. Another review of the same collection in *The Bookman* a couple of months later expanded on the theme, observing that Lawrence

> writes of matters which cannot be subdued to conventional rhythm and rhyme – chiefly the intense thoughts, emotions or gropings of self-conscious men or women set on edge by love or fatigue or solitude. If he trusts to make a general appeal, it is by faithful concentration on the particular. . . . His triumph is, by image and hint and direct statement, to bring before us some mood which overpowers all of a sick, complex man save his self-consciousness. . . . He will be exact in defining an intuition, a physical state, or an appearance due to the pathetic fallacy. . . . Such moods he will some-times follow with a painful curiosity that makes us rather sharers in a process than witnesses of a result.[1]

In tracing the morphology of immediate, lived experience, Lawrence has refused to force the new modern sensibility into old moulds, what Thomas in a review in the *Morning Post*, of the then popular Anglo-Manx poet T. E. Brown, had called 'the old stately, aristocratic forms'.[2] In the numberless reviews that he wrote, virtually daily, to earn a living and support a growing family between 1900 and 1914, we can see Thomas groping for a formula to describe what he felt, in the condition of post-Victorian modernity, to be a necessary new poetics for a changed world. In the concept of a poetry which 'makes us rather sharers in a process than witnesses of a result', he had stumbled on a perfect description of the verse he was himself soon to write, finally liberated from the drudgery of endless hack work by his decision to enlist.

The necessity for such a new kind of writing extended to fiction also, as Thomas had written in reviewing Mrs Laurence Binyon's selection and arrangement of *Nineteenth Century Prose*:

> It was usual, in earlier prose for a man to acquire a vocabulary, sentences, and cadences of a well-defined character, and to throw everything into the moulds thus made. Their mind was thus reflected, but their spirit did not move upon the surface, coming and going, as in some modern prose.[3]

Now, however, he continued, 'There is less and less writing which has even the air of infallibility and universal application.' Clearly detectable in the tones of this argument is the influence of books he was to review enthusiastically a few days later: Arthur Symons's *The Symbolist Movement in Literature*, and W. B. Yeats's *Discoveries*.[4] But the theme was persistent throughout his critical journalism. Reviewing a selection of *Contemporary German Poetry* translated by Jethro Bithell in 1910, for example, he noted of the German symbolists represented there that 'whether using personal experience or not the poets commonly speak in the first person singular of very special and individual incidents and momentary moods, and it is left to the reader to see their significance', in poems which are evocations of 'some particular place, person, or event done in such a manner that they take on a kind of symbolic value, just as things and persons will in real life'.[5]

One poet Thomas singled out, somewhat unexpectedly, as a model of this new sensibility was Whitman. According to his biographer John Moore, Thomas while at Oxford in the 1890s was 'utterly repelled by Walt Whitman, whom he believed to be "an added fiend to Hell"', but, as Moore commented laconically, 'We all go through such phases.'[6] By 1903 at least, Thomas had come to admire Whitman because he 'has alone among our poets met our changed world frankly with a changed style, as if he saw in it nothing in common with Dante's or Spenser's world'.[7] While Thomas's own poetry rarely sought to emulate Whitman's free verse style (his poem 'Health' is one of the few instances, not wholly successfully), Whitman was a recurrent reference point in his struggle to imagine a truly modern poetics. In 1910, for example, in a review of the late James Thomson (B. V.)'s study of the poet, edited by Bertram Dobell, he praised

Whitman's poems because they 'read like improvisations, and seem less works of art than immediate outgrowths of nature'.[8]

Dobell was the recent editor of the seventeenth-century mystic Thomas Traherne's manuscripts, which Dobell had come across on a bookseller's barrow. Traherne was another of Thomas's lifelong enthusiasms, about whom he wrote extensively both in reviews and in prose books such as *The South Country*. Thomas's notebook for the never-completed and unpublished study *Ecstasy*[9] linked Whitman, Traherne and Coleridge as poetic predecessors of the philosophical and psychological explorations of pre-reflective consciousness in William James's *Varieties of Religious Experience*, a book on which Thomas drew in several places. A note in the manuscript, citing the three poets' preoccupation with 'moments of self-surrender', concludes: 'It implies an intuition of the "absolute balance" (Whitman in James, 396)'. The reference is to page 396 of the first edition of *The Varieties of Religious Experience*, where James discusses Whitman's 'chronic mystical perception', his 'intuition of the absolute balance, in time and space, of all this multifariousness . . . that divine clue and unseen thread which holds together the whole congeries of things, all history and time, and all events, however trivial, however momentous', providing 'a root-centre for the mind'.[10] For James, this 'unseen thread' is what he identified, in the second edition of the book, as the 'subliminal region of consciousness', the primary, pre-reflective, sensorial awareness which precedes self-conscious ratiocination.

The skilfully contrived effect of improvisation, of a verse which gives the impression of being extempore and provisional, the immediate, unmediated utterance of the subject, arising from James's 'subliminal region of consciousness', constituted for Thomas the key feature of any modern poetic. In 1910, for example, he wrote appreciatively of Ford Madox Hueffer's *Songs from London* as 'decidedly dramatic lyrics' all of which 'have an unusual sudden directness of attack', and 'a rhythm and a language so bold and fresh as to have at times something of the character of improvisation; and all have movement'.[11] If the American Whitman offered one source of this new poetic, For Thomas, revolutions in fiction-writing in a wider Europe provided another. Thus, reviewing Isabel F. Hapgood's translation of *The Novels and Stories of Ivan Turgenieff* in 1905, he commended the way in which the Russian writer 'prefers to give us the materials, and to laugh, as life does, at maxims and epitomes. . . . We feel constantly that he would never answer a general question about life'. A modern poetic, whether in prose or verse, Thomas indicated, would conform to Turgenev's model, and seem 'constantly to assert that everything human has its value and charm, that it is only a kind of transcription, that events, when properly seen, carry their own special savour and significance', so that it 'seems to be setting down life and allowing it to exhale its own poetry . . . surely not arranging at all'. Without setting out 'to produce certain effects', simply 'record[ing] a number of events', nevertheless, 'in the end, each sequence produces its own effects without any of the labels, the insistence, or the paraphernalia of intentions, of the majority of writers'.[12]

Thomas here gives a specifically twentieth-century inflexion to the famous demand, in Wordsworth's Preface to *Lyrical Ballads*, for a poetry which speaks 'the real language of men'. Like Wordsworth, Thomas believed that such a poetic had an implicit demographic, finding, in preference to the etiolated refinements of a metropolitan, high-bourgeois culture, 'a plainer and more emphatic language' in 'low and rustic life', 'because in that situation the essential passions of the heart find a better soil' where 'elementary feelings' are conveyed 'in simple and unelaborated expressions'. For Thomas too, this poetic had a distinct social and class dimension, in a writing 'on close terms with life and toil', as he wrote in 1909 of both Whitman's *Leaves of Grass* and William Morris, 'with the actual troublous life of everyday, with toil of the hands and brain together'.[13] It was for him no accident that the cadences of a specifically modern sensibility should find their epitome in the works of the ultra-democratic Whitman and the revolutionary socialist Morris, the miner's son D. H. Lawrence, personally known to him through their mutual friend Eleanor Farjeon,[14] and the writer Thomas was largely responsible for discovering and propagating, the Welsh 'super-tramp' W. H. Davies. His review of Davies's collection *The Soul's Destroyer* in 1905 summed up the essence of this new poetic, in speaking of Davies as 'a poet of experience'.[15]

The Narrative Lyric

Thomas's new poetic foreshadows Robert Langbaum's classic account, now 50 years old, of the way in which a poetry where 'immediate experience is primary and certain', and 'the analytic reflection that follows is secondary and problematical', offered through the vehicle of the dramatic monologue 'an appropriate form for an empiricist and relativist age, an age which has come to consider value as an evolving thing dependent upon the changing individual and social requirements of the historical process'.[16] Langbaum detected the origin of this form in Coleridge's 'conversation poems', and its maturity in the dramatic monologues of Robert Browning.

There is, however, *pace* Langbaum, a crucial difference between Coleridge's and Browning's forms. Whereas a poem such as 'My Last Duchess' speaks in the confident present tense of an imagined subject, a fictive voice, the present tense of Coleridge's conversation poems is, supposedly, that of the poet himself, speaking *in propria persona*, at the very moment of their composition. This is no elaborate fictive projection, but an insistently autobiographical self-presentation of the kind which Wordsworth first set out to write in *The Prelude* and which Whitman was to perfect in *Song of Myself*. As Thomas wrote in his study of George Borrow, 'The autobiographical form – the use of the first-person singular – is no mere device to attract an interest and belief', for 'A writer composes out of his experience, inward, outward, and histrionic, or along the protracted lines of his experience.' Borrow's prose writings issue from 'the instinct for proportion and connection which is the simplest, most inexplicable and most essential of literary gifts':

> With the help of this he could write narratives that should suggest and represent the continuity of life. He could pause for description or dialogue or reflection without interrupting this stream of life. Nothing need be, and nothing was, alien to the narrator . . . for his writing would now assimilate everything and enrich itself continually.[17]

It is with this specifically modern narrative innovation in mind that, in his various reviews of Thomas Hardy's poetry, Thomas sought to clarify his own emerging poetics. Thomas's relation to Hardy's poetry, despite many subsequent critical attempts to relate the two writers, remained ambivalent. On the one hand, in a 1909 *Daily Chronicle* review of *Time's Laughingstocks*, he could respond positively to the humane, and humanist, content of the volume, which demanded, he said, 'a time when values and judgments will be truer than they are' (he cites specifically a poem about the callous treatment of an unmarried mother). Thomas's conclusion seems unequivocal: 'His worst tragedies are due as much to transient and alterable custom as to the nature of things. He sees this, and he makes us see it. The moan of his verse rouses an echo that is as brave as a trumpet.' On the other hand, he could simultaneously observe that the prevailing mood of the poetry is 'the sense of the misery and fraudulence of life. The men and women have been happy and are not, and the happiness is now nothing; or they are or ought to be happy, but there is an inexplicable sigh.' The ambivalence of his response to this poetry is summed up in a fraught antithesis which resolves nothing: 'The book contains ninety-nine reasons for not living. Yet it is not a book of despair.'[18]

It was, however, the formal rigidity of Hardy's verse forms which primarily attracted Thomas's disapprobation. Their for him tyrannously Victorian rigidity embodied a metaphysics quite at odds with the fluid, open-ended, improvisational poetry he admired in Whitman and other poets, arising, he speculated, from 'an instinct for finality in form, a need of limitation and strict obedience to rule, or a desire to express but not to explain', which while it 'indulges in many varieties of rhyme and stanza', nevertheless 'it is hard to believe . . . is for any sensuous quality':

> Other poetry allows a great richness and diversity of interpretation. . . . He will not give his readers a moment's liberty. He gives them not only actions and characters, but their results; not only their results, but what is to be thought of them . . . by unmistakable implication. We cannot think of any other poetry so tyrannous; and this in part makes us restive under the conventional form, which adds a grotesqueness by means of the necessary inversion and other poetic license to the philosophic prose diction.[19]

Reviewing the same book a couple of days later, Thomas summed up this formal tyranny by suggesting that, in the construction of Hardy's poems, 'the "President of the Immortals" is the dominant figure'.[20] In a lengthier review, in 1911, of F. A. Hedgecock's *Thomas Hardy: Penseur et Artiste*, he returned to the theme, arguing that Hardy gave 'a ghostliness to [his] characters', which indicated that, 'valuable as they are in the weaving of his patterns of destiny, in themselves they concern him little': 'Thus, he describes two men watching a girl and then one of them departing and the other emerging from the wood close to "the interesting object of their contemplation."' Such omniscient imperiousness bespeaks a preoccupation with the workings of an 'Immanent Will' of which human beings are passive vehicles and victims, which his narratorial stance underwrites:

> The total effect is great. It establishes Mr. Hardy as the chief character in his novels, a 'weird archimage' sitting alone, 'Plotting dark spells and devilish enginery', and enjoying it after his fashion. If men and women are performing for the entertainment of a god, Mr. Hardy has a seat. When the wife-seller returns to the place of the selling, he goes over the day in his mind. . . . 'Then', says Henchard, 'We saw the tent – that must have stood more this way.' Mr. Hardy says: 'He walked to another spot; it was not really where the tent had stood, but it seemed so to him.' The novelist is excessively fond of showing, when he has made someone to do or say a thing, that he himself knows something else in the future or at a distance which will put a different complexion upon the first. In this mood he says about a lover's phrase: 'Foreknowledge to the distance of a year or so, in either of them, might have spoilt the effect of that pretty speech. Never deceive her! But they knew nothing, and the phrase had its day.' So doing, he flushes to anticipate some far-off event and loses much to gain a tenuous irony.[21]

Hardy, then, in adopting a 'spectatorial position, of greater curiosity than sympathy' in relation to human affairs, a detachment which 'may be held to account for the increasing abstractness of his style' (*loc. cit.*), seems an unlikely candidate to exemplify a modern 'poetry of experience'. But this is not the whole story.

Thomas did not review Hardy's *Satires of Circumstance* (1914), whose remarkable elegiac outpourings, 'Poems of 1912–13', might well have qualified the harsher assessment in these reviews. Even they, however, do identify some praiseworthy features. The *Morning Post* review of 9 December 1909 noted that 'many of the lyrics are narrative, nearly all the narrative poems are in stanzas of lyrical quality', and singled out their capacity to evoke a whole life in a contracted lyric space in, for example, 'The Minute before Meeting', where 'the form is a sonnet, and if it is in a sense "a moment's monument", the moment is full of years, and it is an implied narrative', giving Rossetti's famous description of the sonnet a specifically modern twist.

The *Daily Chronicle* review also noted this narratival insistence, though more equivocally, seeing it as in some ways an aspect of a stylistic tyranny, which would 'not give his readers a moment's liberty': 'Many of the poems are narrative. Even when called lyrical they suggest a chain of events. They are full of understandings, forebodings, memories, endings, questionings.' But they also constitute 'an atmosphere from which there is no escape'. 'We wonder', Thomas wrote, 'what subtle reason he had for using a lyric stanza . . . for a narrative full of conversation'. While this sounds like a criticism, Thomas almost answers his own question in the same paragraph: 'The utmost positive effect of the verse is to give brevity solemnity. The poems do not materially differ from his stories except that they are shorter . . . and that they gain a greater solemnity from their more uniform colouring, their greater simplicity, and the lack of explanation.'[22]

Thomas needed the encounter with Robert Frost's *North of Boston*, in a succession of reviews he wrote in 1914, fully to appreciate the potential of the form Hardy had pioneered. A review of Frost's book in the *Daily News* of 22 July 1914 recognized it unequivocally as 'one of the most revolutionary books of modern times', in which the poems, 'in dialogue mainly', were 'revolutionary because they lack the exaggeration of rhetoric': 'poetry because it is better than prose'. A further review, in *The New Weekly* of 8 August of the same year, saw that Frost had 'gone back, as Whitman and as Wordsworth went back, through the paraphernalia of poetry into poetry again', rediscovering, in his 'colloquialisms, the predominance of conversation', a 'drama with a lyric intensity which often borders on magic'. Again, in *The English Review* in August 1914, he praised the volume as 'a collection of dramatic narratives in verse', some 'almost entirely written in dialogue', which had 'got free from the habit of personal lyric': 'The result is a unique type of eclogue, homely, racy, and touched by a spirit that might, under other circumstances, have made pure lyric on the one hand or drama on the other.' Hardy had pioneered a new genre, half-way between the popular forms of ballad and folksong and the personal lyric of the high literary tradition. Lawrence had taken this further, in 'extraordinarily original closepacked poems' which were 'the quintessences of novels', 'not mere sketches or embryos of novels; but, as it were, the tiny but solid beings of which novels are the shadows artificially made gigantic'.[23] But it was the impact of Frost's 'revolutionary' achievement that finally precipitated the kind of dialogical narrative lyric which Thomas himself was shortly to perfect in the poems he began to write in December 1914, starting with his very first, the consummate narrative and dialogue poem 'Up in the Wind'.

It was Not Midnight

At the end of Samuel Beckett's *Molloy*, Moran, compiling his report on the missing Molloy, records that 'I went back into the house and wrote. It is midnight.

The rain is beating on the windows. It was not midnight. It was not raining.'
Moran here returns, in a circular movement, to the start of his own narration,
in the second section of the novel:

> It is midnight. The rain is beating on the windows. I am calm. All is sleeping.
> Nevertheless I get up and go to my desk. I can't sleep. My lamp sheds a soft
> and steady light. I have trimmed it. It will last till morning. I hear the eagle
> owl. What a terrible battlecry! Once I listened to it unmoved. My son is
> sleeping. Let him sleep. The night will come when he too, unable to sleep,
> will get up and go to his desk. I shall be forgotten.[24]

In circling back, at the end of the novel, to this starting point, only to negate
the event it has so persuasively made present, Beckett calls into question the
truth claims of all writing. We have only the author's word for it; or, in this case,
that of the author's surrogate, the fictive internal narrator. The circular movement, that is, pulls the rug from beneath all narrative authority, in a *mise en
abyme* which leaves the reader unsure where he or she stands, or sits, in reading
this text.

It is possible to discern here a ghostly echo of the 'Abstruser musings' at the
start of Coleridge's poem 'Frost at Midnight', which also returns at the end to
its starting point, in a cottage whose 'inmates [are] all at rest' and his 'cradled
infant slumbers peacefully' beside him in a solitude broken only by the 'owlet's
cry'.[25] Beckett's is not, however, an artful modernist deconstruction of
Coleridge's artless, spontaneous overflow of Romantic feeling. Coleridge's
application of the word 'performs' to the frost's 'secret ministry', resonates, for
the poet too is performing a secret ministry, artfully inscribing the processes by
which poetic creation transforms the immediate moment, as evanescent as the
fluttering flame on the hearth, into an abiding fiction that, 200 years later, readers can still share in as if eavesdropping on a continuing present. In inviting us
to interpret the text according to our own moods, to seek and find everywhere
echo or mirror of ourselves, in a present tense we supposedly share with
the speaker, Coleridge's conversation poems establish a central feature of the
poetry of experience, evoked most memorably in D. H. Lawrence's call, in the
American Preface to *New Poems*, for a poetry which inscribes 'the incandescence
and the coldness of the incarnate moment: the moment, the quick of all change
and haste and opposition: the moment, the immediate present, the Now'.[26]
Beckett's eponymous first narrator, Molloy, calls attention to the double-take in
such a way of reading when he confides that 'I speak in the present tense, it is
so easy to speak in the present tense, when speaking of the past. It is the mythological present, don't mind it.'[27]

Most fiction, and much poetry, is written in what Francophone stylistics
call the 'passé historique', specifically reserved for the literary narration of
past events. The English version of Moran's words ('I went back into the house
and I wrote') is cast in the past tense of everyday speech. In its original French,

however, it is formulated in the specific mode of the past historic: 'Alors je rent-rais dans la maison et j'écrivis', rather than 'je suis rentré et j'ai écrit'. Some modernist novels in both English and French have been narrated in what grammarians call the present historic. This verb form is grammatically indistin-guishable in either language from the normal present tense, except in its function of recounting past events as if they were happening at this moment, achieving the effect of vivid immediacy by 'presenting' the past as if it were present. This is actually quite rare in fiction. Modern poems in English, on the other hand, frequently tell their tales in the present historic. Yeats's 'Among School Children', for example, opens: 'I walk through the long schoolroom questioning.' Clearly, Yeats is not walking and questioning in the actual present of the poem, unless he is writing peripatetically, which would be a remarkable and, indeed, somewhat unsocial act. The present tense of the narrated event is not actually coincident with the present of its writing. Yeats's opening lines, however, immediately shift into another, equally problematic present tense, in which 'The children learn to cipher and to sing, / To study reading-books and history, / To cut and sew, be neat in everything, / In the best modern way.' Since this is not an illustration of how modernity prioritizes multi-tasking, it's clear that they are not doing all these things simultaneously. Indeed, they are doing none of them; instead, 'In momentary wonder [they] stare upon / A sixty-year-old smiling public man.' The tense of this determinedly 'modern' learning process is a generic present, describing a continuous, and continuing, activity. Such grammatical nitpickings are not matters which generally arise in discussing poetic language. But Beckett, in formulating the concept of a 'mythological present', has put his finger on a significant aporia regarding the nature of poetic voice: the time in which it exists. The concept allows us to iden-tify a distinctive feature of the poetry of experience, intimately bound up with the question of modernity.

Many of Lawrence's lyrics 'speak in the present tense', following moods, as Thomas observed in the 1913 *Bookman* review cited earlier, 'with a painful curi-osity that makes us . . . sharers in a process'. On inspection, however, these poems, like similar poems by Hardy and Thomas and many modern writers, deploy a peculiar form of that present tense, for which Beckett's formula is sin-gularly apposite. Lawrence's 'Piano', combining the present continuous with the present historic, is an almost perfect exemplification of the 'mythological present':

Softly, in the dusk, a woman is singing to me;
Taking me back down the vista of years, till I see
A child sitting under the piano . . .

Thomas's own most Whitmanesque poem, 'Health', emulates both Whitman and Lawrence by speaking in all the urgency of Lawrence's 'immediate present, the Now'. I want at this point, however, to return to Thomas's reflections on Hardy.

Clean White Pages

By the time he came to write *A Literary Pilgrim in England*, published shortly before his death in 1917, Thomas's attitude to Hardy had mellowed, perhaps because Frost's 'revolutionary' poetry had led him to reconsider Hardy's own poetic innovations. In a short, understated account of Hardy's verse in this book, Thomas inadvertently touched on a characteristic feature of much contemporary verse, including, by this time, his own. It is the unmediated immediacy of time and place he now finds central to Hardy's verse, quoting in full a well-known two-stanza poem:

> [T]he place-names offer many pleasures and provoke several kinds of curiosity. Sometimes the place is given, it appears, out of pure fidelity to the fact. That something happened 'At this point in time, at this point in space', it pleases him to put on record, as when he signs 'Max Gate, 1899', at the end of 'An August Midnight':

> > 'A shaded lamp and a waving blind,
> > And the beat of a clock from a distant floor:
> > On this scene enter – winged, horned, and spined –
> > A longlegs, a moth, and a dumbledore;
> > While 'mid my page there idly stands
> > A sleepy fly, that rubs its hands. . . .

> > 'Thus meet we five, in this still place,
> > At this point of time, at this point in space.
> > – My guests parade my new-penned ink,
> > Or bang at the lamp-glass, whirl, and sink.
> > "God's humblest, they!" I muse. Yet why?
> > They know Earth-secrets that know not I.'

'The general effect of using local names with no significance for the stranger, and no special private value of sound or association for the poet', Thomas observes, 'is to aid reality by suggestions of gross and humble simplicity. It might become a trick or device, but in Mr. Hardy it is not either.' Rather, 'the name gives even a kind of magic reality'.[28] Thomas's resonant phrase, not to be confused with later usages, points to the kind of fictive illusion of real presence for which Beckett's formula is a fitting designation.

There is a further dimension to the mythological present in 'An August Midnight', recalling that in 'Frost at Midnight'. Both Coleridge's and Hardy's poems subsist in a poetic version of what film theory calls 'real time'. 'That something happened "At this point in time, at this point in space"' is not simply 'put on record here': it is enacted again and again. In activating the mythological present, the poem creates its own perpetual instantaneity, in which the act of writing is simultaneous and coextensive with the event narrated. 'On this scene enter', the poem says, and indeed it is precisely at this point that these humble creatures do appear on stage, written in by the poet's pen onto a page that the fly stands on, in the still wet 'new-penned ink' in which these 'guest' performers tread. In a literal sense, these five denizens of the mythological present all meet, all parade, in the still place of a text which inscribes them as *signifiers*. This is not exactly the performative present in which Yeats writes, in 'Easter 1916', that 'I write it out in a verse', or, in 'The Tower', that 'It is time that I wrote my will.' But it has, in an extended sense of the concept, some aspects of the performative. Hardy's whole poem performs the act of writing which brings its narrative into being, in a 'real time' where the temporalities of writing and of narrated event appear to be not only synchronous but, in fact, one and the same, so that 'this point in time [and] space' is resurrected as a unitary experience in the immediate present of the reader. 'It is true that he wishes the poems to be regarded as "dramatic monologues"', Thomas commented of *Time's Laughingstocks* in 1909, 'yet the prevalent tone must be his, and so is the tone of many separate poems. . . . He cannot escape from his own muffled cadences.'[29] Nor can the reader.

There are many instances of the mythological present in twentieth-century poetry, enacting scenarios where, as in Stevens's poem (n. 26), 'the reader becomes the book', and the night is 'like the conscious being of the book'. But that 'like' should give us pause. This is only that perpetually sought-after and elusive chimera of modernity, the illusion of presence. It is, ultimately, a metaphysical claim that is being made in such poems, even as they seem to embody the unreflective, lived experience of 'the moment, the immediate present, the Now'. This is what renders them mythological. Thomas's own poetry is full of evocations of 'the immediate present', most effectively when, as in Hardy's poem, they claim to transcribe the very act of writing which brings them into being. Sometimes, the inscription of the writing act is subtly delayed, as in 'The Penny Whistle', which begins with an act of creation out there, in 'the real world', where 'The new moon hangs like an ivory bugle / In the naked frosty blue.'[30] The subliminal echoes of 'Frost at Midnight' might alert a wary reader to the 'magic reality' constructed in the penultimate stanza's artful parallelism between external events and the act of reading:

> The charcoal-burners are black, but their linen
> Blows white on the line;
> And white the letter the girl is reading
> Under that crescent fine.

The clues are there in black and white, and Thomas is possibly shooting a line about poetic as well as washing lines. It's a consummately understated poem, but, like the washing, it comes clean only at the end. The letter the girl reads is unlikely, in a circularity recalling Coleridge's conversation poems, to be the poem which the poet is supposedly writing here, but the simultaneously parallelism and contrast with her brother's playing on a penny whistle says complex and suggestive things about the 'incandescence and the coldness of the incarnate moment' of artistic creation:

> And her brother who hides apart in a thicket,
> Slowly and surely playing
> On a whistle an old nursery melody,
> Says far more than I am saying.

'Says'/'am saying': two different forms of the present tense. The poem's act of 'saying', in the present continuous in which we still read it, takes retrospective command of the whole scenario. The poem hints at the distance between writer and reader, even as it yearns across that divide, significantly, as in so many of Thomas's poems, a class divide. A similar social and cultural division provides the ground on which 'The Gypsy' is enacted. The poem begins by recounting, in the past historic, an encounter which has a clear sexual undercurrent. The poem moves into the mythological present when it comes to translate that unsatisfactory exchange into its proper coin (the poem itself):

> I paid nothing then,
> As I pay nothing now with the dipping of my pen
> For her brother's music when he drummed the tambourine
> And stamped his feet, which made the workmen passing grin.

The gypsy's 'pink sham flowers', the idea of 'translat[ing] into its proper coin / Gratitude for her grace', the poet's (she alleges) 'lucky face', and his perception of himself, as the poem ends, as 'Like a ghost new-arrived', are all signs pointing to the artifice into which we are being drawn, in the very moment that the poem insists on the immediate reality of the event it reports. It is this very fictionality which underwrites, in the end, the integrity of a poem such as this, ensuring that it creates what Thomas had found so convincing in Frost's narratives, 'drama with a lyric intensity which often borders on magic'.[31]

Perhaps the most magically realist of all Thomas's poems in this vein is 'The Long Small Room'. The room's *mise-en-scène* is all, apparently, past and gone when the poet ceased to occupy it:

> When I look back I am like moon, sparrow, and mouse
> That witnessed what they could never understand
> Or alter or prevent in the dark house.
> One thing remains the same – this my right hand
>
> Crawling crab-like over the clean white page,
> Resting awhile each morning on the pillow,
> Then once more starting to crawl on towards age.
> The hundred last leaves stream upon the willow.

But it is not as simple as that, as is suggested by the latent tension between the ideas of witness and that of the 'tale' which these creatures 'keep / . . . for the old ivy and older brick.' The reader feels compelled to guess what need or accident led to the construction of this poem, without finding an answer, like those accidental witnesses unable to understand, alter or prevent events which are hinted at but never specified. Like them, the poem maintains an enigmatic silence. It is the very indeterminacy of the scene that effects the 'magic' here. Its readers are 'rather sharers in a process than witnesses of a result', excluded from whatever meaning the scene has, whatever events were enacted on its stage. Like the speaker, we look back, uncomprehending, from the mythological present, sure of only one thing linking these imagined and imaginary temporalities, because the poem foregrounds it: the act of writing.

The time scheme is actually quite complex in this ostensibly simple lyric, its complexity focused in that final isolated image, reminiscent of the translated Chinese poetry Thomas had variously reviewed.[32] The crisp generic present of this line, describing a continuing process, is quite distinct from the present participles which depict the writer's writing hand crawling, resting, then 'once more starting to crawl', in a series of discontinuous, disjunctive moments. 'Starting to crawl', recalling the 'sequent toil' that 'crawls to maturity' in Shakespeare's sonnet LX, opens up the prospect of a perpetually repeated attrition ended only in death. The poem had begun in the past tense with the account of a room and a view now superseded, though the room presumably continues to show those willows, in the present, to his successors in the house. Within that past, a future is already latent in the observation that moon, mouse and sparrow 'shall keep the tale', though, strangely, that tale will be kept for ivy and brick which recede into a successively remoter past ('old', 'older'). The poet's present tense then manifests itself only in a further retrospection ('When I look back') which reinstates that lost place, and the 'I am' hovers uncertainly between being a present in the past and one in the here and now, for he was as ignorant then as he is now about what they witnessed there. Like Hardy's sonnet, this poem is 'a moment's monument' in which 'the moment is full of years, and it is an implied narrative'. That 'could' transcends, or telescopes, all these different 'presents', in past, present and future, for the not understanding will persist into the future as it obtained in the past and obtains here in the present. The assertion, then, that 'One thing remains the same' is not quite accurate, unless the poem assumes, as is possible, a sequence of successive, different incomprehensions. It is only when the reader is unsettled by all this interpretative indeterminacy that that harrowing synecdoche reduces the living, breathing poet to a mere function of the writing act, a dehumanized automaton who has to earn his living, day in, day out, by endless, exhausting hack work. Yet it is this same hand which now writes, and has always-already written, the very poem on the clean white page in front of us. It is not fanciful to hear here another echo, for a poet with radical sympathies with the world of labour, of the denunciations by Dickens and Ruskin and Morris of an industrial system that reduces flesh and blood human beings to mere 'hands', simply the functions and instruments of an inexorable production process.

Thomas's essay 'A Return to Nature' records a lengthy exchange with a former city worker whose 'people were oil or grit in a great machine', who rails against men 'too broken-spirited to think of a right to live . . . content only to work', labouring multitudes whom Thomas in his own voice describes as automata that 'move on, or seem to do, on and on, round and round, as thoughtless as the belt of an engine'. Prefiguring the sentiments of 'The Long Small Room', Thomas responds to his interlocutor's despair with an autobiographical counter-claim:

> 'But the journalist and hack writer', said I, 'is worse off. At least your master only asked for your dregs. The hack writer is asked to give everything that can be turned into words at short notice, and so the collar round his neck is never taken off as yours was between six in the afternoon and nine in the morning.'[33]

The professional writer is simply another hand, the clean white page his workplace and prison. The poetry of experience, so expressive of the condition of modernity, emerges, finally, not from some effortless spontaneous combustion, Lawrence's 'incandescence . . . of the incarnate moment', but from the hard graft of manual labour. This poem, indeed, recalls the etymology of the word 'graft' itself, deriving, via Old French *grafe* (a pen) and Latin *graphium* (a stylus), from the Greek *graphein*, to write. Those 'last leaves' streaming on the wind are also, it could be said, the pages of a text whose completion is perpetually deferred.

Notes

[1] *Bookman*, April 1913.

[2] *Morning Post* [hereinafter *MP*], 4 June 1908.

[3] *Daily Chronicle* [hereinafter *DC*], 9 May 1908.

[4] *MP*, 14 May 1908; *DC*, 18 May 1908.

[5] *DC*, 9 May 1910.

[6] John Moore, *The Life and Letters of Edward Thomas* [1939] (London: Allen Sutton, 1983), 37.

[7] *DC*, 26 November 1903.

[8] *MP*, 12 September 1910.

[9] Now in the Berg Collection, New York Public Library. See Stan Smith, 'Edward Thomas's Social Mysticism', *Critical Survey* 11.3 (1999), ed. Peter Widdowson, 67–76.

[10] William James, *The Varieties of Religious Experience: A Study in Human Nature. Being the Gifford Lectures on Natural Religion Delivered at Edinburgh in 1901–1902* (London: Longmans, Green, 1902).

[11] *DC*, 8 February 1910.

[12] *DC*, 13 December 1905.

[13] Edward Thomas, *The South Country* [1909] (London: J. M. Dent, 1932), 117.

[14] Eleanor Farjeon, *Edward Thomas: The Last Four Years* [1958] (Oxford: Oxford University Press, 1979), 123: 'I had read *Sons and Lovers* and *The White Peacock* and had heard Edward envy in the latter observations on nature which he wished he had observed for himself.'

[15] *DC*, 21 October 1905.

[16] Robert Langbaum, *The Poetry of Experience: The Dramatic Monologue in Modern Literary Tradition* (New York: Random House, 1957), 102–3.

[17] Edward Thomas, *George Borrow* (London: Chapman and Hall, 1912), 168, 188, 168.

[18] *DC*, 7 December 1909.

[19] Ibid.

[20] *MP*, 9 December 1909.

[21] *Saturday Review*, 17 June 1911.

[22] *DC*, 7 December 2009.

[23] *DC*, [?] February 1913.

[24] Samuel Beckett, *Molloy, the Beckett Trilogy* (London: Picador, 1979), 162, 84.

[25] *The Poems of Samuel Taylor Coleridge*, ed. Ernest Hartley Coleridge (London: Oxford University Press, 1912), 240.

[26] D. H. Lawrence, *New Poems* (New York: Huebsch, 1920), v. A less 'incandescent' version of the same merging of writer's and reader's presents is the theme of Wallace Stevens's 'The House was Quiet and the World was Calm', *The Collected Poems* (London: Faber and Faber, 1955), 358–9.

[27] Beckett, *Molloy*, 26.

[28] Edward Thomas, *A Literary Pilgrim in England* [1917] (London: Jonathan Cape, 1937), 143–5. 'An August Midnight' is from *Poems of the Past and the Present* (1901).

[29] *MP*, 9 December 1909.

[30] Edward Thomas, *Collected Poems*, foreword Walter de la Mare (London: Faber and Faber, 1936).

[31] That most famous modern poem purporting to enact its own genesis, Ted Hughes's 'Thought-Fox', descends directly from 'Frost at Midnight', 'An August Midnight' and this poem of Thomas's, in making 'this midnight moment's forest' coterminous with 'this blank page where my fingers move'. Hughes's poem insists, along with Lawrence, on the 'nowness' of poetic creation, reiterating the word itself, as 'now / And again now, and now, and now', the thought-fox 'Sets neat prints into the snow'. But for all the urgent immediacy of its present tense, the opening words, 'I imagine', remind us that we are sharers in a merely mythological present. At the poem's close, the previously blank 'page is printed', the present tense incorporating the past in the finitude of a writing act now completed. No more than Hardy's or Thomas's does this poem reproduce the 'real time' of its writing. Their apparent simultaneity is merely 'imagined'.

[32] See, for example, the review of *Twenty Chinese Poems*, paraphrased by Clifford Bax (*MP*, 16 May 1910).

[33] Thomas, *The South Country*, 77–97, 90, 81, 92, 82.

Another 'Last Signal'

(*TH to PW: A Tribute*)

I am the man who noticed with
A raptor's eye; the man who heard
With Wessex the dog's pitch-perfect ear;
Who felt with a woman's generous heart.
Nothing passed me by.

Yes, I was born far lowlier than some.
But stockyard, coop and byre – they didn't
Breed my brain. I am myself, my wayward thoughts
Learned and innocent at once.
Critics can't read me.

I absolve you, Peter, from the critic's taint.
You read, you think, you search, you sympathise,
And as I did, you see, hear, feel, and guess.
What can these modish blockheads tell of tricks
That come of a lifetime's skill?

You live where I should, had I thought
Of dislodging from Dorset; near
Romish Corinium, your Bulwarks,
Their swoops and tumps much like
My homely Rainbarrows.

You've done the things I should have liked to do:
The Cyder Press – the spelling says it all!
Helping the humble bards, Taylors and Clares,
The needy ones. No cash for poetry,
Or the players in Stinsford Church.

You have the eye for what's neglected:
The books that never made it to the top –
Desperate Remedies, Poor Man and Lady,
Ethelberta – I was proud of them.
Their messages were subtle. Only you could read.

You are my listener. From your rough times
To mine, you tune your ear to me. You know
The difficult texts: what counts is love,
In every form. There's no such thing
As a happy ending. So it is.

I wish the stiff-collared gents, the urban know-alls,
Could see as clear as you. Thrush, grass and clouds
Are truth-tellers. I am the man who hears them.
A wave to you, as me-ward once
From Barnes's coffin – *Down with the critics!*
Speak for the inarticulate!

                                        U. A. Fanthorpe

Part II

Personalia

Biographical Sketches of Peter Widdowson

Neville Shrimpton

Peter's first teaching and research posts were in the Department of English at Umeå University in the north of Sweden. Umeå was a very new university when he joined it in 1968, and the English, French and German Departments had been among the first to open soon after the University was inaugurated in 1965. Peter's arrival coincided with a massive expansion of university education in Sweden, with student intakes for English at Umeå rocketing from around 30 to 300 from one year to the next. Everyone had to teach practically everything and to multiple groups. This caused some problems with the teaching of literature, since most of us, Swedes and non-Swedes alike, were language specialists or teachers of English as a foreign language. Peter thus came at a crucial time.

Before Peter, the role of literary specialist in the department had been assumed by an Australian lecturer, Tanya Yakimoff (now Benedictus). When she left, the British Council was asked to try to help us recruit a suitable replacement, and Tanya was persuaded to join their interviewing board. They (She) chose Peter from an impressive array of candidates. Peter and his first wife, Frances, joined a rather motley (*read* eccentric) group of Swedes and Brits. While he was here others, including Paul Binding and Frances herself, became lecturers in the department, or were promoted from student to teacher (Eva Sharp and Per-Arne Oberg). Some remained in the Department for periods in excess of 40 years – Per-Arne (still there), Jan Robbins, Pat Shrimpton and myself. Other braver souls, like Peter and Frances themselves, now with their newly born son, Patrick, strode boldly out into the wider world outside. They were sadly missed and are still remembered. I recently met one of Peter's students who later became a lecturer in Comparative Literature, and she said that he had changed her life. He changed the life of many others too, and not only staff and students.

Our informal meetings in the home (many, many parties), in the coffee bar and elsewhere often had an element of the seminar about them. We taught the novel (long discussions about Hardy among others), British and American poetry, Shakespeare, British and American drama, oral and written proficiency, and many other things. Some of us felt like amateurs at the game of English

Studies, with Peter trying, often in vain, to keep us in check. We certainly all developed, even if we later moved away from the areas that bonded us then. If we developed in good academic fashion, Peter deserves much of the credit for this.

Pat and I have constant reminders of Peter's influence, when we meet students from way back who ask after him and tell us how fondly they remember him and his teaching. We thought that it was a sign of age whenever a new student told us that their mother remembered him. Imagine the shock of hearing, just before we retired: 'Oh yes, you and the Widdowsons, you taught my grandmother!'

Mary Shakeshaft

Peter Widdowson was my Head of School at Middlesex University from January 1986 to August 1992. The School of English was a large one, well over twenty, but while Peter was on exchange in Michigan and I was Acting Head our English Language part-timers were transferred to the School of Modern Languages. After that Peter had only to control a varied group of literary types often at loggerheads over some theoretical point or other, and the ease and good humour with which he did that, preventing many a blood-bath in School meetings, especially when we were working on the following year's timetable or resubmitting our courses, was a joy to observe.

Middlesex was always moving us about: from the red-brick of Tottenham we were moved to our disgust to some huts at Enfield, where Peter strategically took the room nearest the door so he could watch all our comings and goings. This room was a focus for convivial meetings, especially at the end of the day. Peter and I always got on, though we had different approaches to literature, I being of the old London literary history school and Peter – well, this book makes his approach clear. I remember he called me 'the critic on the Clapham omnibus' when I told him the way I tried to explain metaphysical imagery to my students, and once, when at the end of the day, I burst into his office with a new interpretation of a line in 'The Waste Land', he remarked drily, 'Well, that should be good for a paragraph in *Notes and Queries*.'

His secretary remembers Peter as kind and understanding. When he left, the canteen staff insisted on saying their own farewells and presenting him with bars of his favourite chocolate. His lively teaching was appreciated by his students, who at his inaugural lecture not only applauded him vigorously but also stood up and turned their backs on the Vice-Chancellor. We were going through one of our periodic disputes with him at the time – I think it was about being moved to the Enfield campus – and Peter had great difficulty in maintaining a proper professorial gravity.

I am therefore proud and delighted to be able to wish Peter well in retirement, though that word, to quote Donne, 'wrongs' him. I cannot imagine Peter retired.

He was always busy, writing books on numerous modern writers of which I chiefly remember one on Hardy, composing entertaining lectures, appraising his staff, marking endless essays and exam-scripts, writing reports, serving on committees and always having something worthwhile to say there, and yet still finding time for his staff's grumbles and worries. I enjoyed Peter's ironic humour, admired his relaxed style of leadership and was always aware of his concern for his students and staff even when he disagreed with them. I hope he will enjoy his retirement and the freedom it gives to read book not on the syllabus!

Paul Stigant

Literature as History: the title of this Festschrift could not have been better chosen as an evocation and celebration of the years in the 1970s and 1980s that I knew Peter best at Thames Polytechnic. Peter's contribution to the growth and development of what was then the Division of English at Thames was immense. He, along with the team of young staff that worked with him, helped put a small English Department in a very small south-east London Polytechnic on the national Higher Education map. The Division of which Peter became the Head in January 1972 was part of the School of Humanities that also included Divisions of History, Politics, Geography and Philosophy. The multi-disciplinary nature of the School and its main degree in Humanities was critical and formative for the way Peter encouraged the development of his subject be it in terms of teaching, research, new degree programmes or constant, often heated, debate with colleagues across the School.

A vital part of these debates – indeed it stood at the heart of the Humanities degree – was an investigation, a questioning, of the academic disciplines themselves. It was an enquiry not merely of their various methodologies, gene-ses, future directions but also their boundaries and interconnectedness. For Peter the specific literary text(s) under study always remained central in his endeavour to understand his subject and evaluate its relevance, but he was also more than willing to engage with colleagues who argued for other concerns about how to read the text in a diversity of contexts. The result was a fruitful, intense consideration of the literary canon itself, the role of theory in the study of English, and how to locate the author and his/her work historically.

Peter's other great strength and contribution to Thames and the wider academic community in these years was his determination to put our internal debates into the larger, surrounding intellectual considerations of the role of Theory in the development of English as a discipline. *Re-Reading English* emerged from the collective discussions and arguments at one of the many weekend conferences that seemed to pepper some quarters of academic life in the 1970s. It was Peter who had the vision, determination and energy to put the heated debate into print. Just as it was Peter who had the drive and organizational skills to make the journal *Literature and History* more than a good but passing idea. If literature as history, if literature as more than a mere reflection of or commentary upon its times, literature as a dynamic force in the complex processes of change, ever found a voice it was for over a decade in the pages of *Literature and History*. Editing, producing and occasionally writing for its two editions a year may have been a collective enterprise but the journal would never have been born or survived without Peter Widdowson.

Mike Walters

'Don't start with a bloody quote', he'd probably say, but you want to wedge in as many of the old boy's *bonnes phrases* as you can. Eight or nine years before he arrived at Middlesex as Head of the School of English – later subsumed into some hissing acronym – I encountered Peter across a table as the shiny grey-suited delegate from The Future on a CNAA panel: 'I see that *Tom Jones* is one of the nominated Fielding texts; I'd be interested to know why you privileged (if we said that, in 1977) that over *Amelia*.' Gabbling my 'Any fule kno . . .' response, I'm sure I missed the grin.

What Peter found at Middlesex was perhaps not the department he would have chosen. At his interview, copies of *Re-Reading English* were brandished at him like editions of the *Little Red Book* at a Maoist seeking a bishopric. His (ungrinning) concurrence in our view of F. R. Leavis's centrality was therefore disarming. But Peter has always been a good Leavisian, in his left-handed way. I hope that this well-meant observation won't damage his career prospects.

But how elusive were his ironies! Were they present at all, I still wonder, when he posted an item on an English staff notice-board, with the footnote 'I imagine most of you will already have seen this in the *Guardian*'?

At all events, by the end of the 1980s, he'd brought us hurtling into the 1970s with a new 'Studies in Contemporary Writing' programme, whose cornerstone was a course in 'Contemporary British Writing'. Few but Peter could eagerly accost you in the corridor to report that he had walked into the first seminar asking 'Is this Contemporary British Literature?' to be met with corrective howls from his own seminarians. In my own experience, Peter was probably the last of the non-managerial heads of department. That's to say, he 'managed' by encouragement, persuasion and a deft sleight-of-personality. And on a purely personal level, I have cause never to forget his kindness. 'It's what I've got', says Sheriff John Chance in *Rio Bravo*. I'd guess that PJW has rarely been compared to John Wayne, but Peter brought out the best in what he had, trusting people's judgement in taking their own way. This is not to suggest that the rest of us were drunks and teenage folk-singers: the analogy is exclusively *ad hominem*.

Let me end with his beginning – at any rate, with his inaugural lecture. As the Plump Controller of the then polytechnic rose to introduce him and his topic – that stuff about critical terrorism – all the students present stood and turned their backs in objection to some recent infraction of the PC's. Cue an expression on Peter's hired professorial fizz for which I wish I could find a verbal correlative – a palimpsest in which the grin seemed to hover, negative capability made flesh. What a silent movie actor he would have made! So at least I can't conclude with a quotation.

Mary DeJong Obuchowski

Peter spent the 1988–9 academic year at Central Michigan University on an exchange programme. He shared an office with my husband. Laughter often erupted from there during the course of the year, and I encountered Peter's wit and zest for teaching in the coffee room and when he and Jane and son Thomas came to our home.

I have special reason to be grateful to Peter. We hoped to adopt a child from Chile. I had not only to travel to Santiago, but also to stay there for a number of weeks until the legal issues could be resolved. Fortunately I taught only one class that semester but still urgently needed to have it covered. Peter volunteered to teach the portion on Arthur Miller's *Death of a Salesman*. He understood exactly what the students needed and prepared them well for the examination at the end of the drama section. He sent the tests to me, and they were among the best sets of papers I have seen. After my return, the students' praise for Peter was unanimous.

Peter Obuchowski

My wife's recollections of Peter convey the outward circumstances of his entrance into our lives. Though it has been 20 years since our lives crossed paths, I can still recall a few events that I think reveal the kind of human being he is. When he first arrived at Central Michigan University the English Department Chairperson informed him that one of the upper-level courses that he was scheduled to teach had been cancelled and had to be replaced with a freshman composition section. Peter plunged into the class as if it were an eagerly anticipated part of a prearrangement. He simply saw the course as a way of helping *us* out. I could not help but think what a waste it seemed to put this extremely gifted scholar and eloquent teacher into a freshman composition class. The enthusiasm he brought to this teaching assignment was revealed to me one morning when I arrived at the office. There was Peter at his desk grading compositions, hunched over the paper before him like a medieval monk illuminating a manuscript. Wondering what could merit such rapt attention, I discovered that interlinearly he was carefully pencilling in detailed instructions to the student to help him or her clarify the thoughts. Where I would have put a niggardly 'awk' or 'vague' in the margin, he seemed to be composing a writer's guide.

I remember such incidents, but when it comes right down to it, what I recall most warmly is not so much the detail as a distillation of the days we spent in the office. From our very first meeting I felt a kinship with Peter which only increased over the course of those months. So now when I hear his name mentioned I recall with gratitude this incredibly witty, mischievously warm human being who helped me crawl through another school year and who, I know, enriched a year of my life immensely.

Peter Brooker

In those days we woke to the sound of Althusser bathed in ideology. ISAs (Ideological State Apparatuses) were everywhere – under the bed, on TV, calling after you at street corners, and especially lurking at your place of work. Here life at the Poly strove to imitate the world of George Weber in a staff-room created with uncanny accuracy by Posy Simmons.

But of course it couldn't really have been like that: could it? Not like a cartoon in the *Guardian,* at that time published under the name of *Grauniad?* Because, after all, we were serious. Thirty-somethings with a memory of long hair and flares who were particularly serious about two things. Even when there seemed to be three things, like home, spouse and family, or literature, ideology and society, there were still really only two things: the high and the low of what mattered – though you could find your base had gone all superstructural overnight – of, yes, 'Literature' and 'History'. This was when the pencil hit the sharpener and the boot was on the other foot. Not that it was easy. First, 'History' was a problem because it thought it ran the show and because it was itself two things: a department down the corridor and just about everything you could see out of the window. But we were troubled too by the words 'Literature' and 'English', partly because they'd been stuck together as if by ideological glue squeezed out of a long tube of ISA, and partly because we could see they weren't the same when everybody said they were. And then there was that joining word 'and' as in Literature *and* History. Shouldn't it have been 'in' and wouldn't it one day be 'as'? And deep down should the first word have been 'Literature' at all? Why not 'Writing' or 'Signs'? 'Writing' or 'Signs' and 'and' or 'in' . . . 'Culture'?

To be honest all this was food and drink to us, year in year out. It all started in Manchester or more precisely coming home from Manchester where Peter and I had been to a conference when Brian Cox of Cox and Dyson, the editors of the notorious Black Papers had said something we didn't like about teaching English. Polytechnics, where we came from, were a bit uncouth and didn't even make it into Malcolm Bradbury's *The History Man.* But we should have a conference, we said, we could even run a journal. And for 13 years (before the Second Series of *Literature and History*) we did, all of us banging on about Marx and Gramsci and Althusser and Macherey and Williams and Thompson and

Eagleton and about 'literature' and 'history' and 'ideology' and 'signs' and 'and' or 'in'. We talked when we arrived at work and after we left, in and out of offices, over coffee and over lunch – Peter alternating always between his two rolls, cheese and ham, ham and cheese. And we carried it all into lecture and seminars, talking with students, at parties, down the pub, and especially at the Indian on Thursday nights. It was a world of talk and longhand, of pink memo pads, of busy pigeon holes, of the heavyweight imperial typewriter at home before you got your first Amstrad. We had control, we thought, of the means of production of *Literature and History*, helped by a professional typist round the corner and a patient typesetter at the print room and student assistants who entered the details of articles and comments and decisions by pen in a ledger (which still exists). It was a hands-on, in-house, from the bottom-up talking shop, and a model of comradeship.

So we entered the 1980s and the bad times of Thatcherism and went our different ways. Peter was known for *Re-Reading English* and for his work on Hardy, but we continued to write and edit together, in a way I now know was exceptional. One early essay we co-wrote was on one of those words which had occupied us: 'Englishness'. I've read it recently. My own contribution was snappy and opinionated. Peter's was the better part, but it was probably one of the best pieces, and certainly the longest piece, we did, and my guess is we would still think much the same now as we did then.

Peter Widdowson, our contemporary. Who is this? He would be the first to answer that he is what we, in a collection of essays such as the present volume, make of him. His critical mode, in person and on the page is to question such questions, backing up so as to ask again. The mark of this procedure is the set of quotation marks, just as in those quotation marks around key words above, which might just as well be Peter's own.

None of it would have happened, there wouldn't have been a *Literature and History* without Peter, doing two things at once, ham and cheese, cheese and ham, saying and unsaying in quotes, then and now.

Stuart Laing

I first came across the name of Peter Widdowson in the mid-1970s as one of the editors of the new journal *Literature and History*. At that time I was a lecturer in English at the University of Sussex and, in common with many others in university English departments, was both surprised and intrigued to find such a journal being based at a polytechnic. Having been recently a graduate student at the Birmingham Centre for Contemporary Cultural Studies I was very much on the lookout for developments which broke the mould and first met Peter, as I recall, at Thames Polytechnic in the late 1970s at a meeting addressing the relationship between literature, history and politics. Over the next few years, as a member of the CNAA English Studies Board, a contributor to *Literature and*

History and an external examiner at Thames Polytechnic I came both to know Peter himself and to realize the critically important impact that Peter's work, his example and his influence was having on the reputation and achievements of the polytechnics and colleges (then known as 'public sector' higher education).

For Peter himself, I suspect, certainly in hindsight and to some extent at the time (as illustrated by his editorial comment in the tenth anniversary issue of *Literature and History* in 1985), his position as apparent champion of interdisciplinarity and (following his editorship of *Re-Reading English* at the height of Thatcherism in 1982) of literary iconoclasm was full of ambivalence. It was perhaps a function of the particular historical situation in which he found himself as much as any kind of compelling personal crusade. For much of what makes Peter's published work so immensely valuable are the traditional virtues of the highest quality literary historical and literary critical scholarship – attention to the facts of the case, intelligent and dialogic commentary and a thoughtful and discriminating engagement with the current of contemporary aesthetic and cultural ideas and theories. Yet also I now think it was *the way* he played his role at that time that was so important and impressive – for, whether as journal or book editor or as the public face of serious humanities teaching and research in the CNAA institutions, he showed a generosity of spirit and a duty of care to others from which so many lecturers, scholars and students have greatly benefited. He then shared, in an immensely practical way, with Raymond Williams, a commitment to the extension and democratization of public education in the humanities, and in literature in particular. And he shared and still shares with those writers he most attends to (Hardy, Williams, Graham Swift) a full sense of the balancing of the historical determinants of our existence and the human and humane choices they provide for us. A wise teacher, a true scholar and a good man.

Victoria Bazin

Peter Widdowson was head of the English Department at what was, in 1990, Middlesex Polytechnic. He was on the interview panel that appointed me as a temporary lecturer in literature for a period of two years. In those days, English was based in a prefab structure in a car park on the Enfield campus. As you entered this rather fragile structure you would invariably see Peter at his desk working away on his book on Lawrence. He seemed to be the one permanent fixture in that temporary structure.

The English curriculum was spread across three different campuses and we were often flung out to the far reaches of the Northern Line. Not everyone had offices in the prefab, some were based at the leafy Trent Park campus. The different and distinctive degree programmes such as Susanna Gladwin's course in creative writing and publishing or studies in contemporary culture competed with the more traditional English literature programmes and this contributed to a good deal of territorial conflict. Departmental meetings were lively affairs presided over by Peter with unerring good humour. I seem to remember we spent a lot of time debating the name of the department and that the final suggestion, the School of English and Cultural Studies, was chosen because its acronym would be SECS.

What pulled me through that first year of teaching was simply Peter's confidence in my ability to do the job. When he came along to observe one of my seminars, he commended me on the way I had carefully structured the seminar discussion. Rather than pointing out that I had not really given any of the students a chance to express their own ideas about the text, he had offered the kind of critical observation that only resonated with me later, when I was a little more experienced. But I learnt more from Peter by actually seeing him 'in action'. His lecture on modernism on the sprawling first-year survey course, delivered without referring to any notes, told a persuasive and compelling story that held everyone's attention for a full 50 minutes. The way Peter provided both an account of modernism's formal innovations as well as relating it to the rise of English Studies in the academy and the development of a specialized critical discourse was for me, a new way of thinking about modernism.

The image of Peter at his desk writing his book on Lawrence (in his spidery scrawl) is one that illustrates so well his approach to his job. Able to integrate his research into the daily routines of the department, he could be fully present, supportive of and patient with his cantankerous colleagues and the various cohorts of students he taught and supervised. Peter's research was not a separate activity that took him away from that creaky prefab: it was, on the contrary, central to the concerns of the department.

John Hughes

I met Peter after I had read a fair amount of his writing on Hardy, so knew what an important and original intervention in Hardy studies his work constituted. He had come for interview at the then Cheltenham and Gloucester College of Education in the early 1990s. It was an institution very recently in pursuit of its research culture (or its University title, at least), and it seemed a real *coup* that we might bag someone of his eminence and quality. First impressions were of a piece with the colleague we would come to know. He seemed slightly wired, watchful and canny – yet mild and modest, too, his evident social ease fed by a nervous energy naturally seeking and inviting an outlet in humour. Over the next few years many of these traits would translate into the restlessness, pragmatism, and tact that he brought to his post, as he balanced strategic objectives with a horse-handler's (sometimes horse-whisperer's) skill in building an inclusive and productive research team out of the English Department. Along with Simon Dentith and Philip Martin, he fulfilled all desired institutional outcomes, presumably including all the brutal performance targets bullet pointed in senior management argot. Most importantly, he set a tone of inclusivity, and created a vibrant collegial ethos that exemplified the kind of consensual, even-handed, academic values to which he subscribes. It was a golden age, when sabbaticals were suddenly two a penny, but it was noticeable that Peter did not take one himself.

In his plate-spinner's way, Peter's achievements from this time were many. They included, notably, his developing of the Cyder Press, and his founding of the prestigious cycle of Open Lectures, over which he presided for more than ten years. His inimitable facility, as chair and first respondent at these events, to find the right joke, and to set the tone were always a kind of marvel to me. He often says that a good teacher is someone who you can see thinking on their feet, and it was certainly true, time and again that you could almost hear the mental wheels whirring, as Peter (working his knuckles the while, bending up and down from the knees) searched for the right question to unlock the discussion, before somehow plucking it from the ether. Not that there aren't more exasperating aspects of Peter's desire to think on his feet, and to make things new. Along with Simon Dentith, he shares the gift of turning even the most innocuous seeming agenda item into a merciless investigation of current practice and first principles. What alternatives to the seminar? What to do about comma-splicing? What kind of first-year course? To the cynic many such questions appear intractable cul-de-sacs, but it is of a piece with Peter's optimism and practicality, that many of his suggestions have led to important revisions in our practice, including his typically thorough *Grammar and Literary Terms* document for students.

One of his oft-repeated dictums in these meetings, has been to suggest that the seminar was badly titled, on the grounds that it was not a meeting of equals (as he would have its etymology prove). However, his gift as a teacher has always been to treat students as if they were equals. The seriousness, industry and attention that he brings to marking work is a legend in our corridors. However, these painstaking qualities are also always evident in the seminar room, as in a teaching session on Allende's *The House of the Spirits* that I observed a few years ago. Peter's respectful and restrained way with every student – from the sparkiest to the most recalcitrant and halting – is certainly personal to him, but it made me think that he must have imbibed something of this style from his own undergraduate experience, and the enabling influence that he attributes to his own teachers, such as John Lucas.

If I end on a personal note it is because I know I will be talking also for the many students and colleagues who have enjoyed Peter's quiet and generous mentoring (and suffered his proofreading) over the years. I have always associated him with the sketch of the Giant's pair of spectacles, marooned on the eweleaze near Weatherbury, that Hardy penned for the first edition of *Wessex Poems*. In Hardy matters, he has been a senior presence of the most benign and companionable kind. Equally, though, I have relished his Hardeyan readiness to digress from the business in hand for a while, wherever the conversation might go.

Hilary Hinds

Peter is a kind of anti-Macavity, charmingly and disarmingly ubiquitous. Wherever you go, in terms of a new research interest, you find that Peter was not only there first, but he's published something indispensable about it. Consequently, while the writing of Thomas Hardy might be his best known specialism, this is set in a context of quite extraordinary breadth. A few years back, I found myself writing an article about *Howards End*; needless to say, Peter's pithy and thought-provoking study from 1977 quickly established itself as a crucial reference point. A colleague of mine is currently writing a study of literature and terrorism, this decade's unavoidable issue; but Peter got there first, bringing the two topics together in 1988 in an article in *Textual Practice* on 'Terrorism and Literary Studies' (how's that for being ahead of the game?). While this list could be expanded, his breadth of interest is perhaps best exemplified by two of his books. His 1999 book *Literature* engages its topic both theoretically and historically, and through the elucidation of careful and percipient transhistorical case studies, along the way illuminating both its metatopic and its exemplary texts. *The Palgrave Guide to English Literature and Its Contexts, 1500–2000* (2004) relishes its pursuit of the arcane textual and contextual detail, and the framing of concise and resonant entries. The ambition of the task, and its dizzyingly exacting nature, seemed to energize rather than to weary Peter. While preparing the book, he would frequently bounce out of his office with the latest update on his long march through the literary centuries: 'I'm into the 1590s now. What date would *you* give for *Arden of Faversham?*' Both books share Peter's hallmark style: the writing is engaging and crafted, its lucidity the outcome of a scholarly expertise and analytical acuity all the more impressive for being worn lightly.

All this, however, is to tell not even half the story, for Peter is also the most collegial and congenial of workmates, as well as one of the most generous, working alongside junior colleagues with the same energy and enthusiasm which he takes to his professorial duties. He was the senior academic on the interview panel for my post at Cheltenham and Gloucester College of Higher Education (as the University of Gloucestershire then was), but he was also the first into the kitchen that day, making coffee for everyone. Moreover, Peter has without question the quickest wit of anyone with whom I have ever worked, having an anecdote, a customized saw, a quip or a riposte for every occasion. Eight years on, I still miss working with him. In fact, if I had to design my ideal academic colleague, I would come up with someone remarkably like Peter. But on reflection, this just wouldn't be good enough. It would have to *be* Peter, not just be *like* Peter, to fit the bill.

Sandra Courtman

As it turned out, my undergraduate use of Peter's work was a proleptic encounter. When I was set a final year assignment to write on a literary critic that I had found 'useful', I could not foresee that I would complete a Ph.D. under the supervision of this very critic. As his *Hardy in History* was (and still is) one of the most illuminating and accessible pieces of criticism that I had been exposed to, I wrote to its author. Ill-formed questions about literary theory can usually expect little hope of a reply. *Au contraire* (as he would later say with a twinkle) he responded immediately.

Peter's generosity prompted me to respond to the fortuitous call of a *Guardian* advert for a Ph.D. studentship to be supervised by the same 'useful' critic. The interview was held on a stifling day. As he sprinted up the stairs at Dunholme in his infamous *It Ain't Half Hot Mum* shorts, how could I not warm to him immediately? While I was often terrified at the prospect of his meticulous gaze, supervisions were peppered with jokes and smoothed by vernacularisms all designed to put me at ease. I remain grateful for his early advice to keep a research journal as this would turn out to be the key to a struggle with my thesis. In having Peter as a supervisor, I was blessed by his association with many important scholars and few turned down his invitation to speak as part of a series of 'Open Lectures in Culture and Criticism'. Consequently I benefited from discussions with Michael Green, Harry Goulbourne, Sushelia Nasta and many others who value Peter's friendship.

I enjoyed many after-lecture dinners at a local wine bar which had the capacity to veer from the intellectually sublime to abject silliness. Peter, ever mindful of the need to stretch the departmental research budget, would repetitively counsel the speaker to order from 'the light meals' section which he claimed 'are quite sufficient'. When one eminent speaker ignored Peter's advice only to lose control of an enormous rack of lamb, Tara Morgan and I had to dive under the table to stifle our laughter.

It was sometimes necessary to extinguish the spark of humour between Peter and myself because of my tendency to 'corpse' at inappropriate times. Even sitting on opposite sides of the room, unscheduled comedy moments at public lectures provoked a telepathic reflex that I had to learn to control. It would be misleading to suggest that I guffawed my way through the Ph.D. but when I remember Peter, it invokes a mixture of the pain associated with difficult research and the pleasure associated with his wonderful personality.

Emily Wroe

As Peter's former student, it is natural to follow his method of unravelling meaning by starting with the etymology of the name 'Peter' itself. Pronounced *PEE-ter*, of Greek origin and meaning 'rock' or 'stone', Peter was the fisherman apostle who was impulsive, bad-tempered and strong in faith. Jesus said of him 'Upon this Rock I will build my church.' Peter Widdowson is, to a great extent, the foundation of my academic achievements and career. I've only ever known him to be good humoured and I think his daily ritual of currant bun after sandwich says something about him being a man of routine and, as many know from his *Palgrave Guide to English Literature and Its Contexts*, of 'timelines' rather than impulsivity. What he has in generous amounts is faith in his students, and in my case, he believed – more than I did at times – that I could get to the finish line with essays, exams and a doctoral thesis. Entering undergraduate studies via a non-traditional route in my late twenties I was academic-shy but with Peter's support, encouragement and good doses of hilarity ('did I tell you the one about the mobile phone and the loo?') he helped me transform an interest in post-colonial writing, which he fostered, into three degrees. Like all good fisherman he plucked me out of a murky sea – a job at an insurance company – and provided an opportunity to do three years research into Black British Writing, some teaching and work for the Cyder Press.

Working for Peter on Cyder Press publications was a healthy distraction; he single-handedly nurtured its publications and I was proud to help send them out into the world. He commissioned *As Told to a Child* which resulted in a rare and beautiful book much loved by fans of Robert Frost. This experience helped me find my later career in publishing.

Peter's lectures and seminars were sell-out performances and a great mental workout. We'd always leave feeling intellectually energized and enthused to go off and discover more about *Midnight's Children* or *Waterland* or *Beloved* and their literary, historical and cultural contexts. He had this amazing ability to peel away narrative layers, or to *press the text* as he put it, so that you'd come away feeling you'd discovered that elusive 'whole' story. And who would have thought there'd be so much to say about literature and history by way of holes, phlegm and chutney?

To be an eternal Widdowson student would be wonderful thing – so much stimulation and fun – but I continue to experience this every time I pick up a novel. This is why, in addition to his influential body of work, there is no petering out of Peter's way with texts because it lives on in readers like me.

James Green

I first met Peter Widdowson in 2001, shortly after I embarked on what would eventually become seven years of study at the University of Gloucestershire. Peter delivered my very first lecture on the English Studies programme which, if I remember correctly, attempted to introduce the thorny concept of 'Literature' in a little under an hour to a roomful of dazed freshers. Although I'm not sure I can recall much of what was said, despite my frantic efforts to write every word down – disregarding Peter's exhortation for us simply to listen rather than take notes – I immediately warmed to the man who stood before us in that echoing lecture hall, trying both to educate and enthuse.

Peter has written widely on a range of topics and authors, and those who have had the pleasure of being taught by him will know of his deep interest in his subject. His energy and passion for language and ideas is infectious; I and my fellow students always looked forward to seminars with Peter because we would invariably leave them seeing the world anew. More than simply teaching the texts, he instilled in us the desire to challenge and inquire that is the well-spring of true learning. Peter's success as a teacher stems in no small part from his convivial nature, and I will remember him as a man of integrity and generosity whose office door was always open.

As well as mentoring my undergraduate and MA dissertations, Peter was also my doctoral supervisor between 2005 and 2008. Some people thrive on the experience of studying for a Ph.D., but for me these were three very difficult years, and it is for Peter's help and support during this period that I am particularly grateful. Through the days, weeks, and even months when every sentence had to be chiselled out of stone – and I feared that the words had finally run out for good – Peter offered reassurance, encouragement and precious sparks of inspiration that enabled me, somehow, to get the thing finished. During those periods of creative blockage when the thesis seemed to eclipse everything else in my world, I could always rely on Peter's good humour and unswerving optimism to help me recalibrate my perspective. As an incorrigible perfectionist, though, I'd like to thank Professor Widdowson most of all for teaching me the wisdom of Samuel Beckett's dictum: 'try again. Fail again. Fail better.'

Neil A. Wynn

I think I knew Peter Widdowson, although could not recall having met him, before I arrived at the University of Gloucestershire in 2003 and found him on my interview panel. The interview went well, and Peter was in fact one of the reasons I accepted the job. In the course of the questioning, I sensed our paths had crossed in some ways before and that we might have had experiences and interests in common. We both wanted to explore some of those common interests, particularly the work of Toni Morrison and the links between history and literature, and I left the interview with a sense of Peter's sympathetic presence, and optimistic about the possibility of working in the same department as him one day. Once the post was mine and I was 'settled in', I not only became more aware of Peter's significance within the department and the university as a whole, but I realized why it was he had seemed so familiar to me. It wasn't simply the fact that our career trajectories bore some resemblance (although Peter's has been much more illustrious than my own), but that in some ways Peter represented the path followed by a whole generation of academics.

Although we probably hadn't met (or if we had, neither of us could remember exactly where), we clearly shared experiences, friends and colleagues. Peter and I had both entered polytechnics rather than the older more 'established' universities, albeit his in England, mine in Wales. We both taught in Humanities programmes that emphasized the interdisciplinary, and of course Peter famously was involved in establishing *Literature and History*, the journal that so represented some of the newer trends and the influence of figures like Richard Hoggart and Raymond Williams. Some of this influence could be found at the Open University (OU) and I was not surprised to discover that Peter had also taught as a part-time tutor at the institution where I had worked as a full-time postgraduate and temporary lecturer. Indeed, when Peter was clearing out his office he passed onto me old OU Arts faculty units he had used, some of which are still useful today. He also passed on a compilation tape he had made on blues and jazz – an interest, along with cinema, we both shared.

Working in the polytechnics led both Peter and I to the CNAA. There I came across Peter's colleagues Paul Stigant, Peter Humm and Joan Ryan – possibly even Peter himself! Thus it was hardly surprising that when I finally caught up with Peter, I felt I already knew a lot about him and perhaps it was this that made him such an easy colleague to get on with. It might also have been the fact that despite the undoubted significance of his role at Gloucestershire or his research record, Peter had no airs or graces, no sense of academic pretension, no nagging insecurity. Instead Peter was always self-deprecating, modest, humorous, willing to share a tale, compare film reviews, discuss crime writing, or war poetry and historiography, or the problems of compiling dictionaries, and above all, to lend a sympathetic ear.

In those first years Peter was one of the friendly faces that helped me to understand my new employers – the more so after we had moved buildings and Peter was in an office just across the corridor from me. So his retirement came too soon for I still felt I hardly knew him.

Charlotte Beyer

I want to open my tribute to Peter with some recollections of a recent experience. The following snapshot presents, to me, an enduring image of the respect and genuine warmth Peter generated from the students whom he taught.

The occasion is the University of Gloucestershire Graduation Ceremony, November 2008. Peter is awarded an honorary fellowship. The guests respond with enthusiasm. The English students applaud, but more than this, they spontaneously rise to give Peter a standing ovation as they watch him take the stage. Students responded to Peter's teaching, and to his inimitable (not squeaky-clean) sense of humour, his breadth of knowledge, and his humanity. Staff, myself included, also benefited enormously from having Peter as a mentor and colleague.

I consider it a great privilege to have taught modernist literature with Peter over a number of years. His lecture notes on the modernism module tended to be mostly either in yellowed typescript or scrawled handwriting – he was not a 'PowerPoint man' – but he did not really need those notes much anyway, and besides, the students' response amply demonstrated that he did not have to resort to technological wizardry to capture his audience. Occasionally Peter would refer modestly to his knack of lecturing without dependence on a script. He would exclaim, 'Like my old boss Valerie Pitt used to say, "Pop in a penny, and out it comes!"' Peter's lectures, however, were no intellectual penny-pinching exercise. He knew his stuff inside out, but also continued to be intellectually curious, open to new writers, stimulated by new ideas.

Peter is such a generous person, with his time and his knowledge. He also has a great sense of humour. You could chat about life and family and you could share a laugh about almost anything, for example, about the time when his mobile phone stopped working because he had dropped it down the toilet while on a train. Or that other time, when he was stuck in bad weather in the car on the way home, but had forgotten to switch his mobile on, so no one was able to ring him to check he was safe – Peter is not a 'Mobile Phone man'.

Since the award of his Honorary Fellowship, Peter's influence on the department and on the Cyder Press continues, but it is in day-to-day teaching that he is most missed, not least on Friday mornings for modernism.

Peter Childs

'The splendid thing about education is that everyone wants it and, like influenza, you can give it away without losing any of it yourself.' Peter reminds me of this Evelyn Waugh comment because he dispenses enlightenment, but not flu, with the generosity of those who take joy in others' learning. In the capacity of 'observer', I once attended one of Peter's seminars. He sat the students in a large circle and engaged them on the subject of allusion, narrative and history in *Midnight's Children*. 'Engagement' is an over- and misused word these days but Peter engaged the students' minds as fully as I have seen any seminar tutor. His enthusiasm was as infectious as his erudition.

Waugh also remarked that the Second World War wasn't bad, depending on who you were with. This is how I often felt about Peter's presence in the English Department amid the thunder of theory wars and the red-rust creep of audit culture. Peter manages to combine intense scholarly rigour with serious Nietzschean playfulness; learned and ludic is perhaps how his colleagues see him in the round. I will personally treasure moments of debate with Peter that lightened the grey battles of departmental meetings. He injected as much sanity as levity, but it was the latter that kept us collectively sane as we found intellectual solace in his knowledge and judgement but pleasure in his quick wit and mischievous perorations: how the rail network was repeatedly brought to a halt by the wrong kind of Snow and Leavis, and the degree to which by the twenty-first-century post-modernism had disappeared, up its own *ars*.

Peter's unique gift as a colleague has always had for me the texture of glue. He keeps the English staff together, and more. I have seen him hold research seminars together, students together and a department together. His sagacity and *bonhomie* have even held together interminable meetings to discuss exam papers, when the insertion of a semi-colon – surely the meaning would be clearer if a new sentence was started – and the potential for ambiguity – yes, but the question could also be read *this* way – were the subject of an hour's entrenched and embattled dispute. Such internecine sessions depend on the people you are with, and they never seemed bad with Peter.

Debby Thacker

From my first encounters with him, Peter Widdowson redefined, for me, the meaning of the quintessential 'professor'. It might have been his surprising array of many-coloured socks, or perhaps it was the mischievous method by which he found the most fruitful innuendo in the wording of potential examination questions. Whatever it was, rather than the distant figure one might expect, Peter became a model of how to maximize satisfaction and minimize aggravation for a fledgling academic in the changing world of the English university system.

In his hospitality, whether directing me to promising reading matter in his book-lined study or, with Jane and Tom, nurturing colleagues with food and wine in their house and garden in Stroud, or providing a base for 'getting away from it all' in the cottage in Cornwall, Peter continually demonstrated, through example, that the life of an academic was not merely employment, or a head-in-a-book pursuit, but a calling.

Whether it was advising me during my first tentative book proposals, or mentoring me through my first role as research supervisor, Peter was not only there for sage advice, but could also find the perfect anecdote to lift my mood and spur me on. The most turgid or dreaded meetings were rescued by his playfully subversive commentary and 'mis'-readings of official documents, or lengthy debates about the placing of a comma. I knew that Peter would always be a loyal colleague and the perfect example of one who delights in engaging with the 'the life of the mind'.

There was time for seriousness, too, of course, and while Course Leader for English, I was frequently to experience Peter's dedicated support of students, including his uncanny ability to gauge the difference between the lazy and poorly trained writer and the student with, until then, unrecognized dyslexia. This admirable facility, to wear his professional authority so lightly and to combine it with a genuine dedication to teaching, provided me as an academic at the beginning of a career, with encouragement that one could not only combine the seeking of knowledge with a deftness of touch, but also with a devilish sense of humour.

Perhaps the most significant aspect of his influence, though, is Peter's devotion to *le mot juste*. In his own writing, in his fondness for quoting significant wise females in his past, and in his dedication to seeking precision and clarity in countless university documents and assessments, Peter has shown that language can be a tool of insight and craft, but also a playful thing. Of course, while writing this, I am trembling at my possible misuse of the semi-colon and I also know that I should have left behind a trail of suggestive innuendo, but I hope that I will have done enough to declare my fondness and admiration for Peter Widdowson, every inch a professor.

Index